A-level
In a Week

Biology

Year 1 / AS

Eliot
Attridge

CONTENTS

DAY 1

Page	Estimated time	Topic	Date	Time taken	Completed
4	40 minutes	Water			☐
8	60 minutes	Carbohydrates			☐
12	40 minutes	Lipids			☐
16	40 minutes	Proteins			☐
20	40 minutes	Enzymes			☐

DAY 2

Page	Estimated time	Topic	Date	Time taken	Completed
24	40 minutes	Eukaryotes			☐
28	40 minutes	Prokaryotes			☐
32	40 minutes	Methods of Studying Cells			☐
36	60 minutes	Cell Division			☐

DAY 3

Page	Estimated time	Topic	Date	Time taken	Completed
40	40 minutes	Cell Transport			☐
44	40 minutes	Gas Exchange 1			☐
48	40 minutes	Gas Exchange 2			☐
52	40 minutes	Energy from Respiration			☐

DAY 4

Page	Estimated time	Topic	Date	Time taken	Completed
56	40 minutes	Mass Transport			☐
60	40 minutes	Transporting Blood			☐
64	40 minutes	Controlling Heart Rate			☐
68	40 minutes	Plant Transport			☐

DAY 5

Page	Estimated time	Topic	Date	Time taken	Completed
72	40 minutes	Nutrition			☐
76	40 minutes	Modelling Digestion			☐
80	40 minutes	Trophy			☐
84	40 minutes	Dentition and Diet			☐

DAY 6

Page	Estimated time	Topic	Date	Time taken	Completed
88	40 minutes	The Genetic Code			☐
92	40 minutes	DNA Replication			☐
96	40 minutes	Sexual Reproduction			☐
100	40 minutes	Biodiversity			☐
104	40 minutes	Evolution			☐

DAY 7

Page	Estimated time	Topic	Date	Time taken	Completed
108	40 minutes	Disease			☐
112	40 minutes	Immune Response 1			☐
116	40 minutes	Immune Response 2			☐
120	40 minutes	Antibiotics and Stem Cells			☐

| 124 | Answers |
| 135 | Index |

Water

The Importance of Water

As all life on Earth shares a common ancestor, it should not come as a surprise that all life on Earth requires water for survival.

The planet is covered by approximately 75% water which is the only commonly found molecule that exists on the planet in all three physical states of matter (solid, liquid and gas).

Water is a **covalent compound** made up of two hydrogen atoms covalently bonded to an oxygen atom.

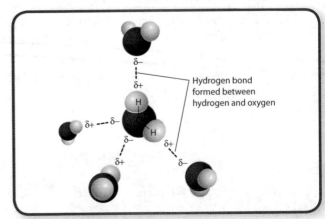

Hydrogen bond formed between hydrogen and oxygen

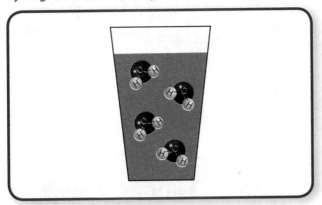

Oxygen is a more **electronegative** atom than hydrogen, which is **electropositive**. This means that the electron shared from the hydrogen atom is pulled closer to the oxygen atom. The water molecule has a slight overall charge, with the oxygen being **δ negative** (delta negative) and the hydrogen being **δ positive** (delta positive).

As water is a **polar molecule** it means that it can form **hydrogen bonds** with other water molecules. Hydrogen bonds are weaker than covalent bonds.

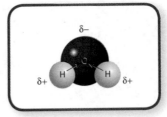

The hydrogen bonds are regularly formed and broken. The water molecules stay close together when in liquid form. This property is called **cohesion**. Cohesion is an important component of plant **transpiration** where a column of water is moved through the plant. Another important property is **adhesion** – attraction of water molecules to other substances.

Water also has a surface tension. At the boundary between liquid water and the air the water molecules are arranged in an ordered fashion. This makes it very difficult to break the surface, acting a little like a film. One consequence of this is that animals that are light enough, such as the water boatman, can walk on the surface of water.

Unlike other compounds, water is unusual in that its solid form is less dense than its liquid form. This means that solid water (ice) floats. The water molecules arrange themselves to form a hexagonal structure when they freeze. The water molecules are further away than as a liquid so the ice is less dense.

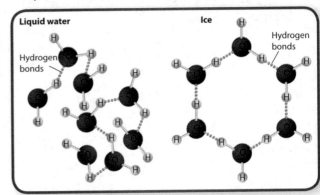

Liquid water — Hydrogen bonds

Ice — Hydrogen bonds

An important consequence of this property is that when water freezes in rivers, lakes and oceans there is often liquid water under the ice. That water can then support life until a thaw occurs. In Earth's history there have been a number of times when a significant proportion of the planet has been covered by ice. Were it not for the difference in density of ice and liquid water life could have been extinguished at an early stage.

Water is a **universal solvent**. Due to the polarity of water molecules, liquid water can dissolve a wide range of polar solutes, such as sodium chloride and proteins. The water molecules surround the charged ions, forming hydration shells. The electronegative hydrogen end is attracted to the positive cation, while the electropositive oxygen end is attracted to the negative anion.

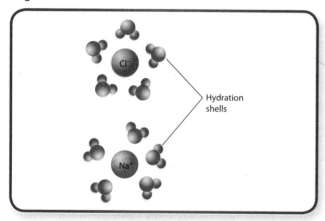

Hydration shells

Water can dissolve a wider range of solutes than any other liquid. Key **inorganic ions** can be dissolved in water, such as Na^+, K^+, Mg^{2+}, Fe^{2+}, Ca^{2+} and PO_4^{3-}.

Water can also act as a solute for non-polar molecules (such as the sugars fructose and glucose). The water molecules form hydrogen bonds with the different parts of the non-polar molecule.

As water is such a useful solvent it also means that a lot of **metabolic reactions** can take place in water. In addition, a wide range of metabolic reactions involve water as a **component** of the reaction.

Reactions that produce water as a by-product are called **condensation reactions**. For example, the formation of maltose from glucose has the chemical equation

$$C_6H_{12}O_6 + C_6H_{12}O_6 \longrightarrow C_{12}H_{22}O_{11} + H_2O$$

This can be written to show the displayed formulae:

CH₂OH CH₂OH CH₂OH CH₂OH

α-glucose α-glucose Maltose

Reactions that take in water as a reactant are called **hydrolysis reactions**, e.g. splitting a dipeptide into its amino acid monomers:

Dipeptide Amino acid 1 Amino acid 2

It takes 4.2 J to heat up 1 g of water by 1°C. This is called the **specific heat capacity**. This is higher than other common substances with similar composition, such as simple alcohols. This means that water can absorb a lot of heat before increasing in temperature. This property helps organisms to survive because it takes a lot of energy to increase the temperature of water, which means that the temperature of large bodies of water will stay within a more constant range. The water effectively is buffering the temperature changes. Organisms living in the water have a more stable environment in which they can operate. Over the whole planet, water absorbs a lot of energy from the Sun and so keeps the global temperatures relatively constant.

The **latent heat of vaporisation** is the enthalpy change (amount of heat) required to transform 1 g of liquid into a gas at a set pressure (usually atmospheric pressure). Water has a relatively high latent heat of vaporisation. In other words, water can take in a larger amount of energy before it will change into a gas. This is important as a lot of heat can be removed from an organism through evaporation of water in sweat, without losing too much water in the process. Sweating therefore cools a body down.

SUMMARY

- Water is a covalent compound formed from one oxygen and two hydrogen atoms.

- The oxygen molecule draws the shared (valence) electron from each hydrogen atom towards it creating a permanent dipole.

- This means that water molecules are polar.

- The oxygen side of the water molecule is δ negative (delta negative).

- The hydrogen side of the molecule is δ positive (delta positive).

- Water molecules form hydrogen bonds with other water molecules. This means the water molecules stay very close together in liquid form.

- Cohesion is the term given to the 'stickiness' of the water molecules due to hydrogen bonding.

- Adhesion is the 'stickiness' of water molecules to other substances.

- Surface tension occurs due to the way the water molecules arrange themselves at the interface between air and water.

- Solid water (ice) is unusual as it is less dense than the liquid form. This is because of the way the water molecules are arranged in the solid form. As the water molecules are more spread out they are less dense than the equivalent volume of liquid water.

- As ice floats it means that living things can survive in the liquid water underneath it.

- Water is referred to as the universal solvent, dissolving more solutes than any other solvent.

- It can dissolve other polar molecules by forming hydration shells around the ions.

- Other compounds dissolve due to the water molecules forming hydrogen bonds with each molecule.

- Metabolic reactions can take place in water and they can also involve water as both a product and a reactant.

- Condensation reactions lead to water as a product.

- Hydrolysis reactions use water as a reactant.

- The specific heat capacity of water is 4.2 J/g °C. This is high and means that water can absorb a lot of heat energy before increasing in temperature. This acts as a buffer for temperature change and living organisms survive as their habitat temperature will not fluctuate to extreme levels.

- Water has a high latent heat of vaporisation so water can be used to remove heat from a body without losing too much water (through sweating).

1. What is the effective charge on the oxygen molecule in water?

2. Why does cohesion occur with water?

3. Draw a water molecule and indicate its polarity.

4. Why is water referred to as being the 'universal solvent'?

5. Why is solid water (ice) less dense than liquid water?

6. Explain what hydrolysis is.

7. How does the latent heat of vaporisation help in removing excess heat from the body?

8. What property of water enables a pond insect, like a water boatman, to walk on the surface of water?

9. What is the specific heat capacity of water?

10. Why is it beneficial to organisms living in the sea that the specific heat capacity of water is so high?

11. Suggest the consequence for life on Earth if the specific heat capacity were low instead of high.

12. What type of bonding takes place between molecules in liquid water?

PRACTICE QUESTIONS

1. The diagram shows two molecules of glucose that can react to form a disaccharide called maltose.

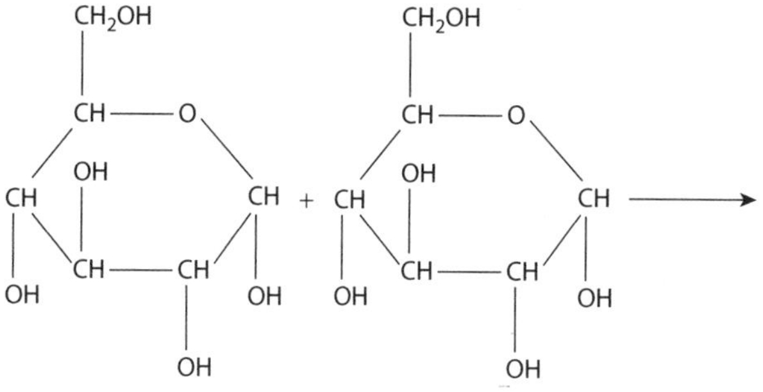

α-glucose   α-glucose

a) (i) What is the name of the reaction that forms the disaccharide? [1 mark]

(ii) Complete the diagram to show the molecule that is formed in this metabolic reaction. [1 mark]

b) The disaccharide can be broken down to re-form the starting glucose molecules.

(i) What is the name of this reaction type? [1 mark]

(ii) What compound is needed in this reaction, other than the disaccharide? [1 mark]

2. Analysis of the sap of a plant shows the presence of dissolved Mg^{2+} and PO_4^{3-} ions.

a) Explain why these ions are soluble in water. [2 marks]

b) Draw a diagram to show the arrangement of water molecules with Mg^{2+} and PO_4^{3-} ions. [4 marks]

Carbohydrates

Carbohydrates are compounds formed from the elements carbon (C), hydrogen (H) and oxygen (O). The general formula for a carbohydrate is $(CH_2O)_n$, the n representing the number of times the base unit is repeated.

For example, with glucose $n = 6$ and the formula for the compound is $C_6H_{12}O_6$.

Carbon can form up to four covalent bonds with other elements which means that it can form chains. Carbohydrates can therefore vary in length.

Based on the chain length, they can be divided into three groups: **monosaccharides**, **disaccharides** and **polysaccharides**.

Monosaccharides

The simplest carbohydrates are monosaccharides. These are made of a single sugar unit.

The number of carbon atoms in the monosaccharide can vary.

Triose Sugars

Triose sugars have three carbon atoms. They are important in cellular **respiration**.

For example:

D-glyceraldehyde

Pentose Sugars

Pentose sugars have five carbon atoms. Two of the most common pentose sugars are **ribose** and **deoxyribose**. These are key components of RNA and DNA, respectively.

For example:

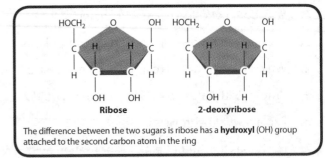

The difference between the two sugars is ribose has a **hydroxyl** (OH) group attached to the second carbon atom in the ring

Hexose Sugars

The formula for a sugar such as glucose $C_6H_{12}O_6$ only indicates what elements are present and in what ratio. The actual shape of the molecule depends on the bonds present. Hence there are a variety of ways to arrange the molecules, forming isomers. Isomers have the same molecular formula but different properties.

There are 16 isomers with the formula $C_6H_{12}O_6$.

Two examples are α-glucose and β-glucose:

α-glucose   β-glucose

Note the difference in the position of the hydroxyl groups

Glucose is a molecule required for aerobic respiration. When it is used in respiration the energy stored in the bonds is released and used in cell metabolism. The glucose molecules have to be transported to the cells that need it. They are small enough to dissolve in the water in blood or the fluid in a plant. The molecules can also pass through the pores in cell membranes.

Disaccharides

The smallest polymers that can be formed have two sugar monomers joined together. Three of the most common disaccharides found in living organisms are sucrose, maltose and lactose. There are many more examples but they are less prevalent.

Sucrose

The sugar that is commonly sold in supermarkets is made of sucrose. Sucrose is made from a glucose monomer and a fructose monomer.

For example:

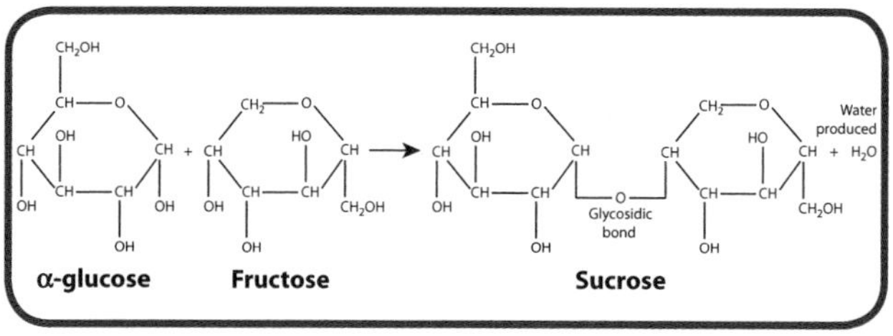

This is a condensation reaction, as water is produced. The link between the two monomers is called a **glycosidic bond**.

The glycosidic bond is between two C atoms on the different monomers, i.e. C—O—C.

Adding water to sucrose reverses the reaction – this is hydrolysis.

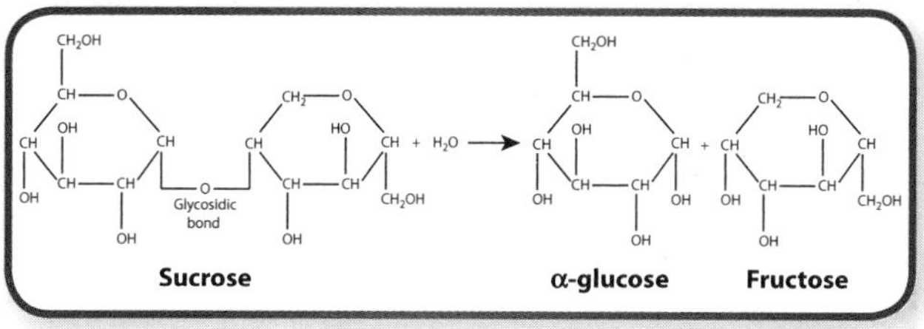

Maltose

Maltose is formed from the condensation of two glucose monomers.

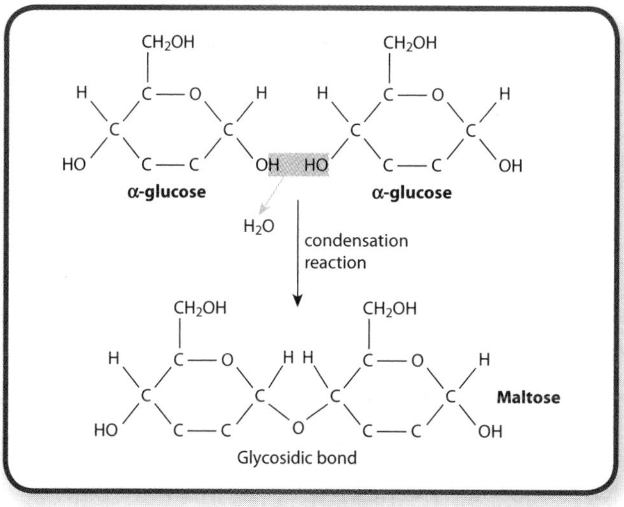

This can be reversed through a hydrolysis reaction.

Lactose

Lactose is a sugar that is found in milk, making up 2–8% of its volume.

It is made by the condensation reaction between glucose and galactose.

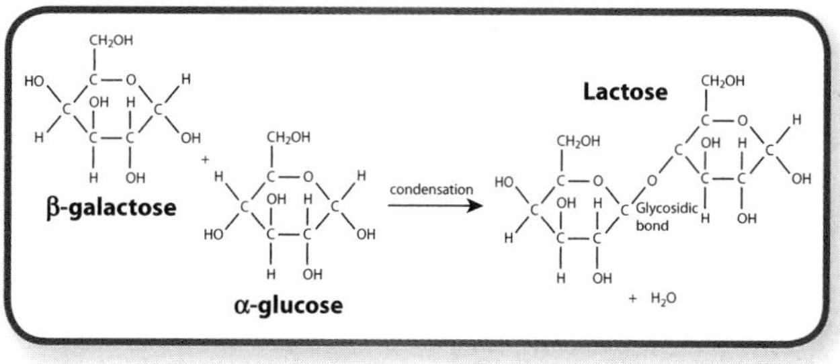

Polysaccharides

Any sugar with more than two subunits is called a polysaccharide. These longer molecules are extremely useful for structural and storage roles in plants and animals. Linking each sugar monomer is a glycosidic bond.

Starch

Starch is the name given to the long-chain polymer of α-glucose monomers. It is a storage carbohydrate in plants. It can be unbranched (amylose) or branched (amylopectin).

Amylose Structure

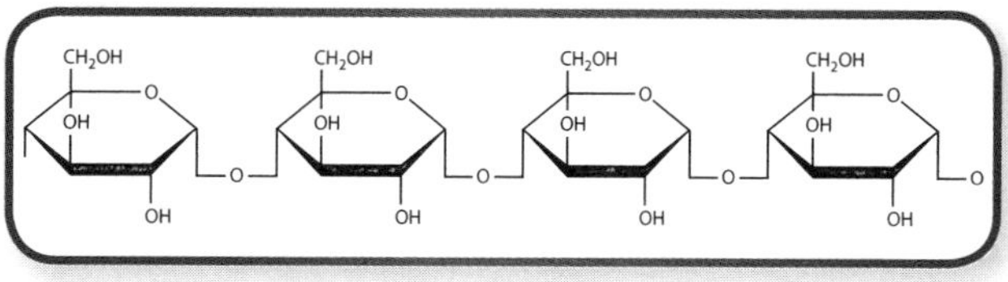

Amylopectin Structure

For example:

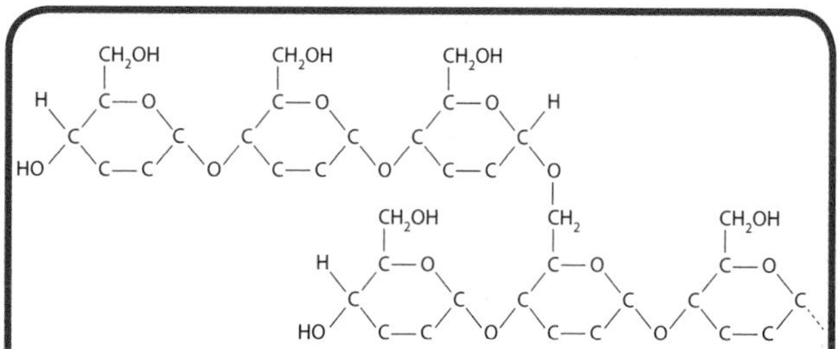

Part of a branched section of a starch molecule

The presence or absence of branching alters the properties of the starch. The starches in many grains used to make bread have a different proportion of each type of starch and this affects processes during the bread-making.

Starch is useful as a storage molecule because it is insoluble and so does not alter the water potential of the cell, unlike individual glucose molecules.

Glycogen
Glycogen is the main glucose storage molecule in animals. It is stored in the liver where it can be metabolised when needed. It has a similar structure to amylopectin but is much more branched. It can be easily mobilised to meet a sudden need for glucose. Like starch, it is also insoluble.

Glycogen

This is where the polymer branches

Cellulose
Like amylose, cellulose is a long, unbranched molecule. Unlike amylose, cellulose is made up of repeating β-glucose molecules. Due to the arrangement of the hydroxyl groups, the only way to join the β-glucose monomers together is by alternately flipping the sugar by 180° to allow the condensation reaction to take place. This makes the polymer much straighter than amylose.

Cellulose

Although the cellulose molecules are unbranched, hydrogen bonds between the individual chains make it very difficult to break the polymer. It is a structural, fibrous polysaccharide.

For example:

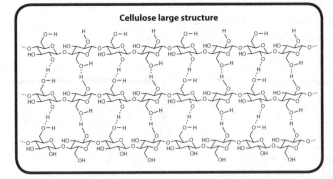

Cellulose large structure

Chitin
Chitin is a structural carbohydrate commonly found in the exoskeletons of crustaceans and insects as well as the cell walls of fungi.

It is formed from the repeating subunits of *N*-acetylglucosamine monomers. Like cellulose, the way the monomers are arranged means that the carbohydrate is very straight, ideal for making structural fibres. Hydrogen bonding between chains strengthens the molecule.

Chitin

QUICK TEST

1. What is a glycosidic bond?

2. What elements are present in a carbohydrate?

3. What property of carbon enables it to form chains?

4. Give three types of monosaccharide.

5. What disaccharide is formed from α-glucose and β-galactose?

6. What sugars comprise the disaccharide sucrose?

7. What are the two structure types of starch?

8. How does the structure of cellulose make it useful as a structural polysaccharide?

- **Carbohydrates are comprised of the elements C, H and O.**
- **The general formula is $(CH_2O)_n$.**
- **Carbon can form up to four covalent bonds with other atoms.**
- **Carbon can form chains of variable length.**
- **Monosaccharides have a single sugar unit.**
  - **Triose sugars have three carbon atoms, e.g. D-glyceraldehyde.**
  - **Pentose sugars have five sugars, e.g. ribose and deoxyribose.**
  - **Hexose sugars have six sugars, e.g. α-glucose and β-glucose.**
- **Disaccharides are two monosaccharides joined by a glycosidic bond.**
- **Glycosidic bonds form between a carbon atom on one sugar and a carbon atom on the other sugar, with oxygen in between (i.e. C—O—C).**
- **This is via a condensation reaction.**
- **Examples include:**
  - **sucrose made of α-glucose and fructose**
  - **maltose made of two molecules of α-glucose**
  - **lactose made of α-glucose and β-galactose.**
- **Disaccharides can be converted back to the original sugars by a hydrolysis reaction.**
- **Polysaccharides are formed by condensation reactions joining more than two sugar subunits.**
- **Examples include:**
  - **starch – a storage molecule in plants; it can be unbranched (amylose) or branched (amylopectin)**
  - **glycogen – a storage molecule in animals**
  - **cellulose – an unbranched polysaccharide in plants, with hydrogen bonds between the chains**
  - **chitin – a structural carbohydrate in the cell walls of fungi and the exoskeletons of crustaceans and insects, with hydrogen bonds between the chains.**

PRACTICE QUESTIONS

1. Maltose is formed from reacting two units of α-glucose together. The diagram shows the two α-glucose monomers.

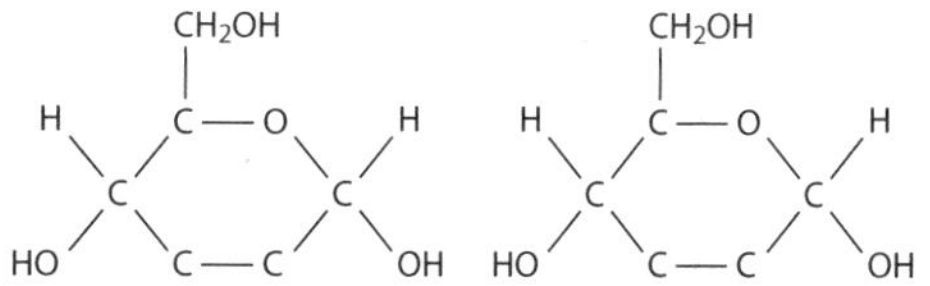

   a) Draw the products of this reaction. **[2 marks]**

   b) What is the name of this type of reaction? **[1 mark]**

2. DNA and RNA are made from nucleotides containing a pentose sugar. The pentose sugar found in DNA is shown on the right.

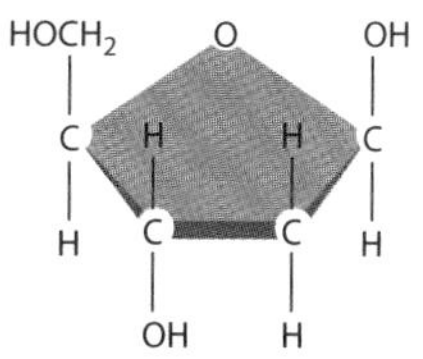

   Draw the equivalent pentose sugar found in RNA. **[1 mark]**

Lipids

Lipids occur in organisms as fats, oils and waxes. They contain the same elements as carbohydrates, but their ratio is different, with molecules having a lower proportion of oxygen compared to carbon and hydrogen.

The molecule shown below is a **triglyceride**.

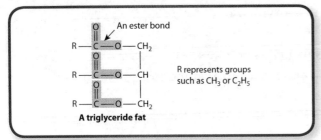

A triglyceride fat

Lipids form through a condensation reaction between three fatty acids and glycerol.

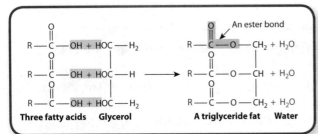

The structure and properties of the triglycerides will vary depending on the length of the carbon chains that make up the molecule (represented in the diagrams by R). The three fatty acids may be the same or different. Each fatty acid forms an **ester bond** in the process, releasing water as a product.

An ester bond is a carbon joined to an oxygen by a double bond and an oxygen via a single bond.

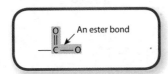

The triglyceride can be broken down into glycerol and fatty acids through a hydrolysis reaction.

Saturated and Unsaturated Fats

The difference between a fat and an oil is that at approximately 20°C, fat is a solid and oil is a liquid. Waxes are similar to fats except that they have a single fatty acid chain attached to a long-chained alcohol group. Waxes are extremely hydrophobic, due to their long non-polar carbon chain.

Lipids are insoluble in water as they are **hydrophobic**.

Saturated Fats

Saturated fats are triglycerides that have been produced from saturated fatty acids. In a saturated fatty acid, all the carbons are joined to four different atoms. There are no double bonds between carbon atoms.

For example, the displayed formula of stearic acid is:

A saturated fatty acid

In reality the molecule would not be in a straight line – the carbon atoms would be arranged in a zigzag.

Fatty acids are often drawn with a zigzag line, omitting the carbon atoms. For example:

Unsaturated Fats

Unsaturated fatty acids have at least one double bond between carbon atoms. The presence of the double bond means the molecule will no longer be as straight – it will have a kink.

For example, the displayed formula of oleic acid is:

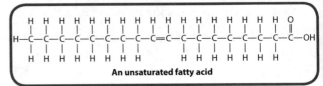

An unsaturated fatty acid

The simplified formula is:

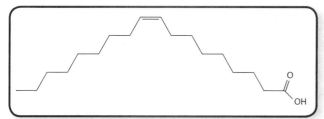

The kink makes it more difficult for the lipids to pack together to become a solid. Hence unsaturated fats tend to be found as oils, particularly in plants and animals.

Saturated fats can be a problem if too many are consumed. They can lead to the build-up of **cholesterol** in the blood vessels, which then causes problems such as **atherosclerosis**, which leads to **cardiovascular disease**.

Uses of Lipids

Triglycerides can be oxidised in respiration, liberating energy for other metabolic processes in the cell. Compared to carbohydrates, the same mass of triglycerides liberates more than twice the amount of energy.

This is because of the low ratio of oxygen atoms in the triglyceride which makes it more reduced than the equivalent carbohydrate. More oxygen has to come from the atmosphere in respiration.

Triglycerides are also a source of metabolic water when broken down through oxidation.

As triglycerides are insoluble it also means that they do not affect the **osmotic potential** in cells.

Beneath the skin, adipose cells are filled with fat. This acts as insulation, helping with temperature homeostasis. The fat also provides support around organs and provides electrical insulation around neurone axons.

All membranes (e.g. cell membrane, nuclear membrane, mitochondrial membrane) are made of **phospholipids**.

A phospholipid is made by the reaction between a triglyceride and phosphoric acid:

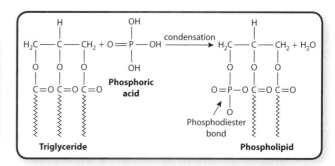

The diagram of a phospholipid can be simplified further to:

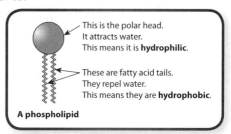

This is the polar head. It attracts water. This means it is **hydrophilic**.

These are fatty acid tails. They repel water. This means they are **hydrophobic**.

A phospholipid

If phospholipids are placed into water, they will naturally arrange themselves into a **liposome**, with the hydrophobic tails on the inside, away from the water, and the hydrophilic heads on the outside. For example:

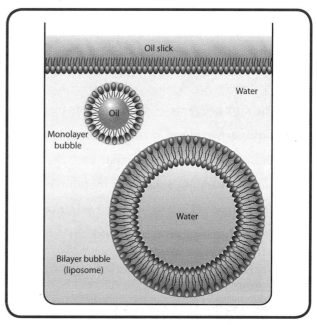

As phospholipids very easily form liposomes it is hypothesised that this property may have led to the formation of the first cells.

SUMMARY

- Lipids are fats, oils and waxes and are comprised of C, H and O atoms.

- The proportion of oxygen to hydrogen and carbon is lower than in carbohydrates.

- Fatty acids react with glycerol to form triglyceride fats.

- An ester bond connects the fatty acid to glycerol:

- This is a condensation reaction producing water.

- Fats and waxes are solid and oils are liquid at 20°C.

- Lipids are insoluble in water as they are hydrophobic.

- Saturated fats have no double bonds between any of the carbon atoms in the chain.

- They can be drawn as a zigzag line:

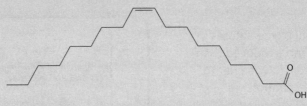

- Too much saturated fat in a diet can lead to cholesterol build-up in arteries and cardiovascular disease.

- Unsaturated fats have at least one double or triple bond between carbon atoms.

- This gives a 'kink' to the lipid molecule:

- The kink prevents unsaturated fats from forming solids easily so these molecules are oils.

- Lipids are oxidised in respiration, releasing energy for metabolism.

- Lipids store more energy than carbohydrates.

- Triglycerides are a source of metabolic water through oxidation.

- They do not affect the osmotic potential in cells.

- Fats aid an organism by providing:
  - temperature insulation
  - electrical insulation around neurones
  - support around organs.

- Phospholipids are formed from a special type of lipid.

- They are formed from the reaction between a triglyceride and phosphoric acid.

- Phospholipids are the main constituent of cell surface membranes and other membranes in cells.

- The phosphate head is hydrophilic (water loving).

- The fatty acid tails are hydrophobic (water hating).

1. In terms of the proportion of carbon, hydrogen and oxygen, what is the difference between lipids and carbohydrates?

2. What is the name of the bond between a fatty acid and glycerol?

3. Draw the bond described in question **2**.

4. What state will a fat and an oil be at 20°C?

5. Why are lipids insoluble in water?

6. How can a triglyceride be broken down into its constituent fatty acids and glycerol?

7. What is a saturated fat?

8. What is an unsaturated fat?

9. Why is an unsaturated fat more likely to be an oil?

10. Give three reasons why triglycerides are useful to an organism.

PRACTICE QUESTIONS

1. A triglyceride is formed by a condensation reaction. Three fatty acids and glycerol are shown below.

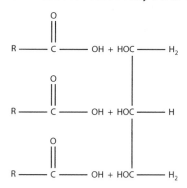

a) Draw the resulting triglyceride. **[1 mark]**

b) On the molecules you have drawn, draw a circle around the atoms that make up the ester bond. **[1 mark]**

c) What does the R on the diagram represent? **[1 mark]**

d) The resulting triglyceride is an oil at 20°C. What does this tell you about the structure of the triglyceride? Explain your answer. **[3 marks]**

e) The triglyceride is reacted with phosphoric acid. What is the name of the type of molecule that is formed? **[1 mark]**

Proteins

Proteins are formed from carbon, hydrogen and oxygen like carbohydrates and lipids. They also always contain nitrogen.

Proteins are polymers comprised of different **amino acids** (the monomers).

The general structure of an amino acid is:

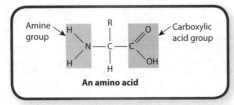

The R represents a carbon chain.

In all life on Earth discovered to date, all proteins present are formed from 20 naturally occurring amino acids. There are some amino acids that are essential for an organism to survive that it cannot manufacture itself. In humans, 10 essential amino acids are needed as children, eight as an adult. These amino acids come from the diet through digestion of other protein.

Protein Construction

Amino acids form through condensation reactions, producing water in the process. In the cell this takes place in the cytoplasm during protein synthesis.

A **peptide bond** joins the two amino acids together.

When lots of amino acids are joined together, a **polypeptide** is formed. The sequence of amino acids will vary depending on the gene that coded for it.

At this stage the polypeptide is not technically a protein. Polypeptides are built into more complicated arrangements, which become the final proteins with individual functions.

Polypeptide to Protein

There are up to four steps in making a protein.

Primary Structure

The primary structure of a protein is the linear sequence of amino acids that make up the polypeptide.

Traditionally amino acids have been represented by three-letter abbreviations, e.g. Ala for alanine, Trp for tryptophan.

The science of **bioinformatics** combines genetic and computer databases to work out the evolutionary link between organisms, by looking at the protein sequences coded by different genes. To make this easier, biologists now regularly use a single letter to represent the amino acids; it's easier to work with a single letter in a program, e.g. alanine = A and tryptophan = W.

This is the primary structure of a polypeptide:

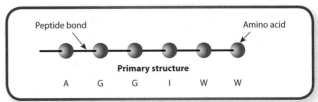

This is a polypeptide made from alanine, glycine, glycine, isoleucine, tryptophan and tryptophan.

Secondary Structure

The amino acids that make up the polypeptide cause it to twist or coil as it forms. The two common structures are the **α-helix** and the **β-pleated sheet**.

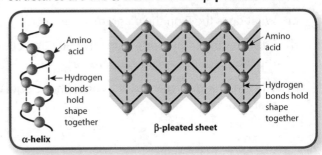

Hydrogen bonding in the secondary structures strengthens the protein. The C=O of one amino acid bonds to the H—N of an adjacent amino acid.

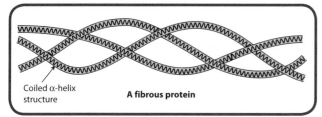

The α-helix structure helps make stronger fibre-like proteins, such as keratin found in hair and nails. β-pleated sheets strengthen in a different way and can be found in proteins such as fibroin (which occurs in silk).

Fibrous proteins have only α-helices. They are not folded any more. More fibres can be linked together.

For example:

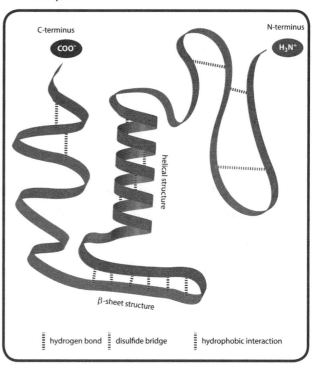

Coiled α-helix structure

A fibrous protein

It is possible to have both types of secondary structures in a single polypeptide. This is because there can be thousands of different sequences of amino acids with different chemical properties making up a polypeptide. One of the largest proteins is titin, which is comprised of up to 34 350 amino acids.

Tertiary Structure
The tertiary structure is where the polypeptide is folded into a specific shape. The shape is kept together by the presence of a number of bonds, which are dependent upon the individual properties of the amino acid's R group. The different types of bonds are:

1. disulfide bridges (sulfur–sulfur bonds)
2. hydrogen bonds
3. ionic bonds
4. hydrophobic and hydrophilic interactions.

For example:

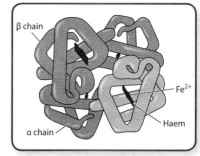

C-terminus · COO⁻

N-terminus · H₃N⁺

helical structure

β-sheet structure

hydrogen bond disulfide bridge hydrophobic interaction

Quaternary Structure
The quaternary structure only exists for those proteins that are made up from more than one subunit. Combining different polypeptides together can result in a wide range of different shapes and functions. Other compounds and elements can also be incorporated as **co-factors**.

The protein haemoglobin is a protein made from four separate polypeptide chains and haem groups, which include iron.

β chain

Fe^{2+}

α chain

Haem

The haem group is a prosthetic (additional non-protein) group and helps the protein bind with oxygen, becoming oxyhaemoglobin.

Uses of Protein
Proteins may be **fibrous** (typically used in structural materials) or they may be **globular**. Globular proteins can be transported in solution, so they are found in the circulatory systems of animals. All enzymes are globular proteins.

SUMMARY

- The elements that form the majority of protein are carbon, hydrogen, nitrogen and oxygen.

- Proteins are polymers made from amine monomers.

- The general structure of an amino acid is:

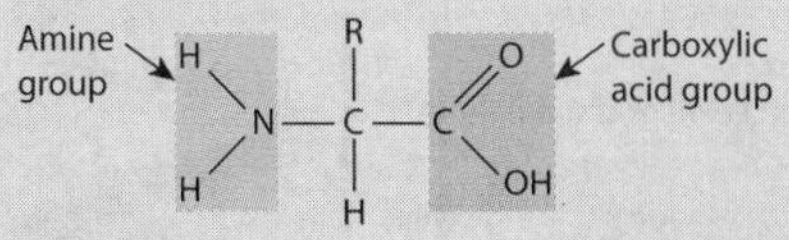

- The side chain attached to the amine and carboxylic acid group is represented by R.

- There are 20 naturally occurring amino acids.

- Ten amino acids are essential to human babies, and eight in adults.

- Amino acids join via peptide bonds:

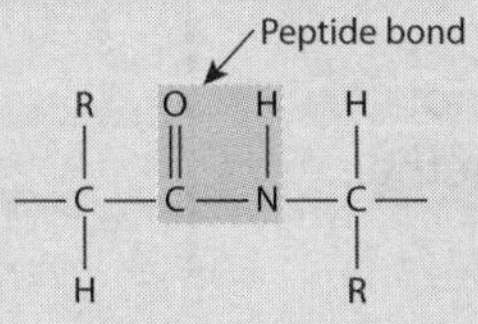

- A polypeptide is a chain of more than two amino acids joined by peptide bonds.

- The primary (1°) structure is the order of the amino acids making up the polypeptide.

- Amino acids are represented by either a three-letter or a single-letter code.

- The secondary (2°) structure is caused by hydrogen bonding leading to the formation of α-helices and β-pleated sheets.

- α-helices are found in proteins that are fibrous.

- The main biological function of β-pleated sheets is to convey specific functions to the protein they occur in such as in the active sites of enzymes.

- The tertiary (3°) structure is where the polypeptide is folded into its final shape as a protein.

- The shape is maintained by:
  - disulfide bridges
  - hydrogen bonding
  - ionic bonds
  - hydrophobic and hydrophilic interactions.

- The quaternary (4°) structure is found in proteins made up from more than one subunit.

- Proteins may be:
  - globular – soluble proteins, e.g. enzymes
  - fibrous – insoluble, structural proteins.

1. What is the name of the bond between two amino acids in a polypeptide?

2. Draw the bond described in question **1**.

3. What groups are present in an amino acid?

4. How many naturally occurring amino acids are there?

5. Where do animals obtain the essential amino acids?

6. What is meant by the primary structure of a polypeptide?

7. What two types of structure are found in the secondary structure of a polypeptide?

8. Give four ways the three-dimensional shape is maintained in the tertiary structure of a protein.

9. How does the quaternary structure of a protein differ from the tertiary structure?

10. Name the two types of protein.

PRACTICE QUESTIONS

1. Alanine and glycine are shown in the diagrams below.

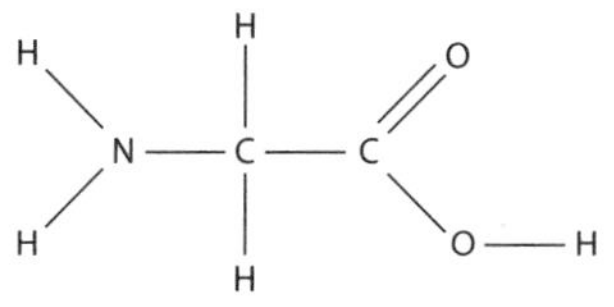

Glycine

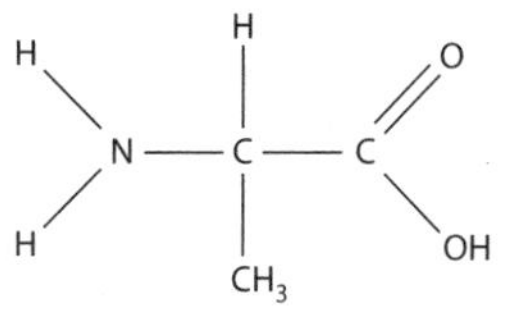

Alanine

  a) Draw the peptide that forms when glycine and alanine are bonded together.   **[2 marks]**

  b) What is the bond that forms between the two amino acids called?   **[1 mark]**

  c) Draw a circle around the atoms that make up the bond indicated in part **b).**   **[1 mark]**

2. A protein is made up of the following amino acids:

  a) How many amino acids are in the polypeptide chain?   **[1 mark]**

  b) Draw the two types of secondary structure of a polypeptide and show the hydrogen
     bonding for each.   **[3 marks]**

  c) Compare the solubilities of fibrous and globular proteins.   **[1 mark]**

Enzymes

Most chemical reactions do not occur spontaneously. Unless there are very high temperatures, pressures or energy input, the reaction will not take place. Conditions like this are not found in cells so another method is needed to get reactions to occur in cellular settings. Enzymes are biological **catalysts** made from globular proteins that are involved in metabolic reactions, enabling the reactions to take place at much lower temperatures and pressures than would normally be needed. They occur far faster than the same reactions without catalysts.

Location of Enzyme-controlled Reactions

Enzyme-controlled reactions can take place inside the cell (**intracellular**) or can act outside the cell (**extracellular**).

The enzyme catalase is found in almost all living organisms and catalyses the decomposition of hydrogen peroxide, H_2O_2, into H_2O and O_2. This intracellular reaction takes place inside the cell where the H_2O_2 first forms.

Amylase and trypsin are digestive enzymes. Amylase breaks down starch into maltose and trypsin breaks down protein into amino acids. Both are secreted by a cell. These are examples of extracellular enzyme action.

Activation Energy

Chemical reactions require an input of energy to initiate the reaction. Enzymes lower the **activation energy**, enabling it to take place. The higher the activation energy the slower the reaction. Lowering it causes an increase in reaction rate.

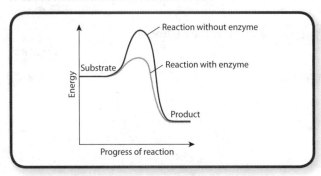

The reactions are extremely rapid, often being increased by a factor of 10 million.

The Lock and Key Model

Every enzyme has an active site. This is a specific region where the substrate molecule binds and is formed when the tertiary folding of the protein is completed.

In the lock and key model, the enzyme acts as a lock, with the active site the keyhole into which the substrate, the key, fits.

Once the substrate binds to the active site an **enzyme–substrate complex** forms.

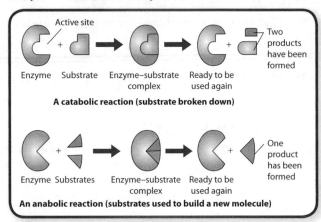

The complex breaks down and the products are released. The enzyme is free to catalyse another reaction.

Reactions that build new molecules are **anabolic** and those that break down molecules are **catabolic**.

For example:

- The breakdown of starch into maltose is a catabolic reaction.
- The formation of glycogen from glucose molecules is an anabolic reaction.

The Induced Fit Model

The induced fit model of enzyme action improves upon the lock and key model. Unlike a real lock and key, the active site is flexible. The substrate is not initially a shape match for the active site. The substrate itself interacts with the active site causing changes in the shape that enable it to fit in correctly. Once the products leave, the active site returns to its original shape.

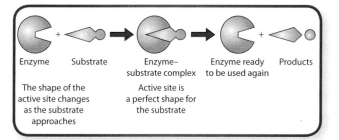

The shape of the active site changes as the substrate approaches

Active site is a perfect shape for the substrate

The induced fit model helps explain why non-competitive inhibitors work. They indirectly prevent the active site from changing shape in the required way.

Reaction Conditions

The rate of enzyme-catalysed reactions is affected by the following four factors:

1. concentration of the substrate molecules
2. concentration of the enzyme molecules
3. temperature
4. pH.

Non-protein Groups

Some enzymes require additional non-protein groups to make them work effectively. Once bound to the non-protein group they are said to be **holoenzymes**.

Co-factors

Co-factors are inorganic substances, such as ions, that have to be present for the enzyme to function correctly. Typically they modify the shape of the active site, increasing the rate of catalysis.

The mammalian form of the enzyme amylase catalyses the hydrolysis of starch to form maltose. To function correctly, it requires Cl^- ions as a co-factor.

Prosthetic Groups

Prosthetic groups are molecules or inorganic ions that are tightly or even covalently bonded to an enzyme. They alter the shape of the enzyme slightly.

Carbonic anhydrase is an enzyme that converts CO_2 and H_2O into bicarbonate (H_2CO_3) and protons (or vice versa). A single Zn^{2+} ion is held in place by three histidine residues (histidine is an amino acid). Again, if the zinc were not present the chemical reaction would not take place.

Coenzymes

Coenzymes are proteins that cannot catalyse a reaction themselves but can bind to the active site and enable the enzyme–substrate complex to form. Most vitamins act as coenzymes, e.g. ascorbic acid (vitamin C).

Effect of Concentration

As enzymes function by forming enzyme–substrate complexes it is logical that if there are too few molecules of either the enzyme or the substrate the reaction will not go ahead. If there are more substrate molecules than the number of enzymes then the number of available active sites becomes a limiting factor. The maximum rate of reaction will only be reached when adding excess substrate leads to no further increase in product formation.

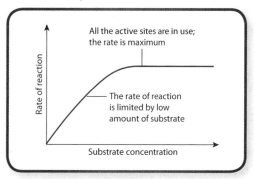

Effect of Temperature

The coming together of the enzyme with the substrate is a random process. The enzyme and substrate move randomly. As the temperature increases, the enzymes and substrates move faster (have more kinetic energy) and have a greater chance of colliding. The successful collisions are the ones where the substrate fits into the active site. At the optimum temperature, the number of successful collisions is at its highest.

Beyond the optimum temperature the heat energy starts to affect the shape of the enzyme. Bonds, such as the disulfide bridges that were formed during tertiary folding, break, altering the shape of the active site. This is a permanent change that cannot be reversed and is called **denaturing**.

At high temperatures well above the optimum there will be a large number of collisions between the enzyme and substrate, but they will be unsuccessful as the enzyme is now denatured.

The optimum temperature depends on the organism and its environment. Some bacteria can survive in hydrothermal vents, where temperatures are extremely high.

Low temperatures do not alter the enzyme structure, just reduce the number of successful collisions, due to decreased kinetic energy of enzymes and substrates.

The relationship between metabolic rate and temperature is often measured as the **temperature coefficient** (Q_{10}). If the metabolic rate doubles with a 10°C increase in temperature, then $Q_{10} = 2$.

Effect of pH

As with temperature, enzymes also have an optimum pH. Changes in pH can affect the shape of the enzyme as the acid or alkali interacts with the bonds formed during secondary and tertiary folding. If the shape of the active site is altered this will prevent enzyme–substrate complexes forming. Unlike the effect of high temperature, the change is not permanent. It can be returned to normal if the pH is adjusted back to optimum.

Enzyme Inhibition

A wide range of compounds can inhibit enzyme action. The effects of these inhibitors can be reversible or irreversible.

Enzymes can also have **competitive inhibitors** added. These are substances with a similar shape to the substrate and so can form an enzyme–inhibitor complex. Unlike the actual substrate, the inhibitor will not break down. The site will remain blocked, preventing the reaction from taking place. Competitive inhibition is temporary, with the inhibitor eventually leaving the active site.

Cyanide is an inhibitor of the enzyme cytochrome c oxidase, which is involved in respiration. Cyanide prevents ATP production as O_2 use is decreased. Cells can only respire anaerobically, leading to a potentially fatal build-up of lactic acid in the blood.

Non-competitive inhibitors can be added that affect the action of the enzyme without blocking the active site. This means the enzyme–substrate complex forms but the product formation is prevented. Often this involves a permanent change in the enzyme shape.

The action of non-competitive inhibitors led to the revision of the lock and key model after a biochemist wondered how a substance that was not involved in the active site could inhibit the active site. This led to the induced fit model of enzyme action.

Metabolic Pathways

Understanding the action of inhibitors is extremely useful. Reactions such as respiration and photosynthesis are often written as being a single chemical reaction. For example, for photosynthesis:

$$6CO_2 + 6H_2O \rightarrow C_6H_{12}O_2 + 6O_2$$

In reality this is a summary of what reactants started the process and what products were eventually formed. In cells there is a metabolic pathway with reactants being catalysed by an enzyme to form an intermediate product that then feeds into a second reaction as a reactant. Each step is mediated by a specific enzyme.

Many genetic disorders are caused by mutations that cause an enzyme to stop working, preventing the end point being reached.

Metabolic poisons (such as potassium cyanide) break the pathway and can potentially kill the organism.

Using metabolic inhibitors enables scientists to piece together the metabolic pathways in living organisms and can ultimately help in the creation of new medical treatments. Some medicinal drugs can be used to deliberately stop metabolic pathways, e.g. ritonavir, which is a protease inhibitor that mimics the target of HIV.

QUICK TEST

1. What is an enzyme?

2. Give an example of a catabolic process.

3. Give an example of an anabolic process.

4. Describe how a competitive inhibitor works.

5. Describe how a non-competitive inhibitor works.

6. Why is an enzyme denatured at high temperatures?

7. How does pH affect the active site?

8. How do enzymes affect activation energy?

9. What is a holoenzyme?

10. Give an example of a coenzyme.

SUMMARY

- Enzymes are globular proteins that catalyse metabolic reactions.
- Enzyme-catalysed reactions can be many times faster than the same non-catalysed reaction.
- Enzyme reactions can be intracellular (inside the cell) or extracellular (outside the cell).
- Enzymes lower the activation energy needed for a reaction to happen.
- The lock and key model is an explanation of how enzymes work.
- The enzyme is a lock, the active site the keyhole, and the substrate the key.
- When the substrate is attached to the enzyme's active site an enzyme–substrate complex forms.
- The complex breaks down and the products are released.
- The induced fit model improves on the lock and key model.
- The active site is flexible (unlike the keyhole in a real lock).
- The substrate itself induces a change in the active site.
- The enzyme–substrate complex is formed and the products then released.
- Co-factors, e.g. ions, typically modify the shape of the active site.
- Coenzymes are proteins that do not catalyse reactions themselves but bind to the active site, helping the formation of the enzyme–substrate complex.
- Enzymes are either anabolic (build new compounds) or catabolic (break down compounds).
- Increasing temperature and concentration increases the rate of reaction up to a maximum at which all active sites are in use, and vice versa.
- At too high a temperature the enzyme will be permanently denatured.
- High temperatures break the bonds formed in tertiary folding.
- pH changes the shape of the active site by altering the secondary and tertiary folding.
- Inhibitors can be reversible or irreversible.
- Competitive inhibitors attach to the active site.
- Non-competitive inhibitors alter the active site's shape from a distance.

PRACTICE QUESTIONS

1. An enzyme catalyses only one reaction. Explain why. **[2 marks]**

2. The lock and key hypothesis explains how enzymes work. An alternative hypothesis is the induced fit model. Describe the induced fit model and explain how it differs from the lock and key hypothesis. **[3 marks]**

3. Scientists have investigated the effects of competitive and non-competitive inhibitors of the enzyme cytochrome c oxidase. Describe competitive and non-competitive inhibition of an enzyme. You may use drawings to illustrate your answer. **[5 marks]**

Eukaryotes

All life on Earth is made of one or more cells. All cells have certain basic features in common, which suggests that all life on Earth shares a common ancestor.

Using **electron microscopes**, biologists can divide life into those organisms that have a nucleus (**eukaryotes**) and those that do not (**prokaryotes**).

The cells belonging to plant and animal life (including humans) are classified as being eukaryotic. A eukaryote is an organism whose cells have membrane-bound organelles, including a nucleus.

Eukaryotic Cells

A typical eukaryotic animal cell and plant cell are shown in the diagrams.

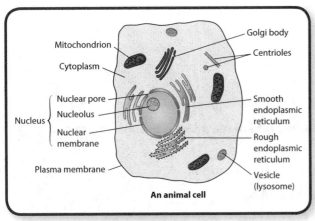

An animal cell

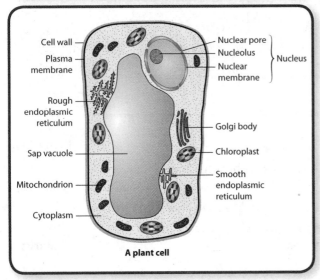

A plant cell

Diagrams of cells always show a cross-section of the cell. It is important to realise that the cell has a three-dimensional structure – the diagrams are of a plane cut into the cell.

Structures Found in All Eukaryotic Cells

Cell Surface Membrane
The **cell surface membrane** of a cell, often called the plasma membrane, is made up of a phospholipid bilayer.

Cytoplasm
The cytoplasm is the site of many chemical reactions. It is a semi-liquid medium that contains all of the cell **organelles** and the building blocks of all molecules needed to sustain life.

Nucleus
The purpose of the nucleus is to store the cell's DNA and all of the molecules including proteins and enzymes needed for it to be decoded and replicated. The nucleus is found only in eukaryotic cells. It is formed of a plasma membrane, called the nuclear membrane or nuclear envelope, and has nuclear pores to allow messenger RNA (mRNA) to leave and nucleotides to enter. DNA is contained within the nucleus but it is not stored as a single strand. Instead it is highly condensed, wrapped around special proteins (called **histones**), forming **chromatin**.

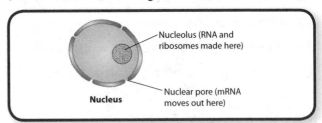

Nucleus

Within the nucleus is the nucleolus. This is an organelle that makes RNA and **ribosomes**.

Ribosomes
Ribosomes occur throughout the cell. They are found in very high concentrations on rough endoplasmic reticulum, as well as freely in the cytoplasm. Ribosomes are structures that enable the 'reading' of mRNA and the building of a protein through the interaction of transfer RNA (tRNA) molecules which carry the amino acids which will form the polypeptide chains.

Endoplasmic Reticulum

There are two types of endoplasmic reticulum, rough (rough ER) and smooth (smooth ER). The endoplasmic reticulum is a series of folded phospholipid membranes. On rough ER ribosomes are embedded on the membrane. Protein synthesis takes place here. With smooth ER the role is to synthesise lipids and to transport them away.

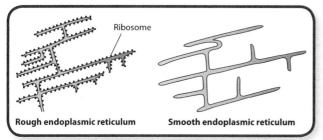

Rough endoplasmic reticulum   Smooth endoplasmic reticulum

Golgi Apparatus

The **Golgi apparatus** (also known as the Golgi body) is where important chemicals are packaged in a membrane so that they can leave the cell. The Golgi apparatus looks like a series of flattened sacs with **vesicles** budding off at the end. Many proteins, carbohydrates and glycoproteins could not pass through the cell membrane without being encapsulated in Golgi vesicles. Transition vesicles move the precursor materials to the Golgi body. Secretion vesicles carry the encapsulated materials to the plasma membrane. The vesicle then merges with the plasma membrane and releases the vesicle contents out of the cell.

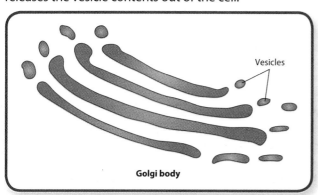

Vesicles

Golgi body

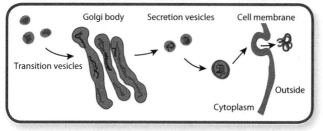

Golgi body   Secretion vesicles   Cell membrane

Transition vesicles

Outside

Cytoplasm

Mitochondria

The mitochondria are the organelles where aerobic respiration takes place. A mitochondrion is made up of a double plasma membrane which is folded on the inside to form finger-like structures called cristae. The cristae increase the surface area for reactions to take place. In the space inside the mitochondrion is a fluid called the matrix. Reactions take place in the matrix and on the membranes of the cristae, generating ATP, the main energy molecule in a cell. ATP is required for most processes in a cell that need energy.

Lysosomes

Lysosomes are a specialised type of vesicle. They are membrane bound and contain digestive enzymes. These break down proteins and lipids when they are not needed, and have to be contained otherwise they would destroy the cell.

Centrioles

Each cell has two centrioles. These are made of microtubules and the purpose is to aid in cell division. They move to the opposite poles of a cell during mitosis and meiosis as the spindle develops and then help pull the chromosomes into each half of the cell.

Structures Found Only in Plants
Cell Wall

Plants have a cellulose cell wall outside the plasma membrane. This provides structural integrity to the cell.

Chloroplasts

Chloroplasts are the sites of photosynthesis in a cell. A chloroplast has an outer double plasma membrane which encloses a substance called the stroma.

The light-independent reactions of photosynthesis take place in the stroma. In addition there are a series of membranes called thylakoid membranes that are arranged as stacks, called grana (a single stack is a granum). The second reaction in photosynthesis takes place in the thylakoid membranes.

Vacuole

Plant cells also have a large sap-filled vacuole. This is involved with storing chemicals and adjusting water levels in the cells.

SUMMARY

- All life is made of one or more cells.

- Organisms can be divided into eukaryotes and prokaryotes.

- Eukaryotes are organisms that have membrane-bound organelles, including a nucleus.

- Animals and plants are eukaryotic.

- A typical animal cell includes:
  - plasma membrane/cell surface membrane – **made from a phospholipid bilayer**
  - nucleus – **stores the DNA**
  - nucleolus – **organelle that makes RNA and ribosomes**
  - cytoplasm – **a semi-liquid containing organelles and the building blocks for metabolic reactions**
  - ribosomes – **structures that enable the reading of mRNA**
  - rough endoplasmic reticulum – **site of protein synthesis**
  - smooth endoplasmic reticulum – **site of lipid synthesis**
  - mitochondria – **site of aerobic respiration**
  - Golgi body/apparatus – **molecules are packaged into vesicles that can pass across the cell surface membrane**
  - centrioles – **involved in cell division.**

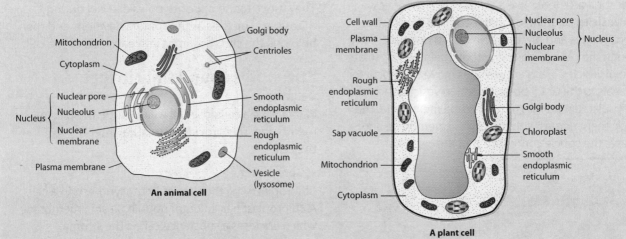

An animal cell

A plant cell

- A typical plant cell has the same organelles as an animal cell, but in addition has:
  - a cellulose cell wall – **tough and rigid, providing structural integrity and support, and a barrier to infection; also involved with transport of substances between cells**
  - chloroplasts – **site of photosynthesis**
  - large vacuole – **filled with sap; involved with storing chemicals and adjusting water levels in cells.**

1. How is the DNA held in a eukaryotic cell?

2. What role does the rough endoplasmic reticulum carry out?

3. What is the purpose of the smooth endoplasmic reticulum?

4. What is the Golgi apparatus?

5. Give three differences between plant and animal cells.

6. Draw a typical animal cell.

7. Draw a typical plant cell.

8. What is the main feature of plant and animal cells that distinguishes them as being eukaryotic?

9. Which organelle is the site of photosynthesis?

10. Where does aerobic respiration take place?

PRACTICE QUESTIONS

1. **a)** Draw the rough endoplasmic reticulum. **[1 mark]**

    b) How does the structure of rough endoplasmic reticulum differ from smooth endoplasmic reticulum? **[2 marks]**

2. **a)** What is the purpose of the nucleus? **[1 mark]**

    b) Draw a nucleus. **[3 marks]**

3. Draw a diagram to show how the Golgi body produces secretion vesicles. **[2 marks]**

4. Look at the diagram of an animal cell.

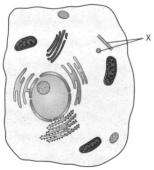

An animal cell

a) What features identify this as being an animal cell and not a plant cell? **[3 marks]**

b) What is part X? **[1 mark]**

Prokaryotes

Prokaryotes are organisms that do not have membrane-bound organelles. They include the bacteria. They are extremely small, only viewable using very powerful optical microscopes or electron microscopes. Their genetic material is not held in a nucleus, but floats freely in a loop.

Prokaryotic Cells

There are a wide variety of cell types and structures present in the prokaryotes.

A diagram of a typical prokaryotic cell is shown below.

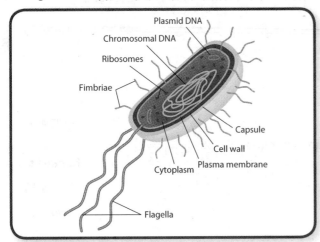

Structures Found in All Bacteria

Chromosomal DNA

One of the defining features of a prokaryote is that its DNA is not housed in a nucleus. The DNA of a prokaryote is typically in a single, circular chromosome, called a **nucleoid**. The chromosomal DNA is not associated with any proteins.

Cell Wall

The cell wall present in bacteria is made of **peptidoglycan** (also known as **murein**), which is a substance composed of disaccharides and amino acids. The purpose is to provide structural integrity for the bacterium while at the same time allowing transport of substances through to the cell membrane. The cell wall can absorb a stain called Gram stain. Cells with a thick cell wall absorb a lot of the stain and are identified as being **Gram positive**; those with a thin cell wall are **Gram negative**. Bacteria can be sorted into groups based on this difference.

Plasma Membrane

As with eukaryotes, bacteria have a plasma membrane made from a phospholipid bilayer. This is evidence towards all organisms sharing a single, common ancestor.

Cytoplasm

The cytoplasm is the site of all metabolic reactions in bacteria and contains all the microstructures, although none of them will be membrane bound.

Ribosomes

One distinguishing feature of prokaryotes from eukaryotes is the size of the ribosomes. Bacterial ribosomes float freely in the cytoplasm. These are smaller than the ribosomes present in eukaryotic cells. Measured using **Svedberg units** (S), the ribosomes can be sorted according to how far they move when centrifuged. Prokaryotic ribosomes are 70S compared to eukaryotic 80S.

Structures Found in Only Some Bacteria

Plasmid DNA

A plasmid is a smaller, circular DNA molecule that is separate from the chromosomal DNA. It can replicate independently and can be passed between bacteria. A bacterium may have none, one or many plasmids.

Capsule

Some bacteria have a capsule surrounding the cell wall. It is a gelatinous structure made from polysaccharides. It helps prevent bacteria from being ingested by **phagocytes** (a type of white blood cell), and also helps them adhere to surfaces.

The capsule also provides protection for the bacterium. The presence of a capsule can make a bacterium more virulent, i.e. become more likely to cause disease.

Flagella

Some bacteria have a single flagellum, some multiple flagella or some none at all. The flagella have a filament composed of a protein called flagellin and a hook that connects the flagellum to the bacterial cell. The flagella are used for movement.

Fimbriae

Also known as pili, fimbriae are thread-like structures that are present in some bacteria. They are involved with helping the bacteria to attach to surfaces, such as host cell membranes, and help them cause infections.

Viruses

Viruses are a type of disease-causing particle made up of a strand of RNA or DNA, a protein coat, and, in more complex viruses, a surrounding protein envelope. All viruses are therefore **pathogens**. Technically they are not a living organism as they cannot reproduce by themselves and they are not made of cells (they are acellular). They can only be reproduced by specific, living cells, the cell's own machinery replicating the virus.

Viral Shapes

Viruses can only be seen using electron microscopes. When they are observed they often have a wide variety of forms and shapes.

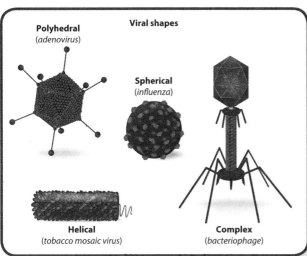

Viral shapes

Polyhedral (*adenovirus*)

Spherical (*influenza*)

Helical (*tobacco mosaic virus*)

Complex (*bacteriophage*)

With each shape of virus, the sole purpose is to ensure that the virus can enter the target cell and be replicated.

Viruses can potentially be manipulated. **Tobacco mosaic virus** (TMV) can be altered to transmit desired genes into cells, a process called gene therapy. The TMV has its own DNA removed and a new set of instructions are added that have the desired gene. The TMV injects the genetic payload into the target cell and the cell now treats the viral DNA as part of its own cell. It transcribes and translates the DNA as it would normally, producing the desired product (e.g. a protein that the patient's cell could not make as the cell's DNA was faulty).

In some parts of the world disease is managed by producing **bacteriophages** (viruses that attack bacteria) instead of using antibiotics (e.g. the Republic of Georgia).

Viruses also have specific proteins which are used to evade detection by the host immune system. The same identifying molecules can be used in vaccines to make the immune system respond to future infection by the virus.

Viral Structures

Genetic Material

The genetic material of a virus occurs as a core made from either DNA or RNA. The DNA or RNA is injected into the host cell and the host treats the genetic information as its own, transcribing and translating it to make new viruses.

Capsid

A protein coat surrounds the genetic material. This is made from polypeptides synthesised by the host cell according to the instructions in the core.

Attachment Protein

Some viruses have modifications to the coat that enable the virus to more easily enter the host cell. These are called attachment proteins.

Virus Reproduction

The stages in the virus reproductive cycle are:

1. The virus detects the host cell by recognising a marker protein on its surface.
2. It attaches to the cell using attachment proteins.
3. The virus injects genetic material (RNA or DNA) into the cell.
4. The cell reproduces the genetic material and reads it, creating new viral parts.
5. The virus leaves the cell, often using part of the cell membrane to complete its structure.
6. The virus will now infect another cell.

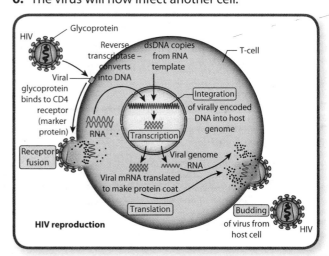

HIV reproduction

Using HIV as an example: this virus has proteins on its surface to enable it to bind to the target cell (an immune cell called a T-cell) by matching with CD4 protein marker on the cell surface. Attachment proteins ensure the virus stays attached to the cell. The HIV RNA is injected into the cell where it is replicated and converted into DNA. The DNA is then incorporated into the host cell's DNA. This is unusual and does not happen with most viruses. The DNA is then replicated and mRNA coding for new HIV is produced. This enters the cytoplasm where it is read and the HIV is assembled. The virus buds off the cell using the cell's own membrane to complete its structure. This is repeated millions of times, and the cell eventually bursts and dies.

SUMMARY

- Prokaryotes do not have membrane-bound organelles, including a nucleus.

- Bacteria are prokaryotic.

- All bacteria have:
  - **chromosomal DNA** – this is a circular loop of DNA (also called a nucleoid) not encased in a nucleus
  - **cell wall** – made of peptidoglycan (also called murein), for structural integrity and to allow substances to enter and leave the bacterium; the cell wall can be thick (Gram positive) or thin (Gram negative)
  - **plasma membrane** – made of a phospholipid bilayer; allows substances to move into and out of the cell
  - **cytoplasm** – the site of all chemical metabolic reactions, and houses the microstructures of the cell
  - **ribosomes** – smaller than those found in eukaryotes (70S instead of 80S); involved in protein synthesis.

- Some bacteria also have:
  - **plasmid DNA** – a circular DNA molecule that replicates independently and is passed on to other bacteria
  - **capsule** – a gelatinous structure surrounding the cell wall; helps to protect the bacterium from the phagocytes produced during the host's immune response
  - **flagella** – with a filament made of flagellin connecting them to the cell; involved in movement
  - **fimbriae (pili)** – thread-like structures that help the bacterium to attach to surfaces such as host cell membranes.

- Viruses are disease-causing particles.

- The shape of the virus maximises the chance of it inserting its DNA or RNA into the host cell without recognition by the immune system.

- Viruses have:
  - **genetic material** – a core made of DNA or RNA
  - **capsid** – a protein coat that surrounds and protects the genetic material; it is created by the host cell
  - **attachment protein** – enables the virus to target and attach to the host cell.

- Viruses reproduce by identifying a target cell via protein markers on the cell surface.

- Attachment proteins ensure the virus attaches to the cell.
- The genetic material is injected into the cell.
- The genetic material is read and used to make new viral material.
- The viral material is assembled and leaves the cell via the membrane.
- Parts of the membrane of the cell may be used to make the protein coat of the virus.
- The virus is free to infect other cells.

QUICK TEST

1. What is the main difference between prokaryotes and eukaryotes?

2. What is a nucleoid?

3. What is the bacterial cell wall made of?

4. If a bacterium is Gram positive, what does that tell you about the cell wall?

5. How does the prokaryotic ribosome differ from a eukaryotic ribosome?

6. What is a bacterial plasmid?

7. Why are viruses not technically alive?

8. What three features do viruses share?

9. How do viruses reproduce?

10. What piece of equipment is needed to view a virus?

PRACTICE QUESTIONS

1. The rod-shaped bacterium *Mycobacterium tuberculosis* is the cause of tuberculosis.

   a) Unlike eukaryotic cells, bacteria like *Mycobacterium tuberculosis* do not have cholesterol in their cell membrane. Cholesterol helps make the cell membrane more rigid. Despite the lack of cholesterol, the bacterial cells still have a defined shape. Explain why. **[2 marks]**

   b) A feature of *Mycobacterium tuberculosis* is that it is impervious to the Gram stain. This is due to an unusual waxy coating containing myolic acid in the cell wall.

      (i) What does the Gram stain indicate? **[1 mark]**

      (ii) Suggest why the inability to take in Gram stain could be an issue when identifying *Mycobacterium tuberculosis*? **[2 marks]**

2. Explain why a simple virus, such as tobacco mosaic virus, could potentially be used to treat certain genetic conditions. **[3 marks]**

Methods of Studying Cells

Cells are very small and cannot be seen with the naked eye. Instead biologists have to use microscopes to visualise the cells.

Optical Microscopes

Optical microscopes focus visible light through lenses to magnify the sample being observed. The **resolution** is the ability to distinguish between two objects as separate entities. At a low resolution it would appear that only one object was present whereas at high resolution the image would show two or more. A very high quality optical microscope enables resolution of parts of a sample that are as close as 200 nm.

A Schematic Diagram of a Light Microscope

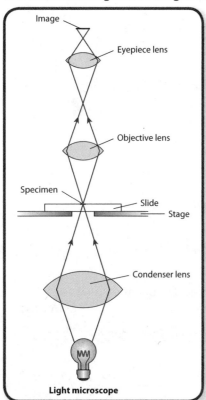

Light microscope

The specimen is placed onto a transparent slide which is held securely on the stage. Light is shone through the specimen having first passed through a **condenser lens** (to focus the light). An **objective lens** is used to magnify the image which is then further magnified by the **eyepiece lens**, which is used to focus the image on the retina of the eye.

Magnification

Overall magnification is a combination of the magnification of the objective lens and the eyepiece lens. This uses the following formula:

Overall magnification =
objective magnification × eyepiece magnification

For example, if the objective lens used was × 40 and the eyepiece lens was ×10 then the overall magnification would be × 400. The specimen would appear 400 times the actual size.

To calculate the magnification of an observed image the following formula can be used:

$$\text{Magnification} = \frac{\text{size of image}}{\text{size of real object}}$$

Preparation of Specimens

Many cell structures are colourless or match the colour of the surrounding organelles and microstructures. To make them easier to see, stains have to be applied, e.g. potassium iodide solution can be added to make starch grains stand out in plant cells or methylene blue added to stain nuclei. Sometimes more than one stain can be applied to make different subcellular parts contrast with each other. This is called **differential staining**.

Limitations of Optical Microscopy

The part of the electromagnetic spectrum that is visible to the human eye is in the range 400–700 nm. This means that optical microscopes can resolve structures as small as 200 nm under ideal conditions. In practice the highest magnification that yields usable results is ×1000.

Due to this limitation the finer ultrastructures of cells could not be observed properly or even at all. This led scientists to confuse artefacts with actual organelles. (An artefact is something that is not naturally present but occurs as a result of the preparative procedure.) To learn more about cell structures a method of seeing further was needed. This prompted the invention of the electron microscope.

Electron Microscopes

Electron microscopes use a stream of electrons directed at the specimen which is at an equivalent wavelength of less than 1 nm. This enables very high magnifications of up to × 250 000 and high resolution (to 0.5 nm).

There are two main types of electron microscope.

Transmission Electron Microscope (TEM)

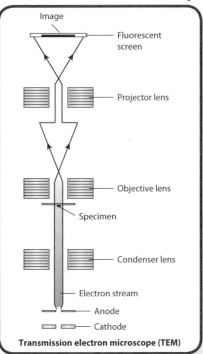

Transmission electron microscope (TEM)

The specimen is prepared and placed in a vacuum within the TEM. The vacuum is necessary as any molecules present in air would scatter the electron beam, distorting the image. Electromagnets that can bend the electron beam, in the same way as a glass lens can refract light, act as a lens. There is no objective lens as the eye cannot see the electron beam. Instead there is a projector lens that focuses the beam onto a sensor or fluorescent screen. A computer then interprets the data gathered from the sensor to create the image.

Scanning Electron Microscope (SEM)

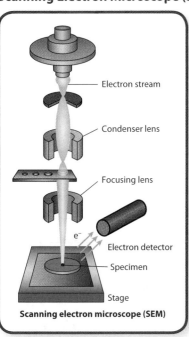

Scanning electron microscope (SEM)

A scanning electron microscope passes an electron beam over the surface of the specimen in a similar way to a computer scanner scanning a document. The beam dislodges electrons from the specimen. The reflected electrons are detected by a detector. A computer interprets the patterns of electrons and compiles an image of the surface of the specimen. This enables very high magnification and resolution of surface structures.

Preparation of Specimens

Both TEM and SEM require the specimen to be dead. This is because the electron beam is very intense and because of the need for a vacuum. The samples also have to be 'fixed' and dried thoroughly so that the electron beam does not destroy them.

With TEM samples, thin sections – 100 nm or thinner – need to be cut. SEM requires that the sample is coated in a thin layer of metal, usually gold or a mixture of gold and platinum.

As in light microscopy, specimens to be viewed using TEM often need stains added to help resolve different structures. The stains used need to interact with the relevant cell structure and absorb the electron beam. Salts of osmium and uranium are often used for this purpose.

Limitations of Electron Microscopy

Whereas optical microscopy can be used to observe living cells, the preparation of material for electron microscopy requires a dead specimen. When a specimen dies the structures start changing, e.g. when oxygen levels drop this causes mitochondria to change appearance. Lipids present in the cell start forming micelles (spherical structures). These are artefacts of the process that could be mistaken as an organelle or ultrastructure that is not present in the live cell. Telling the difference between an artefact and a real structure is difficult. Consequently there is still a lot of research into how to minimise artefacts with different fixation techniques.

Separating Cell Components

The whole cell is often not required for imaging. Instead the cell components can be separated and observed.

Cell Fractionation

The cell tissue is collected and then broken down (e.g. grinding, mincing, freeze-thawing, etc.) in an isotonic buffer solution (to prevent damage via osmosis). The samples are then kept at a low temperature to prevent damage by enzymes. The cells are filtered to remove any connective tissue.

Centrifugation

The cell mixture is placed into tubes and loaded into a **centrifuge**. The high speeds separate the cells based on their density. This allows pure samples of specific cell types to be removed. These can be experimented on or imaged.

The cells themselves can be broken down further using enzymes and a variety of mechanical techniques.

Ultracentrifugation

Broken cell mixtures can be put into an ultracentrifuge that spins at faster speeds (hundreds of thousands times greater than g, the gravitational constant) than a standard one. This causes different cell components to separate into layers based upon their differing densities.

Once the ultracentrifuge has stopped, the required cell fraction can be removed and stored or, after further preparation, used in electron microscopy.

SUMMARY

- Optical microscopes focus visible light through a series of lenses.

- Resolution is the ability to distinguish between two objects as separate entities.

- An optical microscope of the highest quality can resolve features that are 200 nm apart from each other and magnify by × 1000.

- An optical microscope consists of the following parts:
  - light source (e.g. lamp) – passes light through the specimen
  - condenser lens – focuses the light onto the slide and specimen
  - stage – supports the slide
  - slide – holds the prepared specimen
  - objective lens – magnifies the image
  - eyepiece lens – magnifies and focuses the image.

- The magnifying power is found by multiplying the powers of the objective and eyepiece lenses:

  Magnifying power = objective magnification × eyepiece magnification.

- The magnification can be calculated by dividing the size of an observed object by its size in real life:

  $$\text{Magnification} = \frac{\text{size of image}}{\text{size of real object}}.$$

- As parts of cells can be colourless or match the colour of the surroundings, cells have to be prepared before they can be observed.

- Stains which affect particular cell components can be added to differentiate those structures, e.g. potassium iodide and starch grains.

- The limits imposed on resolution in optical microscopy meant that new technology had to be created before scientists could observe cell structures in greater detail.

- Electron microscopes focus a beam of electrons onto the specimen.

- They can resolve to 0.5 nm (magnifying by × 250 000).

- With TEM, samples are placed in a vacuum. This ensures electrons aren't scattered by molecules in air.

- In SEM, a beam of electrons is reflected from the surface of the specimen onto an electron detector.

- Specimens are prepared by being 'fixed' and dried (so the beam does not destroy the specimen).
- With TEM, specimens are sliced into very thin sections.
- With SEM, specimens are coated in a layer of metal (usually gold or a gold–platinum mix).
- Salts of osmium and uranium are used to 'stain' structures to make them stand out from other structures.
- Cell fractionation separates cells from the cell tissue.
- Centrifugation separates the mixture of cells, enabling different cell types to be investigated.
- Ultracentrifugation occurs at faster speeds and separates cell components based on their densities.

QUICK TEST

1. What is meant by the term resolution?

2. How can the magnifying power of a microscope be calculated?

3. What is the formula for calculating magnification?

4. Why are stains added to cells for optical microscope viewing?

5. What is the maximum magnification and resolution of an optical microscope?

6. What is the maximum magnification and resolution of an electron microscope?

7. What is the difference between samples prepared for TEM and SEM microscopy?

8. Describe what is meant by cell fractionation.

9. What is the purpose of centrifugation?

10. A biologist wants to extract mitochondria from cells. What technique should they use?

PRACTICE QUESTIONS

1. Scientists use optical microscopes to look at a variety of samples. Look at the following samples:

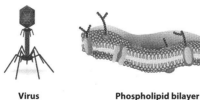 

Virus   **Phospholipid bilayer**   **Animal cell**

a) Which would not be suitable for looking at through an optical microscope? Explain your answer.   **[3 marks]**

b) How does the transmission electron microscope differ from a light microscope?   **[3 marks]**

2. The study of how cells work has been dependent upon the development of new microscopy techniques. Starting with the invention of the first optical microscope, suggest why our understanding of the cell has had to wait for new technology to be invented.   **[6 marks]**

Cell Division

Cells become differentiated to carry out specific roles in an organism, e.g. transmit nerve impulses in neurones, carry oxygen in red blood cells, contract and relax in muscle cells.

A cell can be viewed like a factory manufacturing products. Once differentiated the cell will need to synthesise the cellular organelles (the machinery) and molecules (products) needed to fulfil its role. Unlike a real factory the organelles will regularly be broken down into their component molecules which are then used to build new organelles and compounds.

Organisms grow by cells dividing to produce more cells. The process from the first cell to the formation of a new cell is called the **cell cycle**.

The Cell Cycle

The cell cycle is the coordinated sequence of events that take place during the life of a cell, from cell formation through to cell division.

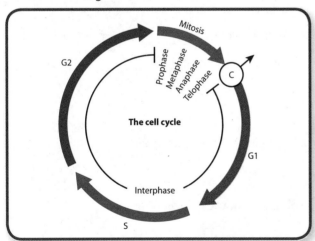

The normal life of a cell where it carries out its function is called the **interphase** (sometimes called G0). Many cells, particularly those that once differentiated never divide (such as red blood cells), will never leave the interphase. The interphase itself takes up approximately 95% of the entire cell cycle.

G1 Phase

Cells that are able to replicate will progress through the cell cycle. The first stage of the cell cycle is called G1 (the G stands for gap). During this phase the cell grows, making new organelles and proteins. It is here that cells that will not differentiate leave the cycle, spending their life in G0. The section of G1 that follows the G0 exit is where the machinery needed to replicate DNA is created. There is no need for cells that will not replicate to form this machinery, hence they leave the cycle before this point.

S Phase

In the S phase the DNA is now replicated (copied) by **semi-conservative replication**.

G2 Phase

The machinery that was created to replicate DNA is broken down by enzymes and new organelles are made which are needed for **mitosis**. In addition, the spindle (made up of microtubules) forms.

Mitosis

When the cell is ready to divide it moves into the mitosis phase. Mitosis is where the genetic material is separated into two separate nuclei. Mitosis leads to growth, tissue repair, and asexual reproduction in bacteria and fungi.

When a cell enters the mitosis phase, a series of events takes place.

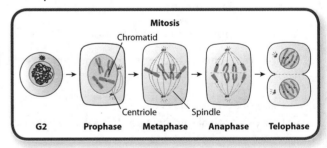

Prophase

This is the phase identified by the chromosomes becoming visible under a light microscope, with methylene blue stain added. The chromosomes are densely packed and form two **chromatids** joined by a **centromere**. The centrioles move to the poles of the cell, forming a spindle made of **microtubules**.

Metaphase

The nuclear membrane is broken down so there is no nucleus. The chromatids of each chromosome line up in the middle of the cell.

Anaphase

The spindle fibres connect the centromeres. The spindle fibres then shorten, separating the chromatids. At this point each is now a chromosome.

Telophase

The shortening of the spindle fibres pulls the chromosomes towards the centriole at the pole of the cell. The nuclear membrane re-forms around each set of chromosomes. The cell membrane narrows at the middle of the cell.

C Phase

This phase is cytokinesis. The cell membrane completely forms around the new cells. The cell divides into two daughter cells, each genetically identical to the other. Each daughter cell will now move through G1 in the next interphase.

Control of the Cell Cycle

The time taken to move completely through the cell cycle varies according to cell type. Cells such as those in bone marrow typically take around 8 hours to divide. The steps in the cell cycle are controlled by molecules called **cyclins** and **cyclin-dependent kinases**.

If this process breaks down, then the cell can undergo uncontrolled cell division. This can lead to the formation of tumours.

Binary Fission

Bacteria do not go through as complicated a cell cycle as eukaryotes. The cells replicate the circular DNA and plasmids (if present) and then this moves to the poles of the cell and cytokinesis takes place, forming the two daughter cells. Each daughter cell will have a copy of the circular DNA and a variable number of plasmids (or even none). Binary fission is a form of **asexual reproduction**. All offspring are genetically identical.

Meiosis

Meiosis is a form of cell division that leads to the production of haploid gametes, reducing the chromosome number by half. The process is very similar to mitosis and takes place in all sexually reproducing organisms. Ultimately meiosis follows DNA replication leading to two rounds of cell division producing four daughter cells, each containing half the number of chromosomes of the parent cell.

Meiosis I

The stages of meiosis I are prophase I, metaphase I, anaphase I and telophase I (with cytokinesis).

In prophase I the chromosomes line up as a homologous pair of chromosomes. One chromosome from each homologous pair is a maternal chromosome, the other is a paternal chromosome. Homologous chromosomes will have the same genes in the same order but may have different alleles (versions) of those genes. During prophase I a process called genetic recombination can take place.

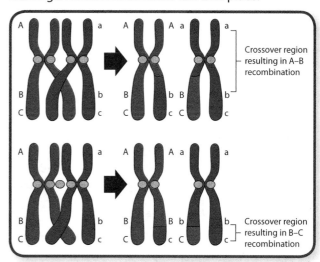

The crossing over ensures that there is greater genetic variation between chromosomes. The alleles carried on each chromosome will vary from the original maternal and paternal allele order.

In the diagram above the paternal chromosome (in blue) has dominant alleles A, B and C. The maternal chromosome (in red) has recessive alleles a, b and c. Crossing over leads to combinations of alleles that are different to those on the paternal and maternal chromosomes, e.g. Abc, aBC, ABc and abC. As there are thousands of genes on a chromosome, this leads to a wide variation in the alleles on the chromosomes formed in meiosis.

In metaphase I the chromosomes line up at the equator and in anaphase I the chromosomes pull apart to the poles of the cell. In telophase I the cell pinches apart and a nuclear membrane forms around each set of chromosomes, with cytokinesis leading to the formation of two new daughter cells.

Meiosis II

Prophase II starts with the two daughter cells. The nuclear membrane breaks down and the chromatids shorten and thicken. In metaphase II the chromatids attach to the spindle fibres and line up at the equator of the cell. In anaphase II the chromatids, now separate chromosomes, start to move to the poles of the cell. Telophase II leads to a new nuclear membrane forming around the new sets of chromosomes. Cytokinesis separates the cells so that there are now four granddaughter cells, each with half the number of chromosomes of the parent cell.

Independent Assortment

Independent assortment means that traits coded for by alleles are not linked together. The separation of the alleles held on different chromosomes is random, so the genetic make-up of alleles of the gametes is random.

Variation

The process of meiosis is completely random, so each cell will get one of the four possible versions of each chromosome. Due to the crossing over that takes place during prophase I the chromosomes will have different combinations of alleles compared to the original maternal and paternal chromosomes. This, together with independent assortment, means that the chromosomes in each granddaughter cell show far wider variation from the parent cell.

When a gamete fuses with another gamete of the opposite sex (fertilisation) the new individual will show considerable variation from the parents. This is a benefit of sexual reproduction over asexual reproduction. The offspring possess a greater variety of alleles.

SUMMARY

- The cell cycle is a coordinated sequence of events.
- The G1 phase is where new organelles and proteins are formed.
- Once formed, many cells leave the cycle and spend the rest of their life in the interphase (or G0).
- The G1 phase continues with the machinery for replication being made.
- Cells entering G0 do not need the replication machinery.
- The S phase is where the DNA is replicated through the process of semi-conservative replication.
- In the G2 phase the replication machinery is broken down by enzymes.
- Mitosis is where the genetic material is separated into two separate nuclei. It has four stages:
  1. Prophase – chromosomes become visible when methylene blue stain is added. The chromosomes form two chromatids joined by a centromere.
  2. Metaphase – the nuclear membrane breaks down and the chromatids line up in the centre of the cell.
  3. Anaphase – spindle fibres attach to the centromere and start pulling the chromatids apart.
  4. Telophase – the spindle fibres shorten, pulling the chromosomes towards the poles of the cell, and a nuclear membrane forms around both sets of chromosomes.
- The C phase is where the cells separate into two daughter cells.
- Each cell enters the G1 phase.
- The cell cycle is controlled by molecules called cyclins and cyclin-dependent kinases.
- Uncontrolled cell division can lead to tumours.
- Meiosis is where the genetic material is separated after two cell divisions (meiosis I and meiosis II) into four separate nuclei, each containing half the number of chromosomes of the parent cell.

- The phases of meiosis are similar to mitosis:
  1. Meiosis I – prophase I, metaphase I, anaphase I and telophase I (with cytokinesis).
  2. Meiosis II – prophase II, metaphase II, anaphase II and telophase II (with cytokinesis).
- During prophase I the arms of homologous chromosomes can cross over, resulting in the exchange of DNA sections between one chromosome and the other.
- Crossing over, together with the random allocation of each chromosome to the four granddaughter cells and independent assortment, means that the chromosomes present in each of the granddaughter cells will show considerable variation from the parent cell.

QUICK TEST

1. What is cell differentiation?

2. In which phase of the cell cycle are new organelles and proteins formed?

3. Why do some cells leave the cell cycle at G0?

4. What process happens during the S phase?

5. What are the four stages of mitosis?

6. What molecules control the cell cycle?

7. What happens if the cell cycle is not controlled?

8. How does meiosis differ from mitosis?

9. What is a homologous chromosome?

10. Describe what occurs during crossing over.

PRACTICE QUESTIONS

1. Look at the root tip squash:

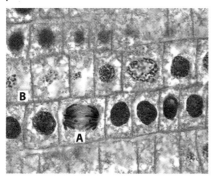

   a) At what stage of mitosis are cells A and B? Explain your answer. **[4 marks]**

   b) What are the stages of meiosis? **[2 marks]**

2. Why do most cells spend their lives in interphase? **[2 marks]**

Cell Transport

The basic structure of all cell membranes, from the cell surface membrane around a cell through to the membranes around the organelles in eukaryotes, is the same.

Cell Surface Membrane

The cell surface membrane is comprised of a phospholipid bilayer. Embedded within the phospholipid bilayer are various proteins that allow substances to move in and out of the cell as well as to identify the cell so that hormones can act upon specific cell types. The cell surface membrane is not a permanent structure. The components can move within the cell surface membrane and the cell can also produce different proteins if needed, changing the properties of the cell membrane. The cell surface membrane is a **fluid-mosaic** structure.

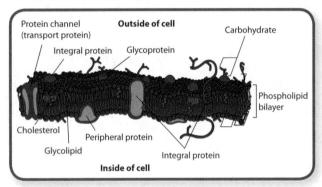

The cell membrane is comprised of the following components:

Phospholipids

Phospholipids have a hydrophilic (water-loving) head, a phosphate group and a hydrophobic tail. These are arranged as a bilayer, with the lipid tails in the centre and the phosphate heads on the outer surface.

Proteins

A number of proteins are part of the membrane. These can be **integral (intrinsic) proteins** or **peripheral (extrinsic) proteins**.

Integral (Intrinsic) Proteins

Integral proteins are a permanent feature of the cell surface membrane. A significant proportion of the DNA of a cell codes for these proteins. Integral proteins all have a section inside the centre of the hydrophobic section of the membrane.

Some integral proteins are **transmembrane proteins** that have channels that connect the extracellular surface to the cytoplasm within the cell. These are involved in the transport of substances through the membrane.

Carbohydrates can be attached to proteins to form **glycoproteins**. These integral proteins are involved in cell to cell interactions. The carbohydrate section extends into the extracellular fluid.

Glycolipids are formed by attaching a lipid to a carbohydrate. They function as markers for cellular recognition.

Peripheral (Extrinsic) Proteins

These are proteins that sit on the surface of the membrane. Some will also have small sections that enter the hydrophobic middle layer of the membrane. These are not permanent parts of the membrane. They are often involved with assisting the transmembrane proteins.

Cholesterol

Cholesterol is an important molecule that makes up around 20% of the cell membrane mass. Its role is to help maintain the integrity of the membrane by restricting the movement of the protein components of the membrane. It also, like glycolipids, helps in cell signalling.

Transport Across the Cell Surface Membrane

The nature of the phospholipid bilayer means that not all molecules will be able to cross it. There are a number of different routes for entry of molecules.

Diffusion

Diffusion is the movement of a substance from an area where it is in high concentration to one in which it is in low concentration. It requires no direct energy to occur – it requires only the random kinetic movement of molecules within the substance. The diffusion will continue until the concentration in both locations is the same. The greater the gradient in concentration, the faster the rate of diffusion.

With cells only those substances that are lipid soluble will be able to pass through the membrane via diffusion. The smaller the molecule the faster the diffusion. Oxygen, water and carbon dioxide can easily diffuse rapidly through cell surface membranes.

Hydrophilic molecules are less likely to pass through the membrane. Water is polar but as it is so small it will freely move across the membrane. Sugar on the other hand is too large. Charged molecules cannot pass through.

Osmosis
Osmosis is a special case of diffusion where water molecules diffuse across a **partially permeable membrane**. The concentrations of the solutes in the water affect the rate of osmosis. When a solute dissolves in water the water molecules tend to surround the solute, forming a shell. This lowers the amount of free water, effectively lowering the concentration of the water.

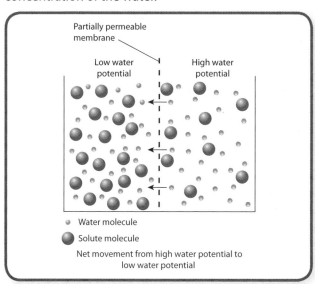

Net movement from high water potential to low water potential

Water potential is the measure of the concentration of free water molecules. The fewer free water molecules there are to diffuse, the lower the water potential and vice versa. Water therefore moves from an area where there is a high water potential to one where there is a low water potential. Osmosis is therefore defined as being the diffusion of water from a region of high water potential to a region of low water potential through a partially permeable membrane.

Facilitated Diffusion
Some of the integral proteins are channel proteins and carrier proteins.

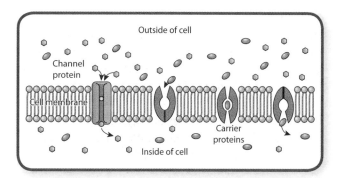

Facilitated transport, like diffusion, is a passive process. **Channel proteins** allow ions to pass through the membrane down a concentration gradient.

Carrier proteins are similar, but the substance that is being diffused first has to bind to a receptor on the protein. This causes a conformational (shape) change that passes the substance through the membrane.

With both types of protein, changes in temperature can have a dramatic effect on the ability to carry out facilitated diffusion, unlike with standard diffusion.

Active Transport
Where a molecule needs to move against a concentration gradient, from low to high concentration, energy is needed to transport the molecule. This process is required in cells which are accumulating high concentrations of molecules, e.g. glucose, amino acids and ions. The energy is supplied in the form of **adenosine triphosphate (ATP)**.

ATP is hydrolysed to form adenosine diphosphate and phosphate, in the process liberating energy that alters the shape of the carrier protein that then allows the molecule to move against the concentration gradient.

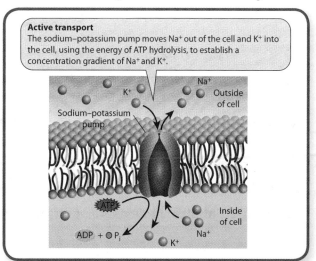

Active transport
The sodium–potassium pump moves Na$^+$ out of the cell and K$^+$ into the cell, using the energy of ATP hydrolysis, to establish a concentration gradient of Na$^+$ and K$^+$.

Co-transport

Co-transport is a secondary type of active transport. This is where one molecule can drive the transport of another molecule against its concentration gradient. For example, in the **ileum**, cells in the lining absorb sodium ions which drive the passage of glucose through as well. This does not directly involve energy. Instead it uses the **electrochemical potential difference** created by pumping ions in and out of the cell.

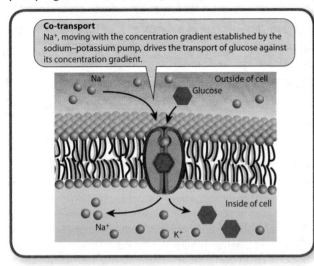

Co-transport
Na+, moving with the concentration gradient established by the sodium–potassium pump, drives the transport of glucose against its concentration gradient.

Na+ · Outside of cell · Glucose · Inside of cell · Na+ · K+

Increasing Transport Rates

Cells can increase the rate of transport by:
- increasing the surface area for substances to diffuse across
- increasing the number of channel or carrier proteins
- increasing the gradient in concentration or water potential.

QUICK TEST

1. Draw the arrangement of phospholipids in a cell surface membrane.

2. Why do the phosphate groups point outwards?

3. What is the difference between integral and peripheral proteins?

4. What are transmembrane proteins used for?

5. What is the purpose of glycoproteins and glycolipids?

6. Why is cholesterol an important component of cell surface membranes?

7. Describe the process of diffusion.

8. How does osmosis differ from diffusion?

9. Why do active transport and co-transport both involve energy?

10. What would happen to transport rates if the surface area of the cell was increased?

11. What would happen to transport rates if the number of carrier proteins was reduced?

12. How does the size of the gradient of substance concentration affect the rate of transport across the cell surface membrane?

SUMMARY

- **Cell surface membranes are comprised of a phospholipid bilayer.**
- **The phosphate parts of the phospholipids are arranged so the heads face outwards, towards the water (they are hydrophilic).**
- **The lipid tails are hydrophobic and point inwards.**
- **Embedded into the phospholipid bilayer are a variety of proteins that can move within the membrane.**
- **Cells can alter the amount and types of proteins present according to need.**
- **Integral (intrinsic) proteins are a permanent feature of the membrane.**

- All have sections embedded inside the membrane:
  - **transmembrane proteins** – proteins with channels connecting the inside of the cell to the outside (intracellular to extracellular)
  - **glycoproteins** – proteins with carbohydrate groups attached, required for cell to cell interactions
  - **glycolipids** – proteins with lipids attached, functioning as markers for cellular recognition.
- Peripheral (extrinsic) proteins are non-permanent and sit on the surface of a membrane.
- Some will have sections that pass into the phospholipid bilayer.
- They assist the function of transmembrane proteins.
- Cholesterol is an important peripheral protein, making up approximately 20% of the cell membrane by mass.
- It helps restrict the movement of the transmembrane proteins.
- Substances can pass through a cell membrane via:
  - **diffusion** – lipid-soluble substances move from high to low concentration
  - **osmosis** – water moves from an area of high water potential to an area of low water potential across a partially permeable membrane
  - **facilitated diffusion** – the substance has to pass through carrier proteins
  - **active transport** – substances are moved against a concentration gradient, from low to high
  - **co-transport** – as one substance is moved with its concentration gradient another is transported against its concentration gradient, driven by the first.
- Increased transport through the membrane depends on:
  - **surface area**
  - **number of carrier or channel proteins**
  - **size of the gradient of substrate concentration or water potential.**

PRACTICE QUESTIONS

1. Singer and Nicholson published their hypothesis for the structure of a cell surface membrane in 1972. Look at the diagram of the cell surface membrane.

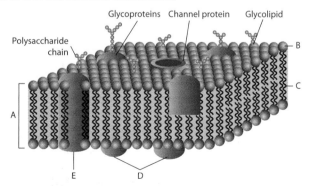

a) Name the structures labelled A, B, C, D and E. [5 marks]

b) What is the function of the glycoproteins and glycolipids? [1 mark]

c) Not shown in the diagram are cholesterol molecules. What are the functions of cholesterol molecules in a cell surface membrane? [3 marks]

Gas Exchange 1

Surface Area to Volume Ratio

The surface area to volume ratio is the amount of surface area per unit volume.

Visualising the organism as cubes:

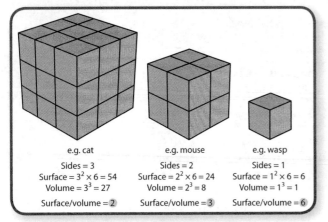

e.g. cat
Sides = 3
Surface = $3^2 \times 6 = 54$
Volume = $3^3 = 27$
Surface/volume = **2**

e.g. mouse
Sides = 2
Surface = $2^2 \times 6 = 24$
Volume = $2^3 = 8$
Surface/volume = **3**

e.g. wasp
Sides = 1
Surface = $1^2 \times 6 = 6$
Volume = $1^3 = 1$
Surface/volume = **6**

The smaller the organism or cell the higher the surface area to volume ratio.

Thus a single-celled organism has a larger surface area to volume ratio compared to a multicellular one.

Diffusion of substances will be faster if the surface area to volume ratio is high. This also places a limit on the maximum size a cell can grow to. If it is too big then there is a risk that substances will not be able to get to the centre of the cell quickly enough for metabolic processes, or be removed before they cause damage to the cell.

This can be demonstrated using agar blocks that contain **phenolphthalein** indicator and an alkali, sodium hydroxide. The blocks will typically be a red/pink colour. The agar is then cut into different-sized cubes. The cubes are placed into a solution of hydrochloric acid (HCl) and left for 5 minutes. The acid decolourises the phenolphthalein making it easy to determine how far the HCl has diffused into the agar.

After being removed from the acid, rinsed and dried, the cubes are cut in half and the distance the acid diffused in each cube is recorded.

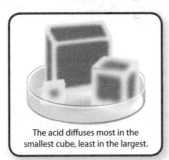

The acid diffuses most in the smallest cube, least in the largest.

Exchanges Across the Surface

Organisms need to take in required nutrients and gases and remove waste products. The process by which the substances enter and leave is called exchange. The internal environment of a cell or organism is different to the external environment. The exchange of substances takes place at the boundary between the external and internal environment. This is usually the cell surface membrane.

Ways Organisms Assist Diffusion

Diffusion is less efficient in cells with a small surface area to volume ratio compared to those with a large one. Smaller cells will enable faster diffusion. Increased diffusion rates can also be achieved by having extensions to the cell, e.g. cells lining the intestine have **villi**, which increase the surface area of the cell.

Maintaining a steep concentration gradient is necessary to ensure that substances move into or out of a cell rapidly. If the substances are allowed to equalise then diffusion slows and stops.

Having moist surfaces enables substances to move faster. Diffusion in a liquid is faster than in a gas.

The distance the substance has to travel is important. The thinner the material the quicker diffusion through it as there is a shorter diffusion distance.

Single-celled Organisms

In single-celled organisms, such as an amoeba, the surface area to volume ratio is very high. The path substances have to travel is very short. This means that exchange of gases and nutrients can be carried out solely through diffusion across the cell surface membrane. This means these simple life forms have no need for specialised cells grouped into organs that are concerned with exchange, as are required by much larger organisms.

Multicellular Organisms

Small multicellular organisms, e.g. liver flukes, continue to exchange materials via diffusion over moist body surfaces. There is no need for specialised transport or exchange systems. The surface area to volume ratio is still high enough to support diffusion.

As the organism increases in size, the surface area to volume ratio decreases. This poses problems for such organisms, which require enough resources to be supplied to keep up with metabolism. The immediate environment of most cells in a multicellular organism is bathed in a **tissue fluid**. This enables diffusion to continue at a fast enough rate to provide enough materials to meet the metabolic processes in the cells.

Gas Exchange

All organisms need to carry out cellular respiration, the process of liberating energy from glucose. Consequently, cellular respiration creates a demand for oxygen so there is enough energy for metabolism.

With single-celled organisms and small multicellular organisms (up to around 25 mm long) the oxygen diffuses into the organism down a concentration gradient, from high O_2 to low O_2. The gradient is maintained as the organism uses the oxygen for respiration. Waste CO_2 leaves by the same mechanism. The external concentration of CO_2 is very low compared to the concentration inside the body cells so CO_2 diffuses out of the cells.

Gas Exchange in Insects

Air enters an insect through openings called **spiracles** on the outside of its body. The spiracles are connected to tubes called **trachea**. The tracheae run deep into the insect's body, ending as **tracheoles**, which are fluid filled. Tracheoles are permeable and connect to cells inside the body, ensuring that all cells can exchange gases. When an insect is undergoing activity the fluid is forced closer to the cells that need oxygen, shortening the distance for diffusion.

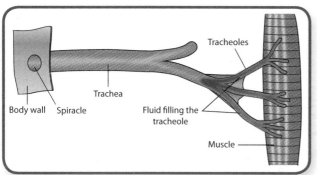

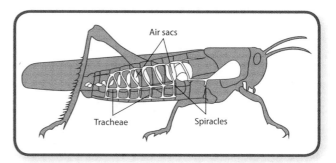

Some larger insects have air sacs that can be squeezed, like bellows, to help the gas enter and leave the spiracles.

The insect's exoskeleton is covered in an impermeable wax that prevents water loss.

Gas Exchange in Fish

Fish live in water and face the problem that the dissolved oxygen content of water is much lower than the amount of oxygen in the air. Fish use a ventilatory system to take in water and pass it through membranous structures supported by cartilaginous or bony struts, called gills, where gas exchange takes place.

Gills have a very high surface area to volume ratio. The gill is comprised of many gill segments that further increase the surface area for gas exchange.

Fish swim continually to ensure water flows over the gills.

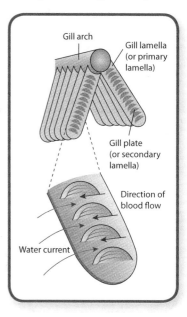

Counter-current Flow

To maximise the diffusion gradient for O_2 and CO_2 a counter-current flow mechanism is used.

A constant stream of oxygen-rich water flows past a fish gill in the opposite direction to the blood flowing through it. This means that the blood flowing through gill capillaries always meets water with an increasing O_2 content. The concentration gradient is always high for O_2 diffusing in and CO_2 diffusing out.

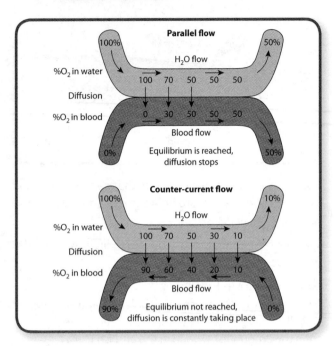

If the water passed through in the same direction, then the gradient would eventually disappear and the oxygen level would be in equilibrium (50%).

The haemoglobin in fish blood also has a very high affinity for oxygen. This means that the fish extracts as much oxygen as possible from water.

Gas Exchange in a Leaf

Plants require CO_2 for photosynthesis. They also require a supply of O_2, even though they can produce O_2 through photosynthesis.

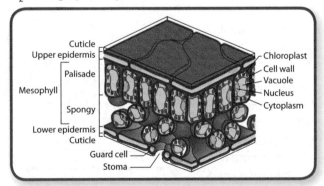

Leaves of **angiosperms** (flowering plants) have a number of **stomata** on the underside of the leaves. The stomata have guard cells either side which open and close to control gas entry and exit.

The cuticle of the leaf is waxy to prevent water loss through the upper leaf surface. Inside the leaf there are air spaces in the **spongy mesophyll** that provide pathways for O_2 and CO_2 to move through. The **palisade mesophyll** contains the main cells where photosynthesis occurs. Photosynthesis takes place in chloroplasts. There are chloroplasts in the cells in the spongy mesophyll, but the majority are in the palisade cells.

QUICK TEST

1. Why is surface area to volume ratio important to living things?

2. Why do single-celled organisms not need a ventilation or circulatory system?

3. Suggest why cells divide into two rather than just increase in size.

4. How does the size of a concentration gradient affect the rate of diffusion?

5. Give three other ways that the rate of diffusion could be increased.

6. Describe the route air travels to get to the cells deep inside an insect.

7. How are gills adapted for oxygen exchange?

8. Describe what is meant by the term counter-current flow.

9. How does air enter a leaf?

10. What is spongy mesophyll?

SUMMARY

- The surface area to volume ratio imposes a limit to the maximum size of a cell.

- The smaller the organism or cell, the larger the surface area to volume ratio.

- If the cell is too large then substances needed for metabolic processes may not get to where they are needed.
- Organisms exchange materials via the cell surface membrane.
- The steeper the concentration gradient across the cell surface membrane, the greater the rate of diffusion.
- Increasing the surface area to volume ratio increases the rate of diffusion.
- The presence of moist surfaces aids diffusion.
- The shorter the distance the substance has to travel, the greater the rate of diffusion.
- Single-celled organisms have a large surface area to volume ratio. Exchange of gases and nutrients is over the cell surface membrane.
- As multicellular organisms increase in size, the surface area to volume ratio decreases. There is a risk that diffusion alone will not provide enough materials for metabolism.
- One way to improve diffusion is to bathe cells in a tissue fluid; another is for cells to have projections such as villi found in intestinal cells.
- Gas exchange in insects requires a respiratory system to ensure all cells receive oxygen.
- Air enters an insect via the spiracles.
- Tracheoles connect to the spiracles and to the cells deep inside the insect's body.
- Some insects have air sacs that behave like bellows to aid the movement of air.
- Fish have to extract oxygen from water.
- Gills have a very large surface area to volume ratio, with gill segments increasing the area.
- Gills use a counter-current flow mechanism.
- Water flows through the gills past blood with the highest oxygen concentration. This ensures that there is always a diffusion gradient from the water to the blood because equilibrium is never reached.
- Leaves of angiosperms (flowering plants) allow entry of air through the stomata.
- The air moves into air spaces in the spongy mesophyll.
- Chloroplasts, the site of photosynthesis, are present in spongy mesophyll and in large numbers in palisade mesophyll.

PRACTICE QUESTIONS

1. Insects such as locusts breathe air.

   a) What property of the body wall of an insect prevents water loss? **[1 mark]**

   b) Suggest what would happen to the fluid filling the tracheoles if the insect were flying rather than resting? **[2 marks]**

2. a) Describe how a gill in a bony fish is adapted to maximising oxygen uptake. **[3 marks]**

   b) Water, unlike air, is very dense and has a low oxygen content. Describe how fish ensure that the maximum amount of oxygen is taken from the water flowing over the gills. **[4 marks]**

Gas Exchange 2

Humans are complex organisms that have a low surface area to volume ratio compared to smaller organisms such as insects and fish. As humans obtain oxygen from the air there needs to be an effective way of getting O_2 to the cells of the body, and expelling waste CO_2. This is achieved via the mechanism of breathing (ventilation) which provides a supply of air to the lungs.

Lung Structure

Lungs are sac-like internal organs that are connected to the outside air via a system of tubes. Gas exchange occurs in the **alveoli**, structures at the end of the smallest tubes, the **bronchioles**.

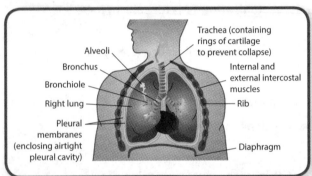

During ventilation, air enters the system via the trachea (the windpipe). This contains rings of cartilage that provide support, keeping the trachea open. At the end of the trachea the air splits into the left or right lung through the bronchi. Each bronchus branches into smaller bronchioles that then further branch into the alveoli (air sacs).

Structure of an Alveolus

The alveoli are arranged in clusters, each served by a bronchiole. Alveoli have elastic connective tissue in their cell walls, allowing the alveoli to increase and decrease in size. Each alveolus has its inner surface coated with a layer of moisture which contains a surfactant. Surfactants reduce surface tension and make it easier to inflate the lungs.

Alveoli are also very thin, around 5 μm thick. This reduces the pathway for dissolved O_2 to pass in and CO_2 to pass out, increasing the rate of diffusion. Capillaries surround each alveolus, bringing deoxygenated blood from the pulmonary artery and

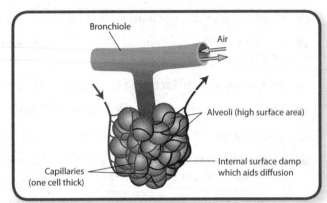

draining into pulmonary veins. This maintains the concentration gradient of O_2 and CO_2. The capillaries are one cell thick, which aids diffusion.

The ventilatory system in humans has a very large surface area to volume ratio. There are around 700 million alveoli in the lungs, which provide a surface area of around 70 m^2 (in an adult) which is a similar area to a badminton court.

Ventilation

The process of ventilation involves air being drawn into and out of the lungs via changes in pressure and volume.

The **pleural membrane**, which encloses the lungs, provides an airtight seal. If this is punctured then breathing will become impossible.

Inhalation

When air is inhaled (breathed in) the following steps take place.

1. The external **intercostal muscles** contract. This causes the ribs to move upwards and outwards.

2. The diaphragm, a muscle underneath the lungs, contracts, causing it to flatten.

3. The volume inside the pleural cavity has increased. Even though there will have been some air in the lungs, the same number of particles will occupy a larger volume, so the pressure will be lower.

4. The air outside the lungs is at a higher pressure, so will flow down a pressure gradient from high to low pressure.

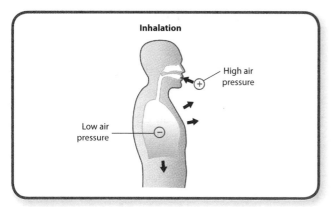

Inhalation

High air pressure

Low air pressure

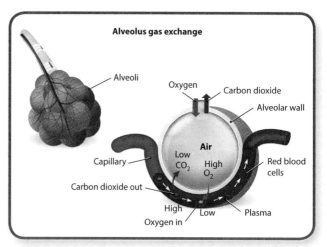

Alveolus gas exchange

Alveoli

Oxygen

Carbon dioxide

Alveolar wall

Capillary

Low CO_2

Air

High O_2

Red blood cells

Carbon dioxide out

High Oxygen in

Low

Plasma

Exhalation

Exhalation (breathing out) is the reverse process.

1. Intercostal muscles relax, leading to the ribs moving down and inwards.

2. The diaphragm relaxes, moving upwards, forming a dome shape.

3. The volume of the pleural cavity is now lower than before. The particles are now in a smaller volume so will be at a higher pressure than the outside air.

4. Air inside the lungs leaves down a pressure gradient, high to low air pressure. This time the high pressure is in the lungs, not the outside air.

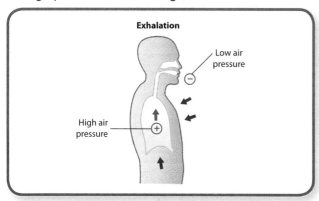

Exhalation

Low air pressure

High air pressure

The movement of air in and out of the lungs is purely due to pressure changes. It is not the same as the process of blowing or sucking.

Gas Exchange in the Alveolus

Atmospheric air contains 21% oxygen. Red blood cells arriving at the alveolus have lost most of their O_2 and so a diffusion gradient exists, with the O_2 diffusing across the alveolus cell membrane into the capillary and attaching to the haemoglobin. Carbon dioxide is

transported in the blood plasma. The blood arriving at the alveolus is high in CO_2. Atmospheric air contains approximately 0.04% CO_2; the percentage in the plasma is far greater, so there is a steep CO_2 diffusion gradient from the plasma to the inside of the alveolus.

Measuring Ventilation

Ventilation can be measured using a device called a **spirometer**. This device measures the volume of air in a single breath.

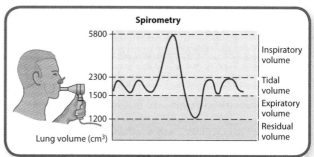

Spirometry

5800

2300

1500

1200

Lung volume (cm^3)

Inspiratory volume

Tidal volume

Expiratory volume

Residual volume

The **tidal volume** is the volume of air breathed in and out during ventilation. The breathing rate is the number of inhalations per minute. Typically a resting adult will breathe 12 to 20 times per minute. When measuring ventilation using a spirometer the tidal volume is first determined. The nostrils of the test subject are closed and breathing occurs normally through the spirometer. This establishes the tidal volume. The test subject is then encouraged to draw in as much as they can possibly draw in, the **inspiratory volume**. This volume will be more than the established tidal volume. The subject is then encouraged to breathe out for as hard and as long as possible. The volume exhaled will be more than the normal exhalation and is the **expiratory volume**.

The three volumes – tidal, inspiratory and expiratory – are added together to give the **vital capacity**. This is the maximum volume of air that can be expelled from the lungs after a maximum inhalation. A healthy adult has a vital capacity of between 3 and 5 litres.

The **residual volume** is the volume of the lung that will always contain some air. It is not possible to completely remove all air through ventilation. The vital capacity + residual volume represents the total volume of the lung.

Pulmonary Ventilation Rate

Multiplying the breathing rate by the tidal volume gives the volume of gas exchanged in a minute. This is called the **pulmonary ventilation**:

Pulmonary ventilation = tidal volume × breathing rate

The vital capacity, tidal volume, breathing rate and pulmonary ventilation measurements can all be affected by different conditions.

Age, sex and height can all affect normal measurements. Exercise can alter the measurements, as can a number of pulmonary disorders, e.g. lung cancer.

SUMMARY

- Mammals carry out ventilation using lungs.
- Lungs are sac-like internal organs.
- They are connected to the mouth via the trachea.
- The trachea branches into two bronchi.
- The end of a bronchus branches into bronchioles.
- The bronchioles are differentiated into alveoli.
- An alveolus is a grape-like structure that is surrounded by a network of capillaries.
- The capillaries are one cell thick, to aid diffusion.
- The alveoli have a very large surface area and are very thin (around 5 μm).
- There are around 700 million alveoli in the lungs, providing 70 m² surface area.
- The internal surface of each alveolus is coated in a layer of moisture.
- The moisture is a surfactant that reduces surface tension and increases diffusion.
- Ventilation involves inhalation and exhalation.
- Inhalation occurs when:
  - external intercostal muscles contract
  - the ribs move upwards and outwards
  - the diaphragm contracts, flattening
  - the pleural cavity volume increases
  - air flows into the lungs from high to low pressure.
- Exhalation occurs when:
  - intercostal muscles relax
  - the ribs move inwards and downwards
  - the diaphragm relaxes, forming a dome shape
  - the pleural cavity volume decreases
  - air moves out of the lungs from high to low pressure.

- Gases move in and out of the alveoli based on the concentration gradient.
- Ventilation is measured using a spirometer.
- The tidal volume is the volume of air breathed in and out in normal breathing.
- Inspiration and exhalation are measured by getting the subject to draw in their biggest possible breath and then exhaling.
- Residual volume is the amount of air that always remains in the lungs.
- Pulmonary ventilation rate = tidal volume × breathing rate.

QUICK TEST

1. Describe the route air travels from the mouth to the alveoli.

2. What are alveoli?

3. Describe how alveoli contribute to efficient ventilation.

4. Give two advantages of the liquid lining the inner surface of alveoli.

5. Describe the steps involved in inhalation.

6. Describe the steps involved in exhalation.

7. In which direction will CO_2 move in the alveoli?

8. Explain your answer to question **7**.

9. What is meant by the term tidal volume?

10. What is the residual volume of a lung?

PRACTICE QUESTIONS

1. The following passage is about the human ventilatory system.

   a) Fill in the missing words.

      The _____i_____ contains rings of cartilage to prevent collapse. When the human breathes in, the _____ii_____ contract and the _____iii_____ move upwards and outwards. The _____iv_____ flattens and moves down.   **[4 marks]**

   b) Explain why air moves into the lung when inhaling and why it moves out when exhaling.   **[2 marks]**

2. Emphysema is a disease of the lungs. The alveoli are progressively damaged, preventing them from taking part in gas exchange. It is caused by smoking. Suggest how this disease would affect tidal volume.   **[2 marks]**

Energy from Respiration

Oxygen Uptake

Oxygen is required for **aerobic respiration**. Knowledge of tidal volume can be helpful but it is even more useful for medical professionals to be able to measure a patient's oxygen consumption – how much oxygen is being used in metabolism. It's no good having a normal tidal volume if the oxygen being exchanged is not being respired. Oxygen uptake, or **VO_2max**, is the maximum rate of oxygen consumption. It is the most relevant measure of the effectiveness of the **cardiovascular system**.

It is measured through a subject undertaking incremental exercise on a treadmill or exercise bike to near exhaustion while wearing a spirometer connected to a device that records the actual O_2 and CO_2 concentrations.

Experimental determination of VO_2max is difficult as the test subject needs to be fit enough to carry out the test. If there are medical issues (such as respiratory or cardiac disorders) it could put them at a high level of risk.

Knowing the amount of oxygen the body requires enables scientists to work out how much aerobic respiration is taking place. This means the energy being used by the body can also be calculated.

Energy

The purpose of aerobic respiration is to liberate energy from glucose.

$$C_6H_{12}O_6 \; + \; 6O_2 \; \rightarrow \; 6CO_2 \; + \; 6H_2O \; (+ \; 38ATP)$$

glucose + oxygen   carbon + water
                dioxide

Adenosine triphosphate, or ATP, is the energy currency of organisms. It is derived from nucleotides and is formed from a molecule of ribose (the pentose sugar in RNA), a molecule of the base adenine and three phosphate groups:

This can be simplified to:

ATP is called a nucleoside triphosphate because structurally, it resembles an RNA nucleotide. However, the presence of the three phosphate groups conveys its vastly different function as an energy source.

Uses of ATP
There is only a relatively small amount of ATP present in the human body at any one time, on average around 250 g. The human body constantly hydrolyses and recondenses the molecule, effectively turning over an amount equivalent to the entire body mass every day.

ATP is used throughout the body in processes such as:
- **Metabolism** – ATP is needed for respiration, synthesising new molecules and active transport (moving substances against concentration gradients).
- **Cell structure and movement** – This includes assembly and disassembly of the cell cytoskeleton during mitosis and meiosis, and moving large molecules in and out of cells via **exocytosis** and **endocytosis**.
- **Cell signalling** – ATP is involved in nerve transmissions and signals inside cells using **phosphorylation**, where phosphate groups are attached onto proteins.

Hydrolysis of ATP
ATP can be hydrolysed to form adenosine diphosphate and an inorganic phosphate molecule:

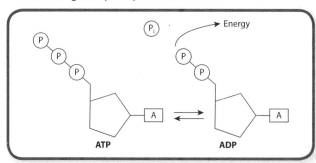

ATP   ADP

The reaction can be written as:

$$ATP + H_2O \rightarrow ADP + \text{inorganic phosphate, } P_i$$

The reaction is catalysed by the presence of the enzyme ATP hydrolase and releases approximately 34 kJ of energy. The ATP hydrolysis to ADP and P_i is coupled to anabolic reactions. Anabolic reactions are where new molecules are made from smaller molecules, consuming energy in the process.

Uses of P_i
The inorganic phosphate, P_i, released can be used to phosphorylate other compounds. Phosphorylation is the addition of a phosphate group (PO_4^{3-}) to a molecule. Phosphorylation can switch many enzymes on and off, altering their function and activity. The addition of P_i to sugars is the first stage of their catabolism. Sugars with a phosphate group attached can no longer diffuse back through their original transport protein.

Condensation of ADP + P_i
ATP is resynthesised by the condensation of ADP and P_i, catalysed by the enzyme ATP synthase:

$$ADP + \text{inorganic phosphate, } P_i \rightarrow ATP + water$$

This condensation reaction is coupled to catabolic reactions, those where molecules are broken down into smaller molecules that are either used to release energy or used in other anabolic reactions. It requires 34 kJ of energy.

The ATP is resynthesised during photosynthesis or during respiration.

Respiratory Disorders
Aerobic respiration can only take place when there is enough oxygen. If oxygen is in short supply, the body will initially move to using anaerobic respiration:

$$C_6H_{12}O_6 \rightarrow 2C_3H_6O_3 \; (+ 2ATP)$$

glucose   lactic acid

The amount of ATP produced is much less than through aerobic respiration, so cells cannot function if anaerobic respiration continues for too long.

If the lungs are damaged either through injury or through illness, the amount of oxygen taken into the body can drop. Alveoli are sensitive to the products in cigarette smoke. This reduces the ability of the alveoli to carry out gas exchange. Smoke also contains carbon monoxide which can bind preferentially to the haemoglobin instead of oxygen, reducing the carrying capacity of the blood for transporting oxygen. Cancer and diseases such as tuberculosis affect large areas of the lungs, reducing the lung capacity and the ability to take in enough oxygen.

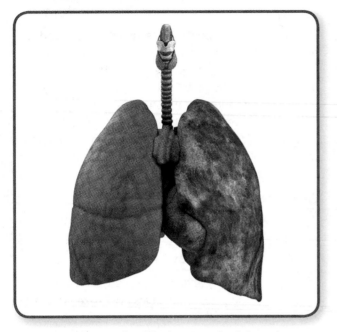

The image shows a healthy lung on the left and one affected by cigarette smoke on the right.

Emphysema causes the walls between alveoli to break down, reducing the surface area to volume ratio for gas exchange.

QUICK TEST

1. What is VO_2max?

2. Why is VO_2max a better way than tidal volume to measure ventilation?

3. Who would be unsuitable for testing VO_2max?

4. Draw a molecule of ATP.

5. How does ATP differ from a DNA adenine nucleotide?

6. Give the three main ways ATP is used in the body.

7. Write the equation for the hydrolysis of ATP.

8. What is inorganic phosphate used for?

9. In terms of energy, why is anaerobic respiration not as useful as aerobic?

10. How does lung cancer affect oxygen uptake?

SUMMARY

- Measuring actual O_2 consumption gives an indication of how much energy is being used by the body.

- VO_2max is a measure of the maximum rate of oxygen consumption.

- It measures actual O_2 consumption rather than just the volume of air breathed in.

- Testing VO_2max requires that the person being tested is fit and healthy.

- The person exercises to near exhaustion while wearing a spirometer.

- Aerobic respiration is glucose + oxygen $\rightarrow$ carbon dioxide + water (+ 38ATP).

- $C_6H_{12}O_6 + 6O_2 \rightarrow 6CO_2 + 6H_2O$ (+ 38ATP).

- An ATP molecule can be represented as:

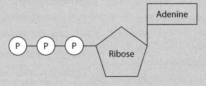

- Structurally it is very similar to an RNA nucleotide but its three phosphates give it a very different function, as an energy source rather than a component of RNA.

- The body hydrolyses and condenses an amount of ATP equivalent to the mass of the whole body every day.
- ATP is used for:
  - metabolism
  - cell structure and movement
  - cell signalling.
- Hydrolysis of ATP leads to the formation of ADP + inorganic phosphate, P_i, releasing 34 kJ in the process.
- $ATP + H_2O \rightarrow ADP$ + inorganic phosphate, P_i.
- Condensation of ADP + P_i to form ATP takes in 34 kJ.
- ADP + inorganic phosphate, $P_i \rightarrow ATP + H_2O$.
- P_i is used to phosphorylate other compounds, such as sugars.
- Respiratory disorders affect the amount of energy available for metabolism in the body.
- Anaerobic respiration is glucose $\rightarrow$ lactic acid and yields only 2 ATP, so is very inefficient.
- $C_6H_{12}O_6 \rightarrow 2C_3H_6O_3$ (+ 2ATP).
- Lung damage or injury reduces the amount of oxygen taken in.
- Cigarette smoke contains carbon monoxide which reduces the carrying capacity for oxygen.
- Damage to the lungs from diseases such as tuberculosis and cancer reduces the surface area available for gas exchange.
- Emphysema is a condition where the walls of alveoli break down, leading to much reduced surface area, so gas exchange is reduced.

PRACTICE QUESTIONS

1. Cyclin-dependent kinase (CDK) helps manage the cell cycle. The enzyme only becomes active when it binds to another enzyme called cyclin. At the same time, ATP is required to phosphorylate the target protein.

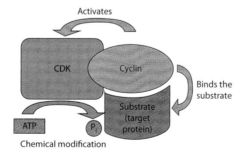

a) Explain what is meant by the term phosphorylate. [2 marks]

b) What type of reaction does ATP undergo in this reaction? [1 mark]

c) The CDK–cyclin complex initiates the next stage of cell division. Explain what would happen if the CDK protein could not be activated by ATP. [1 mark]

d) Once the CDK–cyclin complex has activated a protein, the ATP has to be re-formed. Write the reaction that shows how ATP is re-generated. [1 mark]

Mass Transport

Organisms with a large surface area to volume ratio can absorb substances through the process of diffusion. Once the substances, such as oxygen, have diffused into the cell they can be used for metabolism. If the organism is multicellular and above a certain size, then there is a high chance that the substances will not be able to reach the cells in time. In the same way, wastes produced by the cells would not be able to be removed quickly enough and they could then prevent metabolic processes happening. In these organisms, mechanisms have evolved to ensure that the substances reach their destination and waste products are removed. Mass transport systems ensure that all the substances move in the same direction and at the same speed. A wide variety of mass transport systems are found in large multicellular organisms, e.g. the mammalian **circulatory system**, the mammalian **lymphatic system** and the **vascular system** of plants.

With the formation of mass transport systems, other functions are enabled. Waste materials can be transported, as well as chemicals used in cell signalling (e.g. hormones) and immune responses.

The greater the metabolic rate, the greater the demand placed on mass transport as large quantities of substances have to be moved efficiently and effectively to all cells making up the organism.

Types of Circulatory System
The circulatory system in animals is an example of a mass transport system. There are two types of circulatory system, open and closed. These often reflect the complexity of the organism.

Open Circulation
Open circulatory systems are common in crustaceans, insects, molluscs and other invertebrates. **Haemolymph**, a blood-like substance, leaves a heart and can remain away from the heart for some time. It does not circulate – it is contained in the body cavity. It also allows hydraulic control of the body or parts of the body (e.g. wings in a butterfly after emerging from the chrysalis). Heat can be removed very efficiently, which means insects can survive in very hot environments.

Closed Circulation
Closed systems are where the blood is kept in a loop. The blood cells cannot escape the blood vessels (unless they are broken or cut). Organisms with closed circulatory systems have a finer control over where the blood flows, by contracting or dilating blood vessels. They can also increase blood pressure to increase the transport when necessary.

Insect Circulation
Haemolymph is pumped by a dorsal, tube-shaped heart into the **haemocoel** (body cavity) and surrounds all cells. Haemolymph returns through openings called **ostia**. The haemolymph differs from blood by typically not having blood cells or respiratory pigments for oxygen. This is because oxygen is transported by the tracheal system instead. It is 90% plasma, with a high concentration of amino acids, proteins and sugars. The remaining 10% is comprised of different cell types (haemocytes) that are involved in clotting and immune defence.

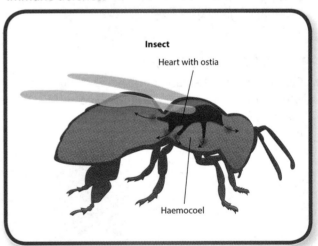

Insect
Heart with ostia
Haemocoel

Earthworm Circulation
Earthworms have a closed circulatory system, but also fluid in the coelom that can carry oxygen and food. Oxygen diffuses across the outer surface into the coelom fluid. Earthworms have five blood vessels that act like hearts. These pump blood, containing cells and haemoglobin with dissolved gases, through the two main blood vessels.

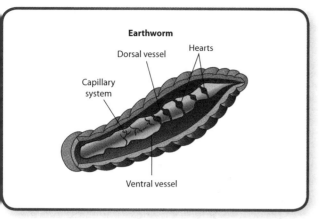

Earthworm

Dorsal vessel
Hearts
Capillary system
Ventral vessel

Fish Circulation

Fish have a single, closed circulatory system. This means that the blood flows through the heart once per circuit of the body. Blood is pumped from the heart to the gills, where it picks up O_2 and loses CO_2. The blood pressure drops, having passed through the gills. This means that the rate of delivery of O_2 to the body cells is not as high as it could be.

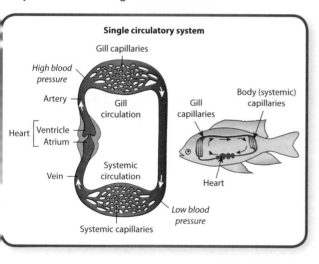

Single circulatory system

Gill capillaries
High blood pressure
Artery
Gill circulation
Gill capillaries
Body (systemic) capillaries
Heart [Ventricle / Atrium]
Vein
Systemic circulation
Heart
Low blood pressure
Systemic capillaries

Mammalian Circulatory System

Mammals (and birds) have a double, closed circulatory system with a heart divided into two halves. Double circulation means that the blood passes through the heart twice for every circuit of the body.

In a double circulation there are two regions that blood flows through. The first runs through the lungs and is called the **pulmonary circuit**. The other runs through the rest of the body and is called the **systemic circuit**. High blood pressures can build up to meet increased metabolic demands (e.g. during exercise).

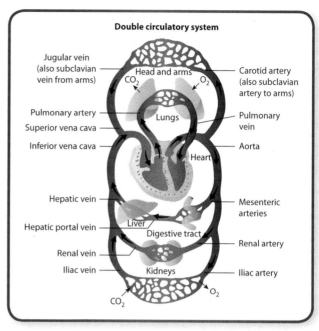

Double circulatory system

Jugular vein (also subclavian vein from arms)
Head and arms
CO_2
O_2
Carotid artery (also subclavian artery to arms)
Pulmonary artery
Lungs
Pulmonary vein
Superior vena cava
Inferior vena cava
Aorta
Heart
Hepatic vein
Mesenteric arteries
Hepatic portal vein
Liver
Digestive tract
Renal artery
Renal vein
Iliac vein
Kidneys
Iliac artery
CO_2
O_2

Blood Vessels

The mammalian closed circulatory system relies on blood vessels to transport the blood through. These have different structures, dependent upon their function.

Arteries

Arteries are vessels that transport blood at high pressure away from the heart to the capillaries within the tissues.

They have thick walls to cope with the pressure; the arteries close to the heart have the thickest walls. The wall of an artery is made of elastic and connective tissue (such as collagen) and is called the **tunica externa**.

The middle layer of the artery (the **tunica media**) is comprised of layers of elastic fibres and smooth muscle tissue to allow the artery to stretch and contract. On the inside of the artery is a thin layer of **squamous endothelium** (very thin cells). The centre

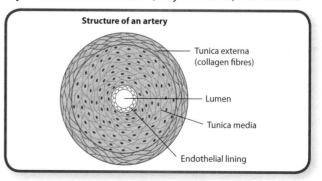

Structure of an artery

Tunica externa (collagen fibres)
Lumen
Tunica media
Endothelial lining

of the artery is the **lumen**. It is narrow to increase pressure. As the blood travels at high pressure, there is no need for valves in arteries as the force of the blood ensures it travels in one direction only.

Veins

In veins blood pressure is greatly reduced. This means veins do not need protection from high pressure.

Compared to arteries veins have a thin tunica externa layer made of connective tissue (collagen) and a thinner tunica media of elastic and smooth muscle fibres. The inside of the vein is lined with a thin layer of squamous endothelium.

Veins also have one-way semi-lunar valves that prevent the backflow of blood, which is more likely to occur due to the low pressure. If blood direction reverses, the valve is forced shut, preventing the blood from moving backwards.

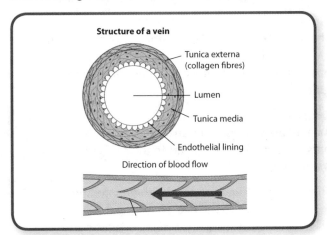

Structure of a vein

- Tunica externa (collagen fibres)
- Lumen
- Tunica media
- Endothelial lining

Direction of blood flow

Capillaries

The capillaries are the smallest blood vessel. They are small, thin tubes that are made of **endothelial tissue**, one cell thick.

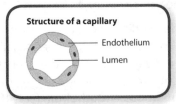

Structure of a capillary

- Endothelium
- Lumen

This gives a smaller diffusion pathway. The diameter of the capillary is around 4–10 μm. Red blood cells are around 7–8 μm wide so can only just pass through. This means that blood flow through the capillaries is very slow (around 1 mm/s). This slow passage gives time for exchange of gases and nutrients to and from the cells.

Capillaries form large networks around tissues and organs. The higher the metabolic rate, the more extensive the network.

Connecting to Capillaries

The arteries and veins are connected by smaller connecting vessels called arterioles and venules, respectively.

Arterioles

Small arteries branch into smaller vessels, arterioles, which have muscular walls usually comprised of only one to two layers of smooth muscle. They regulate the flow of blood into different tissues, branching into the capillaries in the capillary beds.

Venules

Blood that leaves a capillary bed first enters the venules. Like the arterioles, these connect the capillaries to a main blood vessel. Venules connect to the veins.

QUICK TEST

1. Why do organisms have mass transport systems?

2. What is the name of the blood-like substance transported in open circulatory systems?

3. Give the names of two groups of animals which have open circulatory systems.

4. What are two advantages of an open circulatory system?

5. What is the composition of haemolymph?

6. How does a closed circulatory system differ from an open one?

7. What happens to the blood pressure in fish as the blood moves around the fish's body?

8. What are two advantages of the double circulatory system present in mammals?

9. Draw the structure of an artery, vein and capillary.

10. What is the purpose of valves in veins?

SUMMARY

- Mass transport systems allow substances required for metabolism to be moved from the exterior environment to deep inside an organism.
- In open circulatory systems, a blood-like substance (the haemolymph) leaves a heart.
- The haemolymph does not circulate. It allows hydraulic control of body parts and removes heat efficiently.
- Closed circulatory systems involve blood leaving and returning to the heart in a loop.
- Blood cannot leave the tubes of the circulatory system (unless they are cut).
- Organisms can dilate or contract blood vessels, giving fine tuning of the system.
- Blood pressure can be increased to increase blood flow when needed.
- Insect circulation involves haemolymph being pumped into the haemocoel.
- Haemolymph returns through openings called ostia.
- Haemolymph is 90% plasma, with amino acids, proteins and sugars.
- The remaining 10% is comprised of haemocytes used for clotting and defence.
- Earthworm circulation is closed.
- Earthworms also have a fluid in the coelom that carries oxygen and food.
- Fish have a single, closed circulation.
- Blood flows through the heart once for every circuit of the body.
- Blood pressure decreases as it moves through the circuit, from the heart to the gills.
- Mammals have a double circulatory system.
- Blood passes from the heart to the lungs and then returns.
- It then passes to the rest of the body.
- Arteries transport blood at a high pressure away from the heart.
- They have a thick tunica externa and tunica media and a small lumen.
- Veins transport blood at low pressure to the heart.
- They have valves to prevent backflow of blood.
- The tunica externa is thinner, as is the tunica media, but the lumen is large.
- Capillaries are the smallest blood vessel and are made of endothelial tissue one cell thick.
- Arterioles and venules transport blood to and from capillary beds.

PRACTICE QUESTIONS

1. **a)** Using your knowledge of the structure of veins, suggest what must have failed in the veins of someone suffering from varicose veins and why the symptoms (bulges in the vein visible through the skin) occur. **[3 marks]**

   b) How does the circulation of a human differ from that in a fish? **[2 marks]**

Transporting Blood

Blood Composition

Blood is a complex liquid that transports a wide variety of substances – nutrients, waste substances, gases, hormones and components of the immune system. It is involved in temperature regulation through heat distribution. It defends against infections and clots to prevent blood loss if a vessel is broken or cut.

It is made up of cellular components suspended in a straw-coloured solution called **plasma**.

Plasma

Between 50 and 60% of the total blood volume is made up of plasma, which is the non-cellular part of the blood. Water makes up the majority of plasma (91%). It contains proteins, **electrolytes**, hormones and dissolved gases, such as CO_2. The water in the blood transports platelets and blood cells (red and white), helps distribute heat and gives the blood its volume.

Substances Transported in Plasma

The main substances transported in plasma are:

- **Proteins** – some are used to buffer the pH of the blood. The majority of the protein in the blood is **serum albumin**. It binds a variety of ions, hormones and fatty acids travelling in the blood. Its main function is to regulate **oncotic pressure** (osmotic pressure in blood).
- **Water** – dissolves substances for transport.
- **Glucose** – needed for respiration.
- **Lipids** – triglycerides and fatty acids needed for respiration and for membranes.
- **Amino acids** – needed to assemble new proteins or for respiration.
- **Salts** – adjust the water potential of blood so water is not lost through osmosis.
- **Hormones** – chemicals that act as messengers.
- **Antigens** – substances that are recognised by the white blood cells and induce an immune response.
- **Antibodies** – produced by **lymphocytes** (a type of white blood cell) to destroy **antigens**.
- **Urea** – a waste molecule made in the liver from the breakdown of excess amino acids.

Cellular Components

The remaining constituents of blood are the cellular components. These are the red blood cells (which make up the majority of the cellular components, 97–98%). The red blood cells transport O_2 bound to haemoglobin and a very small amount of CO_2 generated through respiration (not from ventilation). The remaining 2–3% are white blood cells (part of the immune system) and platelets (small membrane-bound cell fragments that are important in clotting).

Red Blood Cells

Approximately 96% of the dry content of a mammalian red blood cell is made up of haemoglobin. The presence of haemoglobin in red blood cells increases the carrying capacity of O_2 by around 70 times compared to O_2 dissolved in plasma. Having haemoglobin is very effective in transporting O_2.

Haemoglobin

Many animals are adapted to their environment by possessing different haemoglobins.

Haemoglobins are a group of globular protein molecules that transport oxygen in the red blood cells of all vertebrates as well as the tissues of some invertebrates. This points to a common ancestry between all vertebrates.

Haemoglobin A is a quaternary globular protein. It is made up, in humans, of four subunits. These are identified as being $\alpha_2\beta_2$, i.e. two α units and two β units. In addition, there are four non-protein haem prosthetic groups tightly associated to the protein.

Carbonic Anhydrase

Carbonic anhydrases are a group of enzymes that catalyse the conversion of carbon dioxide and water into bicarbonate (HCO_3^-) and protons (H^+ ions). This is a reversible reaction. They are useful for maintaining the acid–base balance in the blood and tissues as well as transporting carbon dioxide out of tissues.

For example:

$$CO_2 + H_2O \xrightarrow{\text{Carbonic anhydrase}} H_2CO_3 \rightarrow HCO_3^- + H^+$$

This reaction is extremely fast, limited only by the diffusion rate of the water and CO_2.

The reaction taking place inside the alveoli in the lungs, or inside plant cells, is the reverse:

$$HCO_3^- + H^+ \rightarrow H_2CO_3 \rightarrow CO_2 + H_2O$$

Oxygen Dissociation Curves

Oxygen dissociation curves can be plotted to show how haemoglobins and other pigments can bind to oxygen.

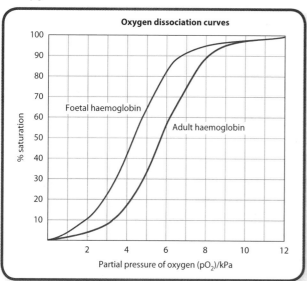

The position of foetal haemoglobin on the left of maternal haemoglobin means that foetal haemoglobin becomes saturated with oxygen at the lower partial pressures of oxygen found in the placenta compared to in the mother's lungs.

Tissue Fluid

For diffusion to take place effectively, cells of tissues need to be surrounded by a fluid. This is an extracellular fluid called **tissue or interstitial fluid**. It is found in the spaces (or interstices) between cells. It is very similar in composition to plasma. It lacks the materials that cannot pass from the capillary to the tissue bed (e.g. albumin protein, red and white blood cells, fibrinogen).

Capillary Beds

All cells need to be close to a capillary. Tissues are surrounded by a network of capillaries, called a **capillary bed**. Blood moves from the arterioles to the capillaries. Some proteins in the capillaries are unable to leave the capillaries. This creates a situation where

the water potential inside the capillary is less than the water potential in the tissue, the oncotic pressure. Consequently water would be expected to move from the tissue back into the capillary. Even though the blood pressure is lower, there is still enough pressure (called hydrostatic pressure) to force the plasma through the pores in the capillaries into the tissue fluid against the oncotic pressure. Water, ions, hormones and small solutes can move into the tissue fluid and consequently into the cells.

At the other end of the capillary bed, tissue fluid containing dissolved waste products moves into the pores of capillaries leading to the venules, becoming plasma again.

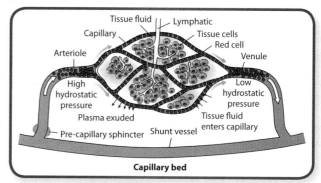

Capillary bed

A pre-capillary **sphincter** at the start of the capillary bed can be closed temporarily, restricting blood movement through the capillary bed. Blood travels in a shunt vessel instead.

Lymphatic System

Mammals have another transport network, called the lymphatic system. It is involved in the immune system. Lymphatic vessels from this system connect to the tissues. They collect tissue fluid that is not reabsorbed back into capillaries. The lymph fluid that is produced has a similar composition to blood plasma with the main difference being the presence of white blood cells, rather than red.

The Mammalian Heart

The mammalian heart is an organ that has the purpose of pumping blood around the body. It is made up of a number of tissues, the main one being cardiac muscle. The cells of cardiac muscle are able to contract and relax without getting fatigued. Each cell is **myogenic**, which means it has its own inherent rhythm.

External Structure of the Heart

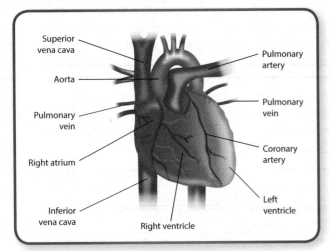

The coronary arteries supply blood to the cardiac muscle itself, providing the cardiac cells with the energy needed to contract. If a coronary artery becomes blocked (as with coronary heart disease) the cardiac cells will die and a heart attack will occur.

Internal Structure of the Heart

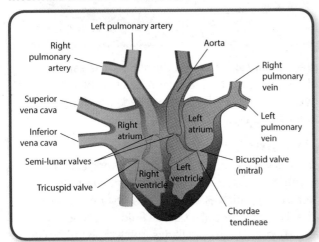

The heart has four chambers: the right and left atria are above the right and left ventricles.

The Cardiac Cycle

Blood enters the right atrium from two veins, the superior vena cava (from the head) and the inferior vena cava (from the rest of the body). A tricuspid valve prevents the backflow of blood when the ventricle below contracts. Chordae tendineae (heart strings) connect to the valve. These help prevent the valves being forced backwards, which is very dangerous, from the high pressure created by **ventricular contraction**.

The ventricles have much thicker walls than the atria. The blood then passes through a semi-lunar valve into the pulmonary artery. This is the only artery that transports deoxygenated blood. Semi-lunar valves exist in blood vessels leading away from the heart and prevent backflow of blood. The elastic recoil of the arteries and the relaxation of the ventricles (which reduces pressure) closes the semi-lunar valve.

The blood moves through the lungs, discharging CO_2 and acquiring O_2 before returning to the heart via the pulmonary veins. These are the only veins to transport oxygenated blood.

The blood passes from the pulmonary vein into the left atrium. Separating the left atrium from the left ventricle is the bicuspid (mitral) valve. This, like the tricuspid valve, has chordae tendineae to prevent the force of ventricular contraction forcing it backwards.

Once in the left ventricle, the blood passes through another semi-lunar valve, this time in the aorta. This is the largest artery in the body and has to deal with the highest pressure blood passing through it.

The blood then carries out a circuit of the body before returning to the heart via the vena cava.

QUICK TEST

1. Approximately what percentage of the blood volume in mammals is made up of plasma?

2. Describe the structure of mammalian haemoglobin.

3. What is carbonic anhydrase?

4. Write the reaction catalysed by carbonic anhydrase in alveoli.

5. Draw the oxygen dissociation curves for foetal and adult haemoglobin.

6. Suggest why there is a difference between the two curves in question **5**.

7. What is oncotic pressure?

8. Why does water leave the blood at the start of a capillary bed and re-enter at the end?

9. What is tissue fluid?

- Blood is involved in temperature regulation of the body and in clotting if the body is cut or broken.
- Plasma makes up between 50 and 60% of the total blood volume.
- The plasma carries a number of different molecules, including proteins, water, glucose, lipids, amino acids, salts, hormones, urea, antigens and antibodies.
- The cellular components include red blood cells (which carry oxygen attached to haemoglobin) and white blood cells (part of the immune system).
- Haemoglobin is a protein molecule in all vertebrates and some invertebrates that binds to oxygen.
- The similarity in haemoglobin points to all life having a single, common ancestor.
- Haemoglobin is a quaternary globular protein with two α units and two β units ($\alpha_2\beta_2$).
- Carbonic anhydrase is an enzyme catalysing the conversion of CO_2 and water into bicarbonate (HCO_3^-) and protons (H^+) in tissues, and the reverse reaction in the lungs and in plant cells.
- Oxygen dissociation curves can be drawn to show how haemoglobin binds to oxygen under certain conditions.
- Tissue fluid is formed from plasma that leaves the capillaries in capillary beds.
- It lacks the albumin proteins and red and white blood cells found in blood plasma.
- The pressure of the blood in the capillary attached to the arteriole is high enough to force the fluid against the water potential gradient.
- When the blood moves from the capillary to the venule the oncotic pressure is greater than the blood pressure so water diffuses back into the capillary.
- The lymphatic system is a separate mass transport system that transports white blood cells and plasma.
- The cardiac cycle is the sequence in which the blood travels through the heart.
- Right atrium → tricuspid valve → right ventricle → semi-lunar valve → lungs.
- Lungs → left atrium → bicuspid valve → left ventricle → semi-lunar valve → rest of body.

PRACTICE QUESTIONS

1. The diagram on the right shows a number of vessels in the human body.

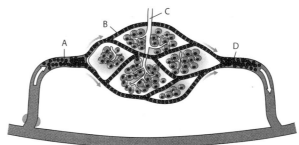

a) What are the names of vessels A, B, C and D? [4 marks]

b) Explain how tissue fluid is formed around the cells. [2 marks]

c) Describe the make-up of the fluid found in vessel C. [2 marks]

Controlling Heart Rate

Cardiac Cycle

Blood has to be moved continuously around the body. To achieve this, the heart pumps the blood using a combination of **systole** (contraction) and **diastole** (relaxation) of the atria and ventricles. When the muscular walls of a chamber contract it causes the volume of the chamber to decrease, increasing the pressure of the blood in the chamber. Blood then flows from high to low pressure. Blood pressure is measured using a **sphygmomanometer**.

Stage 1: Ventricular Diastole, Atrial Systole

Both ventricles relax at the same time, creating lower pressure compared to the atria. The atrioventricular valves (tricuspid and bicuspid valves) partially open. Muscles in the atria contract, forcing the blood through the atrioventricular valves and causing the semi-lunar valves to close in the vena cava and pulmonary vein, preventing backflow of blood.

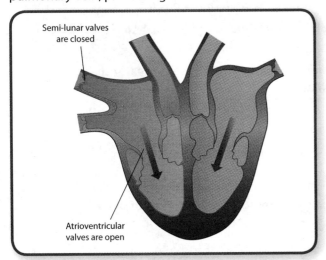

Semi-lunar valves are closed

Atrioventricular valves are open

Stage 2: Ventricular Systole, Atrial Diastole

The atrial muscles in both atria relax and the simultaneous contraction of the muscles in the ventricle causes an increase in blood pressure, causing the atrioventricular valves to close, preventing backflow of blood. This creates a 'lub' heart sound. Blood is forced

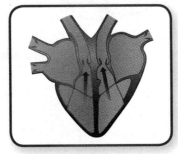

into the aorta (from the left atrium) and the pulmonary artery from the right atrium through semi-lunar valves. Blood travels through the lungs via the pulmonary artery and veins, while the blood leaving the aorta travels through the systemic circulatory system.

Stage 3: Atrial and Ventricular Diastole

The ventricle and atrium muscles relax for a short time and the higher pressure in the aorta and pulmonary vein causes the semi-lunar valves to shut, preventing backflow of blood. This makes a 'dub' sound. The higher pressure in the vena cava and pulmonary vein causes the atria to refill with blood.

The cycle goes back to stage 1 and repeats for the life of the mammal. The entire sequence is one cardiac cycle and lasts for around 0.8 seconds (based on a heart beating 75 times per minute).

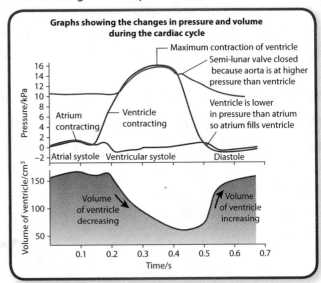

Graphs showing the changes in pressure and volume during the cardiac cycle

Maximum contraction of ventricle

Semi-lunar valve closed because aorta is at higher pressure than ventricle

Ventricle is lower in pressure than atrium so atrium fills ventricle

Atrium contracting

Ventricle contracting

Atrial systole   Ventricular systole   Diastole

Volume of ventricle decreasing

Volume of ventricle increasing

The heart rate will vary according to the metabolic needs of the mammal. If it is sleeping or hibernating, then metabolism slows so the heart rate will slow. If it is doing exercise, then the heart rate will increase to support the increased need for glucose and oxygen by respiring muscle cells. Hormones, such as adrenaline, can increase the heart rate to prepare for fight or flight.

Controlling the Heart

Cardiac muscle cells each have their own inherent rhythm. Left to their own devices, they would all beat at different rates. Pacemaker areas of the heart coordinate the contraction of cardiac muscles to ensure they do so at the same time. Electrical signals from the cardiac centre of the medulla oblongata in the brain alter the activity of the pacemaker, changing the strength and rate of heartbeats. The sympathetic nerve stimulates an increase in heart rate, while the vagus nerve stimulates a decrease. They are **antagonistic** to each other. They are also part of the **autonomic nervous system** and not under conscious control.

When blood pressure is high, the heart rate is lowered. When it is low, the rate is increased. The heart rate can also be controlled by the higher centres of the brain – for example, emotion, stress and anticipating an event can all cause impulses to be sent from the sympathetic nerve, increasing the heart rate.

The nerves are connected to the **sinoatrial node (SAN)** which is in the wall of the right atrium.

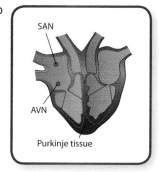

When stimulated, the SAN initiates a wave of electrical excitation across both atria (not just the right). This causes the cardiac muscle in the atria to contract, the right atrium slightly before the left atrium.

The wave of electrical energy reaches a second pacemaker, the **atrioventricular node (AVN)** which is located in the right atrium, above the tricuspid valve. This conducts the electrical activity through **Purkinje fibres**.

Purkinje fibres pass into the septum of the heart deep into the walls of the left and right ventricles, causing them to contract from the bottom of the ventricle upwards. This ensures that blood is efficiently ejected from the ventricles. The entirety of Purkinje fibres is known as the **Bundle of His**.

Interpreting a Normal ECG

The cardiac cycle can be monitored by interpretation of an **electrocardiogram (ECG)** trace. An **electrocardiograph** monitors the small electrical impulses normally generated by the heart.

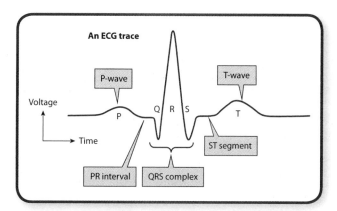

The first event is the P-wave, the depolarisation of muscle fibres in the left and right atria in response to SAN triggering.

There is a delay (the PR interval) caused by the AVN to allow filling of the ventricles. There is then the QRS complex, where the muscle fibres of the ventricles are depolarised, triggering the main pumping contractions. The ST segment shows the beginning of the repolarisation of the ventricles and should be flat. Finally, the T-wave represents repolarisation of the ventricles.

Interpreting Abnormal ECGs

Tachycardia

When someone has an extremely rapid heartbeat above the normal resting rate of between 60 and 100 beats per minute (bpm) they are said to be showing **tachycardia**. An ECG showing tachycardia will show a greater number of wave events over the same time period.

Brachycardia

Conversely, a resting heart rate that is less than 60 bpm is showing **brachycardia**. An ECG showing brachycardia will show fewer wave events per minute than a normal resting ECG over the same period.

Fibrillation

Atrial fibrillation is when the heart starts quivering irregularly. If the cardiac muscle is not contracting together then the cardiac cycle will not be followed. This increases the chance of blood remaining in a chamber and clotting, causing strokes, heart failure and other conditions.

The ECG from someone in atrial fibrillation will show the stages in the ECG being mixed up randomly as parts of the heart contract and relax out of sequence.

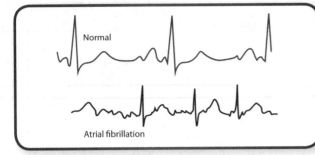

The SAN needs to be reset using a device called a defibrillator. This shocks the heart, resetting the contractions of the cardiac muscle so they follow the electrical signals of the SAN.

Ectopic Heartbeat

Everybody experiences times when the heart 'misses a beat'. Ectopic changes are the name given to these small changes in heartbeat that cause extra or skipped heartbeats. The top ECG shows an extra beat, the bottom ECG a missed beat.

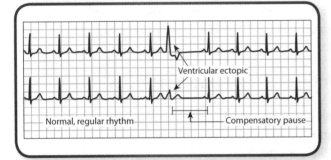

SUMMARY

- The heart pumps blood continuously around the body.

- The atria and ventricles go through a series of systole (contraction) and diastole (relaxation).

- These can be represented by a series of stages:
  - Stage 1: Ventricular diastole, atrial systole
  - Stage 2: Ventricular systole, atrial diastole
  - Stage 3: Atrial and ventricular diastole

- The cycle repeats for the entire life of the mammal.

- Each cardiac cycle lasts for around 0.8 seconds.

- Cardiac muscle cells contract with an inherent rhythm.

- Pacemakers ensure that the cardiac muscle contracts at the same time.

- The part of the brain that sends signals to the heart is the medulla oblongata.

- Signals from the sympathetic nerve cause an increase in heart rate.
- Signals from the vagus nerve cause a decrease in heart rate.
- They are antagonistic to one another.
- The sinoatrial node (SAN) is in the wall of the right atrium.
- It causes a wave of contractions across the atria.
- The atrioventricular node (AVN) is positioned in the right atrium above the tricuspid valve.
- It sends a signal through the Purkinje fibres, causing the ventricles to contract.
- The cardiac cycle can be monitored using an electrocardiogram (ECG).
- The ECG is subdivided into P, Q, R, S and T sections.
- Changes in the ECG can identify problems with the heart.
- Tachycardia is an extremely rapid heart rate.
- Brachycardia is a heart rate lower than 60 bpm.
- Fibrillation is where the heart starts quivering irregularly.
- Ectopic heartbeats are skipped or extra beats, not part of the normal cycle.

PRACTICE QUESTIONS

1. A doctor was treating a number of patients for heart problems.

   An ECG from a healthy patient is shown below:

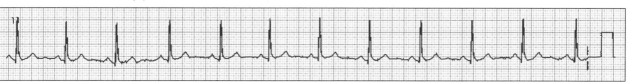

   The following ECGs are from patients with heart conditions.

A

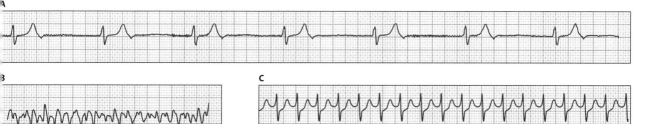

B

C

   a) Explain which patient needs to receive urgent medical treatment first. **[4 marks]**

   b) Which trace shows brachycardia? **[1 mark]**

   c) Which trace shows tachycardia? **[1 mark]**

   d) What happens during the QRS complex stage of an ECG? **[2 marks]**

Plant Transport

As with animals, as plants increase in size and complexity a system for transport is needed. Plant cells require transport of nutrients and dissolved gases for metabolic reactions. Waste materials also need to be removed. In large plants the surface area to volume ratio is low.

Root Structure and Function

The roots of green plants take in water, oxygen and mineral ions and excrete carbon dioxide into the soil environment. This is achieved through the presence of root hair cells that have a high surface area to volume ratio.

The root hairs extend into the spaces between soil particles. There is a high water potential in the soil compared to the lower water potential in the root hair cell, so water moves from the soil into the root hair via osmosis. Water potential is a measure of potential energy in water. Pure water has the highest water potential and so will move via osmosis into water with a lower water potential (e.g. water containing dissolved solutes).

As the root hair cells absorb water, the cell sap becomes more dilute. This increases the water potential compared to adjacent cells. The water moves from high to low water potential into adjacent cells, via osmosis.

This process repeats, leading to the net movement of water from the root hair cell to the cortex.

Active Transport

For mineral ions, the concentration is likely to be higher inside the root than in the soil. If allowed to diffuse, they would move from the plant into the soil, which is not desirable. Active transport moves the mineral ions against the concentration gradient using carrier proteins in the cell membranes and the energy obtained through respiration.

Movement from Root to Xylem

Once water has passed into the plant via osmosis it then has to be moved up the plant.

The Vascular System

Vascular plants, such as green flowering plants like daffodils, have a system of **xylem** tubes that carry the water and dissolved mineral ions up the plant.

Water moves across the cortex of the root through the epidermis before entering the xylem.

There are three pathways by which water can be transported across the cortex:

- **Apoplast route** – The **apoplast** is the gap outside the plasma membrane of cells. In this theory the water travels without entering the cells themselves.
- **Symplast route** – The **symplast** is the inner side of the plasma membrane in which water can freely diffuse. **Plasmodesmata** (cytoplasmic strands connecting one cell to another) allow the direct flow of larger molecules, such as sugars, amino acids and ions, between the cells.
- **Vacuolar route** – Here water moves through the **tonoplast** (the membrane bounding the sap vacuole) first, then through the sap vacuole itself in each cell.

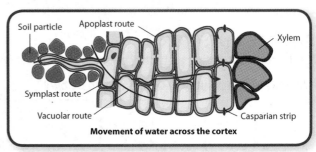

Movement of water across the cortex

Casparian Strip

Before reaching the xylem vessels, water has to pass through the epidermal cells that surround it. The cells of the epidermis contain a band of cell wall material. This is made of a different material from normal cell walls. It prevents water from moving through the apoplast. The water must move through the middle of the cell via the symplast or vacuole to enter the xylem.

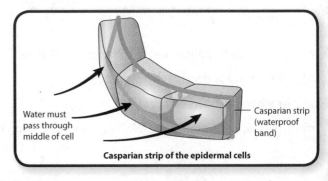

Casparian strip of the epidermal cells

Xylem

The tissue that transports water in vascular plants is called xylem (its name is derived from the Greek for 'wood'). The water passes into xylem vessels that connect the root hair cells to the leaves, in a continuous tube, creating an unbroken column of water. This is because of the cohesive property of water (the water molecules stick together). The water also adheres well to the walls of the xylem vessel.

Xylem is made up of long cells with lignin lining the inner walls for strength and to make the walls waterproof. The ends of the cells have perforated plates, allowing water to move up in a continuous stream. Pits at the side allow water to enter and exit, so cells throughout the plant can access water and minerals.

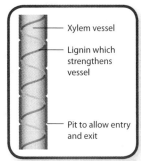

- Xylem vessel
- Lignin which strengthens vessel
- Pit to allow entry and exit

Root pressure gives the initial upward force to the water in xylem vessels. The water then moves up the plant by capillarity. Capillarity is a physical process. Water molecules travelling in very small-diameter tubes will have cohesion for other water molecules so if one water molecule moves the ones attached will also move. The adhesion of water also means that the molecules are attracted to the xylem vessel surface, pulling other water molecules up with them.

Transpiration creates a very negative water potential in the mesophyll of the leaves. As the water potential of the xylem is higher, the water moves from high to low water potential and so up the plant and through the leaves.

Xylem vessels die once they have matured, through a process of controlled cell death. The connection of xylem vessels through the plant produces a complete xylem system, through which water can be transported.

Translocation

A separate system of tubes, called **phloem**, transport sugars and amino acids. The transport of these chemicals is an active process, called **translocation**. Sugar produced through photosynthesis is moved from the sites of photosynthesis (the green leaves and stem) to areas that require sugar for metabolism, called metabolic sinks (e.g. the terminal buds and roots).

Phloem

Sugars are transported in phloem tissue. This consists of two types of living cells, sieve tubes and companion cells.

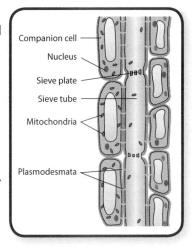

- Companion cell
- Nucleus
- Sieve plate
- Sieve tube
- Mitochondria
- Plasmodesmata

The end of each sieve tube has a sieve plate perforated with pores. Sieve tubes have cytoplasm and only a few mitochondria. Sugars pass through the sieve tubes through cytoplasmic streaming. Cytoplasmic streaming involves the protein actin that helps move the cytoplasm. Sieve tubes are alive but have no nucleus. They are connected by cytoplasmic connections (plasmodesmata) with the companion cells. This allows the sieve cell to share the cytosol, sugars and other materials. The companion cell has a nucleus and mitochondria and effectively carries out the metabolic activities that the sieve cell would normally carry out if it had a nucleus. If the companion cell were to die then the sieve cell would also die.

Transpiration

Transpiration is the loss of water from the plant. Water can be lost through the stem and leaves. The majority of water is lost from the leaves by evaporation through pores called stomata (singular stoma). Each stoma has two guard cells bordering it which open and close it.

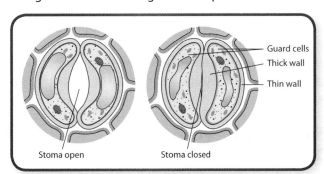

- Guard cells
- Thick wall
- Thin wall

Stoma open   Stoma closed

Water leaves the plant as the water potential in the mesophyll in the underside of the leaf becomes saturated with water vapour. This means the water potential may be higher than the surrounding air, so water diffuses from the higher water potential in the leaf to the lower water potential in the surrounding air.

The guard cells open in the presence of light. Potassium (K^+) ions are transported into the cell via active transport from adjacent cells. The carbohydrate malate is produced from starch and accumulates with the K^+ ions. This decreases water potential in the guard cell so water from adjacent cells moves in. The guard cell has a cell wall that is thin in one location and thick in the other. The increase in hydrostatic pressure causes the opening of the stoma.

The reverse process causes the stoma to close. Depending upon water potentials, the stomata can also be partially open.

Transpiration rates can vary according to the environmental conditions. Warm, dry conditions will lead to faster transpiration than cool, humid conditions.

Measuring Transpiration Rate
To measure transpiration rates a **potometer** is used.

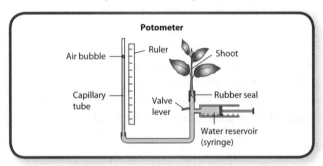

Potometer

Air bubble — Ruler — Shoot
Capillary tube — Valve lever — Rubber seal
Water reservoir (syringe)

A living root is cut and quickly put into water (to prevent bubble formation which would break the transpiration stream). The potometer is immersed in water to fill the capillary tube and air bubbles removed. The shoot is then connected to the potometer via a rubber seal and the valve opened to allow water flow. The volume of water taken up by the shoot in a given time frame is recorded. The molecules of water lost by the plant by transpiration are replaced by an equal number due to cohesion.

Plant Adaptations
Plants live in a wide variety of habitats. They can survive due to special adaptations.

Xerophytes
Plants living in dry environmental conditions are **xerophytes**. They survive by having a thick cuticle to reduce evaporation, a reduced number of stomata, smaller and fewer leaves to reduce surface area, hairs on the plant surface to minimise turbulence, aerodynamic shapes to reduce the force of the wind (which could increase evaporation), deep root networks to absorb water, and a store of water in a modified structure (e.g. the stem of a cactus).

Hydrophytes
Plants living in aquatic conditions are **hydrophytes**. They have leaves with air pockets called lacunae that allow the leaf to float on the water. Roots are minimal or may even be completely missing. Leaves will have a large surface area to facilitate transpiration. There is typically no waxy cuticle as the plant does not need to minimise water loss. In a plant that is fully submerged stomata will be absent as there is no air. In plants that float, stomata are only on the upper surface.

Experimental Evidence of Translocation
Scientists have used a number of experimental techniques to understand transpiration and translocation. By radiolabelling solutes their passage through the plant can be tracked using autoradiography. Aphids, a small insect that feeds on cell sap, have also been used to track translocation as, although they feed on the sap, this does not kill or permanently damage the phloem tubes. Aphids do not suck the sap – it enters the aphid via a water potential gradient. Studies with aphids indicate that the phloem is under pressure. Analysis of the sap harvested by aphids also showed its composition, as well as the rate of translocation.

QUICK TEST

1. How are root hairs adapted for water uptake?

2. Describe, in terms of water potential, how water moves from the root hair cell to the cortex of the root.

3. What are the three pathways water takes when moving across the root cortex?

4. What is the purpose of lignin in xylem vessels?

5. If the companion cell were to die, what would happen to the sieve tube?

6. Give two properties of water that enable it to move in a transpiration stream.

7. What is the name given to plants that survive in extremely dry conditions?

- Green plants take in water, oxygen and mineral ions through the roots.
- Water moves into the root via osmosis due to the higher water potential in the soil.
- The cell sap becomes more dilute and the water potential increases compared to neighbouring cells.
- The water moves to the next cell via osmosis.
- The process repeats until the water has arrived at the cortex of the plant.
- Active transport moves ions into the plant against a concentration gradient.
- Vascular plants have a network of xylem tubes to transport materials up the plant.
- The Casparian strip is a band of cell wall material that is waterproof.
- It prevents water from travelling any way other than through the symplast or vacuole to enter the xylem.
- Xylem is lined with lignin, strengthening it and making it waterproof.
- Pits in the side allow water to enter and leave.
- Water is cohesive (so travels in a continuous tube) and adheres to the sides of the xylem vessels.
- Transpiration creates negative water potential in the leaves, so water is drawn up through the plant.
- Sugars and amino acids are transported by translocation through phloem.
- Phloem is made of living cells – sieve tubes and companion cells.
- Sieve cells have no nucleus and share cytoplasm with companion cells.
- Sugars pass through the tubes via cytoplasmic streaming.
- Transpiration is the loss of water from a plant from the stem and leaves.
- Stomata are pores which are opened and closed by pairs of guard cells.
- Plants have adaptations to enable survival in extremes of water availability.
- Xerophytes live in dry environments. They have thick cuticles, reduced stomata and fewer leaves.
- Hydrophytes live in aquatic conditions. They have lacunae to make leaves float, minimal or no roots, leaves with large surface areas and no waxy cuticle.

PRACTICE QUESTIONS

1. The diagram on the right shows a cross-section of a grass that lives in dry, windy conditions.

   a) State three features, with reasons, that show the grass lives in dry, windy conditions. [3 marks]

   b) What is the name of plants that live in dry, windy conditions? [1 mark]

   c) What equipment could be used to measure the transpiration rate of the grass? [1 mark]

Nutrition

All organisms need energy for metabolic processes and nutrients that can be metabolised for maintaining cells, growth, fighting disease and reproduction. In animals, nutrition involves ingesting food and then digesting it.

Digestion

Digestion is the process of breaking down large molecules into molecules that are small enough to be passed across the cell surface membrane. Digestion takes place in the mouth, stomach and small intestine. In mammals, the process of digestion relies on a number of enzymes.

Carbohydrate Digestion

The simplest carbohydrates are monosaccharides. As they are small they are able to pass through the cell surface membrane. When in a cell they dissolve and can therefore affect the osmotic balance of the cell. Typically, organisms rapidly convert monosaccharides into longer chain polysaccharides so that they no longer affect the water relations of the cells; they are osmotically neutral. When an organism consumes polysaccharides they will have to break them down into their component monomer units.

Carbohydrases

Carbohydrases is the name given to the group of enzymes that catalyse the breakdown of carbohydrates into smaller subunits. Amylase is an example of a carbohydrase. It catalyses the hydrolysis of starch into sugar molecules.

final section of the small intestine). This means that the enzyme is adapted to work efficiently in the mouth at a pH range of 6.7–9.0. The pH of the acidic environment of the stomach is too low and can denature salivary amylase.

The product of starch digestion by amylase is maltose. Maltose is a disaccharide made of two glucose subunits.

Disaccharidases

Carbohydrases that catalyse the breakdown of disaccharides are called **disaccharidases**. The product of starch breakdown by amylase is maltose. Maltose has to be broken down into glucose molecules by maltase. In the ileum, the enzyme maltase is membrane bound on the brush border of cells lining this part of the small intestine. The maltose molecules bind to the active site and glucose monomer units are released. The glucose units then pass through the cell surface membrane via co-transport with sodium ions.

Fat Digestion

Lipids are broken down in the digestive system by **lipases**. Lipase hydrolyses the breakdown of fat molecules (triglycerides) into glycerol and free fatty acids. These can then be used for metabolism. For effective digestion, the surface area of the fats needs to be increased. Bile salts are produced by the gall bladder and they emulsify the fat droplets into much smaller ones. The droplets have a much greater surface area.

The lipases then are able to catalyse the hydrolysis of the lipids into glycerol and fatty acid molecules.

Digestion of the polysaccharide amylose/starch

Insoluble starch/amylose

The reaction is a hydrolysis

The enzyme is called amylase

Soluble maltose

There are two amylases in humans – **salivary amylase** and **pancreatic amylase**. Both catalyse the breakdown of starch. Salivary amylase breaks down the starch in the mouth, pancreatic amylase in the duodenum (the

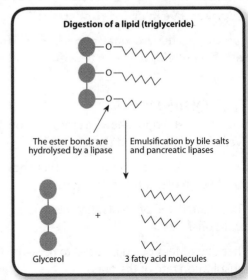

Digestion of a lipid (triglyceride)

The ester bonds are hydrolysed by a lipase

Emulsification by bile salts and pancreatic lipases

Glycerol   +   3 fatty acid molecules

Protein Digestion

Protein is required in the diet as it is a source of amino acids. The amino acids can be used to create new proteins for growth and repair. Dietary protein is ingested and, after being macerated by the teeth, it passes through the oesophagus into the stomach. There are a variety of different ways to break down proteins, depending on where the enzymes bind to break the protein down. The enzymes are very specific and this means that biologists can use a collection of enzymes, with known specificity, to break a polypeptide down and work out its primary structure. They are called **proteases**, or **peptidases**. They are secreted as inactive forms which then have to be activated by phosphorylation before they will work. This is to prevent the enzymes breaking down essential proteins in locations other than where they are needed.

Endopeptidases

Enzymes that catalyse the breakdown of the protein from the non-terminal ends (i.e. within the protein molecule itself) are called **endopeptidases**. An example is trypsin. Trypsin is an enzyme that breaks the peptide bond between the amino acids arginine (Arg, R) and lysine (Lys, K).

Lysine or arginine

A long polypeptide

Trypsin digestion

The peptide bond between the lysine or arginine is broken, leaving two new polypeptide fragments.

Chymotrypsin works by breaking the peptide bonds between phenylalanine (Phe, F), tryptophan (Trp, W) and tyrosine (Tyr, Y), unless followed immediately by proline (Pro, P).

Exopeptidases

Exopeptidases catalyse the breakdown of the peptide bond occurring at the terminal ends of the protein. There are two ends, an NH_2 amine end and a carboxylic COOH end. Aminopeptidase breaks the peptide bond at the amine end while carboxypeptidase breaks the peptide bond at the carboxylic acid end of the protein.

Dipeptidases

Cells in the small intestine can produce dipeptidases. These are specialised exopeptidases that catalyse the breakdown of dipeptides into the single amino acid monomers. The amino acids are then transported across the cell surface membrane of the cells lining the small intestine.

Co-transport of Glucose and Amino Acids

Glucose and amino acids have to be transported across the cell plasma membrane. The cells that line the ileum have cell extensions, called villi. The villi themselves have a brush layer, which massively increases the area available for absorption.

The glucose or amino acid molecules attach to a binding site on the carrier molecule. When Na^+ binds it induces a conformational change in the shape of the carrier protein, which draws both into and through the protein, in the same direction.

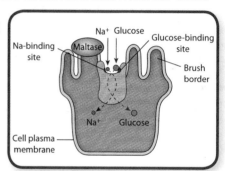

Transport of Fatty Acids

Fatty acids have to be transported across the cell plasma membrane via structures called micelles. Micelles are about 200 times smaller than emulsion droplets.

Micelles are spherical structures made from lipids. Like phospholipids, there is a hydrophilic head and the fatty acid chains form a hydrophobic tail. They self-arrange with the tails towards the centre. Unlike liposomes, formed from phospholipid bilayers, micelles only have one spherical layer. They transport fatty acids that are not water soluble to the brush layer of the villi. It is the contents of the micelle that enter the cell, not the micelle itself. Once the micelle is close to the surface membrane of the cell the contents diffuse across, as they are non-polar. Some will also be moved across into the cell through active transport.

SUMMARY

- Organisms require energy for metabolism and nutrients for maintaining cells, growth, fighting diseases and reproduction.

- Animals ingest food and then digest it.

- Digestion is the process of breaking down large molecules into molecules that are small enough to pass into cells through the cell surface membrane.

- Digestion depends on a number of enzymes.

- Carbohydrates are broken down by carbohydrases.

- The simplest carbohydrates are monosaccharides.

- Monosaccharides can pass through cell membranes, unlike larger carbohydrates.

- They can dissolve in water and therefore can affect the osmotic balance of a cell.

- Organisms can convert monosaccharides into larger polysaccharides so they can be stored and will not affect the osmotic balance of the cell.

- Amylase, a carbohydrase, breaks down starch into maltose molecules.

- Maltose is a disaccharide made of two glucose subunits.

- Maltase is bound to the cell membrane in the ileum, breaking down maltose into glucose.

- The glucose, once formed, is transported across the cell surface membrane via co-transport with sodium ions.

- The enzyme lipase hydrolyses triglycerides into glycerol and free fatty acids.

- To increase the efficiency of this process, bile salts produced by the gall bladder emulsify the fat droplets into smaller ones with a much greater surface area.

- Protein is broken down by enzymes called proteases or peptidases, which are inactive and have to be activated by phosphorylation before they will work.

- The proteases are very specific and those that target the peptide bonds between specific amino acids are called endopeptidases.

- Scientists can use different combinations of proteases to work out the primary structure of a polypeptide.

- Exopeptidases catalyse the breakdown of the peptide bonds at the amine or carboxylic acid terminals of the polypeptide chain.

- The single amino acid monomers produced can then be transported across the cell surface membrane of the brush border of the villi in the small intestine.

- Glucose and sodium are co-transported across the cell surface membrane of cells in the ileum.

- When both are present a conformational change occurs in the carrier molecule, drawing them into the cell.

- Fatty acids have to be transported across the cell surface membrane in structures called micelles.

- Micelles are spherical structures formed from a single phospholipid layer.

QUICK TEST

1. Give three reasons why organisms require nutrients.
2. Define digestion.
3. What type of enzyme catalyses the breakdown of carbohydrates?
4. What molecules does amylase break starch down into?
5. Where is the enzyme maltase located in the digestive system of mammals?
6. What do lipases break fats down into?
7. Where in the molecule do proteases (or peptidases) act on protein?
8. What is the difference between an exopeptidase and an endopeptidase?
9. Describe how glucose and sodium ions are transported into the cells lining the ileum.
10. How are fats from digestion transported across the cell surface membrane?

PRACTICE QUESTIONS

1. The diagram shows the digestive system of a human. Digestion relies on a number of different enzymes. The table shows some of the properties of digestive enzymes.

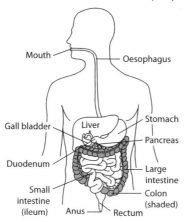

Enzyme	Optimum pH	Role
Pepsin	1.5	Breaks down protein
Lipase	8.0	Breaks down fats
Maltase	6.3	Breaks down maltose

a) Which enzyme is located in the stomach? [1 mark]
b) What does lipase break fats down into? [1 mark]
c) Where in the body is maltase found? [1 mark]
d) Pepsin is produced in an inactive form.
   (i) What process activates an enzyme? [1 mark]
   (ii) Explain why this process is necessary with peptidases. [2 marks]

Modelling Digestion

It is possible to create models of digestion that enable theories of how digestive processes take place to be tested.

Visking Tubing

Visking (dialysis) tubing is a type of seamless tubing that can be used to model absorption across the lining of the intestine. Non-medical grade laboratory visking tubing is made of cellulose, while medical visking tubing for dialysis is made from plastic. It is a partially permeable membrane that will only allow particles below a set size to pass through.

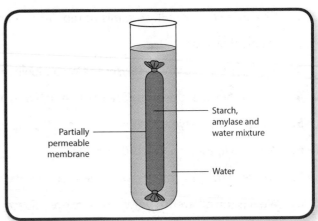

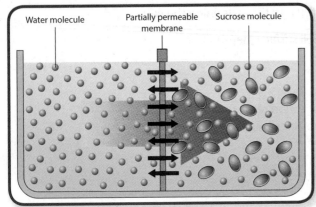

This means that if a sucrose mixture is added to the visking tubing and the tubing placed into a beaker of water, water will move from the beaker into the visking tubing. This is due to the process of osmosis.

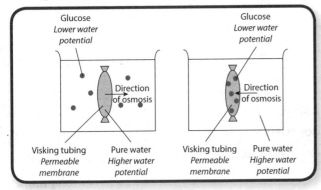

Similar experiments can be set up to model movement of water during digestion. For example, if the visking tubing is filled with starch solution and amylase added, over time the maltose formed will leave the visking tubing and enter the water surrounding the tubing. This can then be tested for the presence of sugar.

Food Tests

The presence of different food nutrients can be tested for by different chemical reactions.

Iodine–Potassium Iodide Test

Iodine can be dissolved in a solution of aqueous iodinised potassium iodide (I_2/KI) solution. This leads to the formation of triiodide anions, I_3^-. In the presence of starch the I_3^- forms a complex with the starch. The colour of the I_2/KI solution changes from brown to an intense dark blue/purple colour. At acidic pH levels the test ceases to work because the starch molecule becomes hydrolysed.

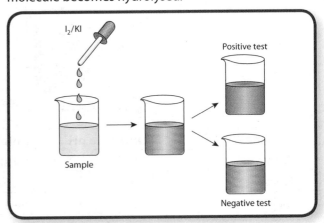

Benedict's Test

Sugars can be classified as being reducing or non-reducing. **Reducing sugars** have the ability to act as a reducing agent, donating electrons in a redox reaction. If a reducing sugar donates electrons then it becomes oxidised. **Benedict's reagent** contains soluble Cu^{2+} ions, from copper (II) sulfate, one of the components of Benedict's reagent. When reducing sugars are present, the Cu^{2+} ions are reduced to form insoluble copper oxide (with Cu^+ ions). Sodium carbonate and sodium citrate are present in the reagent to ensure it is alkaline and the Cu^{2+} ions are in a complex so do not reduce to Cu^+.

Reducing sugars typically have either an **aldehyde** group or a **ketone** group, which is readily oxidised.

All monosaccharides are reducing sugars. Examples include glucose, galactose and fructose. Most disaccharides are also reducing sugars, e.g. lactose and maltose.

The disaccharide sucrose, formed from glucose and fructose monomers, is the most common non-reducing sugar.

Benedict's test involves adding a reagent to a sample of liquid food. The mixture is then heated for approximately 5 minutes. Benedict's reagent is blue in colour. If non-reducing sugars are present the colour will remain blue. If the non-reducing sugar is then hydrolysed (broken down) into its constituent monosaccharides the Benedict's test will then be positive.

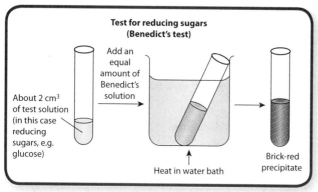

Test for reducing sugars (Benedict's test)

Add an equal amount of Benedict's solution

About 2 cm³ of test solution (in this case reducing sugars, e.g. glucose)

Heat in water bath

Brick-red precipitate

In the presence of reducing sugars, the colour changes to green, yellow, orange or brick-red, depending on the amount of reducing sugars present.

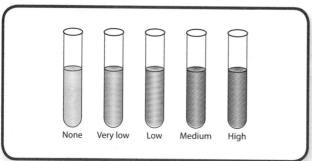

None   Very low   Low   Medium   High

Biuret Test

Proteins are tested for by using the **Biuret test** (pronounced bye-you-ray). Biuret reagent contains Cu^{2+} ions which form a blue colour when in aqueous solution. A strong alkali is added, e.g. sodium hydroxide, followed by copper sulfate solution. The Cu^{2+} ions form a complex with peptide bonds, if present. When this happens, the colour changes to purple. The colour is visible with the unaided eye but it can also be detected using **spectroscopy**, which makes the test quantitative.

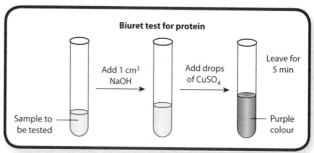

Biuret test for protein

Sample to be tested

Add 1 cm³ NaOH

Add drops of CuSO₄

Leave for 5 min

Purple colour

Emulsion Test

Lipids are soluble in alcohol. A sample of solid food is crushed and then dissolved in ethanol. If the sample is liquid, it is added directly to the alcohol. After being left for around 5 minutes the solids sink to the bottom and the alcohol, containing dissolved lipids, is decanted off into a second test tube. Deionised water is added and the mixture shaken.

If lipids are present a cloudy, white emulsion will form.

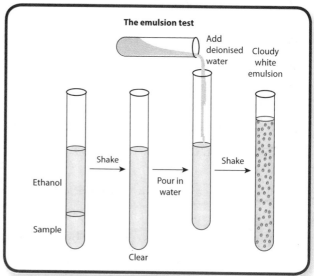

The emulsion test

Add deionised water   Cloudy white emulsion

Ethanol

Sample

Shake

Pour in water

Clear

Shake

SUMMARY

- Visking tubing, or dialysis tubing, is a type of seamless tubing made from cellulose.
- It is partially permeable, so has a large number of pores of a specific size.
- Only those molecules smaller than the pore size may pass through.
- If visking tubing is filled with a solution of sucrose the sucrose molecules will not be able to pass through the pores.
- This creates a gradient of water potential.
- Water will flow by osmosis from an area of high water potential (outside the visking tubing) into an area of low water potential (inside the visking tubing).
- Visking tubing can be used to model digestion.
- A starch solution can be added to the visking tubing.
- When amylase, a carbohydrase, is added it catalyses the breakdown of starch into maltose.
- The maltose can leave the visking tubing whereas the starch cannot.
- The water in the surrounding solution can be tested for the presence of starch and maltose.
- Starch is tested for by the iodine–potassium iodide test.
- In the presence of starch I_3^- ions form a complex with it, changing colour from brown to deep blue/purple.
- The test does not work at acidic pH levels as the starch becomes hydrolysed.
- Sugars can be tested for by heating a sample in the presence of Benedict's reagent.
- Reducing sugars (all monosaccharides and most disaccharides) have an aldehyde or ketone group.
- They can reduce other substances by donating electrons.
- Benedict's reagent, a mixture of copper (II) sulfate, sodium carbonate and sodium citrate, is a blue colour.
- The Cu^{2+} ions react with reducing sugars to form Cu^+ ions in copper oxide.
- This causes a change from blue to brick-red.
- The colours in between (green, yellow and orange) give an indication of the amount of reducing sugars present.
- The sodium carbonate keeps the pH alkaline.
- Sodium citrate forms a complex with the Cu^{2+} ions to ensure they do not automatically convert to Cu^+ ions.
- The presence of proteins is identified using the Biuret test.
- Biuret reagent is blue and turns purple if peptide bonds are present.
- The presence of fats is tested for by the emulsion test.
- The sample is mixed with ethanol and left for 5 minutes.
- The alcohol/lipid mix is decanted off.
- Water is added to the decanted mixture – if it turns a cloudy milky white, fats were present.

QUICK TEST

1. What is non-medical lab grade visking tubing made of?

2. What feature of visking tubing means it is useful for studying digestion and osmosis?

3. What is meant by the term 'gradient of water potential'?

4. A glucose solution is added to a tube made of visking tubing. The tube is placed in a beaker of distilled water. What will happen to the visking tubing?

5. Another tube made from visking tubing is filled with distilled water. It is added to a beaker containing glucose solution. Describe what happens to the visking tubing.

6. Describe the test for starch.

7. Which ion is involved in the starch test?

8. What is the role of sodium citrate in Benedict's reagent?

9. A sucrose solution is tested with Benedict's reagent. Explain what will be observed at the end of the experiment.

10. What colour does Biuret reagent turn in the presence of protein?

PRACTICE QUESTIONS

1. An experiment is set up to identify the food groups present in a chicken tikka masala meal.

   a) Describe the test that can be carried out on the rice component of the meal. **[2 marks]**

   b) The meat is removed. Suggest the appropriate food test that could be carried out on the meat and describe how to carry the test out, including the results of a positive test. **[3 marks]**

   c) Describe the test used to assess for fats in the meal. **[3 marks]**

Trophy

Autotrophs

Organisms that can produce complex organic compounds (e.g. carbohydrates, fats and proteins) using simple substances available in their environment are called **autotrophs**. Autotrophs can be divided into two groups – **photoautotrophs** and **chemoautotrophs**.

Photoautotrophs

All green plants and algae are photoautotrophs. They use light as an energy source for their metabolic reactions and convert atmospheric carbon dioxide into organic molecules.

Chemoautotrophs

Some organisms are able to obtain energy by the oxidation of electron donors in their environment. Typically these are bacteria and blue-green algae that live in deep sea hydrothermal vents. The types of electron donors include methane and sulfur oxide. One theory for how life initially started is based on these life forms.

Heterotrophs

Heterotrophs can only obtain organic molecules from consuming other organisms. They break down the complex organic molecules produced by autotrophs into simpler compounds. Ultimately autotrophs provide all the energy and nutrients for heterotrophs. The majority of types of living organisms are heterotrophic. Heterotrophs can be divided into a number of different types depending on how they obtain their food.

Saprophytic Nutrition

Saprophytes are organisms that land on a food source and secrete digestive enzymes onto the food. Digestion is external, with the enzymes breaking down the large food molecules into small molecules. These are then absorbed into the body of the organism.

For example, fungi produce threadlike structures called **hyphae**.

The enzymes are produced inside the fungal cell and transported inside vesicles (to prevent self-digestion). The vesicle merges with the cell membrane, expelling the enzyme contents. This is called **exocytosis**.

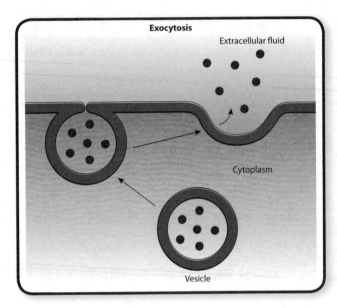

Holozoic Nutrition

Holozoic nutrition is evolutionarily more complex than saprophytic nutrition. Instead of secreting the digestive enzymes, the organism engulfs the food, so digestion takes place internally, within the organism. This is an advantage as all of the available nutrients are likely to be absorbed, whereas with saprophytic nutrition there is a chance that another organism will be able to take in the digested food before the saprophyte does.

Almost all animals exhibit holozoic nutrition. The simplest form of holozoic nutrition is exhibited by single-celled organisms, such as *Amoeba*. An amoeba digests food by surrounding it in a process called phagocytosis.

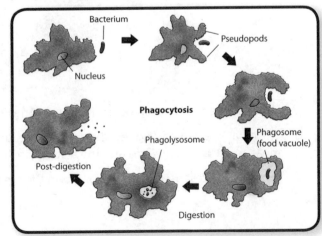

As organisms get larger a digestive system is needed, linked with a circulatory system to ensure all cells can obtain the nutrients needed for their metabolic processes.

As multicellular organisms evolved, they developed simple, undifferentiated sac-like guts with a single opening (e.g. a hydra). This method has the advantage that the digestive enzymes can be stored in the tube, maximising their effectiveness.

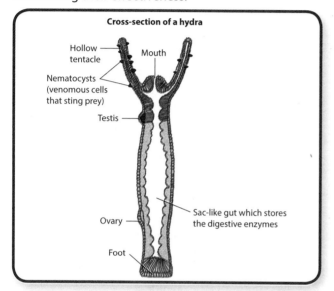

Cross-section of a hydra

- Hollow tentacle
- Mouth
- Nematocysts (venomous cells that sting prey)
- Testis
- Ovary
- Foot
- Sac-like gut which stores the digestive enzymes

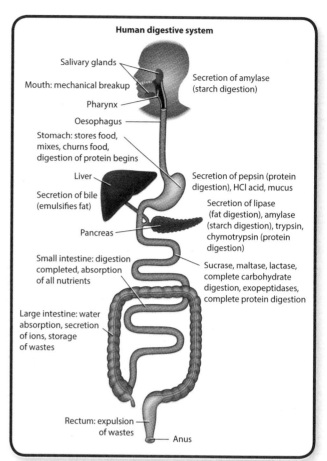

Human digestive system

- Salivary glands
- Mouth: mechanical breakup
- Secretion of amylase (starch digestion)
- Pharynx
- Oesophagus
- Stomach: stores food, mixes, churns food, digestion of protein begins
- Liver
- Secretion of bile (emulsifies fat)
- Pancreas
- Secretion of pepsin (protein digestion), HCl acid, mucus
- Secretion of lipase (fat digestion), amylase (starch digestion), trypsin, chymotrypsin (protein digestion)
- Small intestine: digestion completed, absorption of all nutrients
- Sucrase, maltase, lactase, complete carbohydrate digestion, exopeptidases, complete protein digestion
- Large intestine: water absorption, secretion of ions, storage of wastes
- Rectum: expulsion of wastes
- Anus

Eventually these organisms evolved tube guts with different openings for entry of food (**ingestion**) and for removal of waste (**egestion**). This also meant that cells along the tube could be differentiated to engage with different food molecules.

An example is the earthworm.

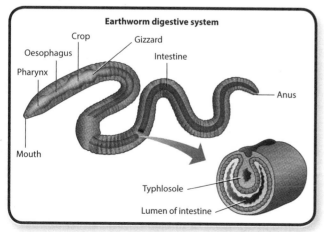

Earthworm digestive system

- Crop
- Gizzard
- Oesophagus
- Intestine
- Pharynx
- Anus
- Mouth
- Typhlosole
- Lumen of intestine

Omnivores

The mammalian digestive system evolved from the simple tubes. The human digestive system is adapted to the breakdown of a wide variety of nutrients, obtained from a mixed omnivorous diet.

A wide variety of different enzymes are produced at different stages along the digestive system, which is still effectively one single tube with an opening at each end. By having a long tube, there can be variation in the conditions for digestion (e.g. pH) so that different enzymes can act on different food molecules.

Herbivores

Ruminants (which include cows and sheep) eat grass which is indigestible to omnivores. They often have a multiple compartmentalised stomach. Unlike mammals like humans, ruminants can pass the food in the first rumen back to the mouth to chew it again (which breaks the food down further). The omasum filters the large fibres back into the rumens. Bacteria and protozoans in the rumens and omasum break down the plant material. The final section, the abomasum, is the cow equivalent of a human stomach. It contains enzymes and acid to break down the food particles ready for absorption in the small intestine.

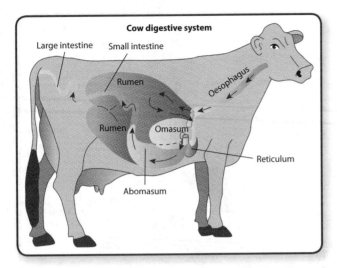

Cow digestive system

Large intestine   Small intestine

Rumen

Oesophagus

Rumen   Omasum

Reticulum

Abomasum

Carnivores

The digestive system of a carnivore, such as a cat, is simpler than that of a herbivore or omnivore.

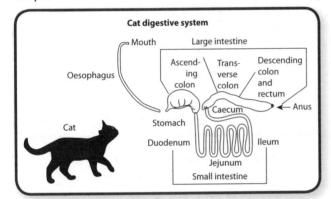

Cat digestive system

Mouth   Large intestine

Oesophagus

Ascending colon   Transverse colon   Descending colon and rectum

Caecum   Anus

Cat

Stomach

Duodenum   Ileum

Jejunum

Small intestine

This is because meat is relatively easy to digest. There is no need for extra stomach compartments or a lengthy small intestine.

Parasitic Nutrition

Parasites are highly specialised organisms that obtain their food at the expense of the host organism. The parasite takes advantage of the fact that the host has already digested food. This means that parasites evolved without some of the features of other heterotrophs.

An example is *Taenia saginata* (beef tapeworm). *Taenia* are tapeworms that live inside the intestine of a heterotroph. It has a head which has suckers and hooks that embed in the lining of the intestine and prevent the tapeworm from being dislodged. It has a series of sections (proglottids) that absorb the digested nutrients that pass through the small intestine. It does not have a digestive system. The host therefore is deprived of some of the food it has eaten and digested.

Lice, such as *Pediculus humanus* (human head louse), are wingless insects that have evolved to obtain their nutrition parasitically. They bite the skin and inject saliva containing an anticoagulant into the blood. They then take in the blood, which contains the dissolved nutrients they need.

QUICK TEST

1. What is meant by the term autotroph?

2. What are the different energy sources for photoautotrophs and chemoautotrophs?

3. How does a heterotroph obtain its energy?

4. A fungus is saprophytic. Describe how a fungus feeds.

5. Describe how an amoeba feeds.

6. What advantage is there in possessing an internal tube for digestion?

7. What is unusual about the digestive system of a cow, compared to that of a human?

8. Which organisms aid digestion of plant material in a cow?

9. How does the length of a carnivore's digestive system compare to that of a similarly sized herbivore?

10. How do parasites feed?

SUMMARY

- Autotrophs are organisms that can produce complex organic compounds using simple substances in their environment.
- Heterotrophs can only obtain organic molecules by consuming other organisms.
- They break the complex organic molecules consumed into smaller molecules that can then be used in metabolism.
- Saprophytes land on a food source and secrete digestive enzymes onto it.
- Fungi produce threadlike structures called hyphae.
- Hyphae secrete enzymes in vesicles that break the food down.
- The smaller digested products are then absorbed into the hyphae via diffusion.
- In holozoic nutrition, the organism engulfs the food.
- Digestion takes place inside the body of the organism.
- Single-celled organisms engulf the food with pseudopods, creating a phagosome.
- The phagosome merges with a lysosome containing digestive enzymes, becoming a phagolysosome.
- Once digested, any unused material is ejected from the body.
- In simple multicellular organisms internal tubes evolved.
- This led to cells becoming specialised to handle different roles in digestion.
- Eventually organisms evolved complex digestive systems.
- Omnivores are organisms that eat a mixed diet of plants and animals.
- The digestive system is adapted for the efficient digestion of plant and animal material.
- Herbivores eat only plant material.
- As much plant material is tough the digestive system needs to be adapted to break the materials down.
- Ruminants, such as cows, have a number of chambers (rumens) where bacteria digest the plant material.
- Carnivores eat meat, which is easier to digest than plant material.
- The length of a carnivore's intestines is consequently much smaller than in herbivores or omnivores.
- Parasites obtain food at the expense of their hosts; the host has already digested the food.

PRACTICE QUESTIONS

1. Beef tapeworm, *Taenia saginata*, lives in the intestine of a cow. Look at the photograph of the scolex of the tapeworm.

    a) What are the structures A and B called? [2 marks]

    b) Describe what the structures A and B are used for. [2 marks]

    c) The body of *Taenia saginata* is very thin and elongated. Explain how this helps the parasite to absorb nutrients. [2 marks]

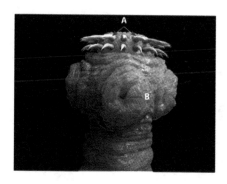

Dentition and Diet

The teeth of mammals vary according to what the animal feeds on. Herbivores require teeth that can grind plant material. Carnivores need to tear meat apart.

Herbivore Dentition

Herbivores typically have flat-topped incisors and canines, typically only on the lower jaw. These are used to pull and tear the plants from the soil. The upper jaw has a horny pad that assists in the tearing of plants. The molars and pre-molars have broad, angled surfaces which are linked to the teeth above or below. The surfaces of the molars and pre-molars have sharp enamel ridges that help grind the tough, fibrous plant material.

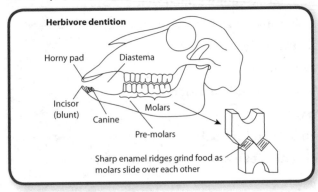

Herbivore dentition

Horny pad — Diastema — Incisor (blunt) — Canine — Molars — Pre-molars — Sharp enamel ridges grind food as molars slide over each other

Carnivore Dentition

Carnivores need teeth to kill their prey and to tear it up. This means that the canines and incisors are often very large, for piercing the skin of the prey. The pre-molars and molars of carnivores are often modified into teeth called **carnassials**. Carnassials are paired upper and lower teeth that are modified to allow enlarged, self-sharpening edges to pass each other in a shearing manner.

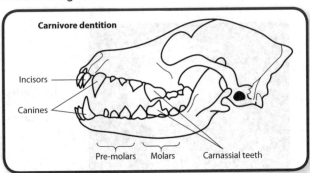

Carnivore dentition

Incisors — Canines — Pre-molars — Molars — Carnassial teeth

Diet

Humans are omnivores and require a balanced diet to avoid health issues.

Fruit and Vegetables

A healthy diet includes fruit and vegetables, which contain vitamins, minerals and dietary fibre. Fibre is necessary for efficient peristalsis within the digestive system.

Carbohydrates

Carbohydrates are needed in the diet as energy sources. Simple sugars release a lot of energy, from aerobic respiration, in the form of ATP. The carbon chains can also be used as carbon skeletons to make new organic compounds. Carbohydrates come from eating starchy foods, such as pasta, rice and potatoes.

Proteins

Protein is needed in the diet to provide a supply of amino acids to build new protein for growth and repair. In an emergency protein can be used as an energy source. Protein comes from meat or certain plant sources, such as beans and soya.

Fats

Fats are a source of energy and provide carbon skeletons for metabolism. Saturated fats are found in butter, fatty cuts of meat, sausages and bacon, cheeses and creams. Most fats from animals are saturated.

Saturated fats are made of fatty acids with only single bonds.

Unsaturated fats are characterised by having at least one double or triple bond in one of their fatty acids. Unsaturated fats are found mainly in plant fats and oils.

The type of fat consumed in the diet has health implications. Saturated fat consumption is associated with cardiovascular disease (CVD).

Saturated fats are processed by the liver to produce cholesterol. Cholesterol is an important constituent of the cell membrane. Its presence in the cell membrane of animals means there is no need for a cell wall. It is also a component of myelin which insulates neurones.

There are two types of cholesterol, LDL (low density lipoprotein) cholesterol and HDL (high density lipoprotein) cholesterol. LDL cholesterol's role is to deliver cholesterol to the cells of the body to be used for manufacture of cell membranes or for synthesising metabolic chemicals called **steroid hormones**. HDL cholesterol's role is to control the LDL cholesterol, via negative feedback. It is produced to travel around the circulatory system and convert excess LDL cholesterol into HDL.

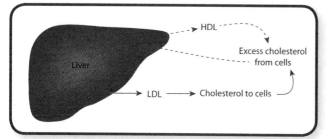

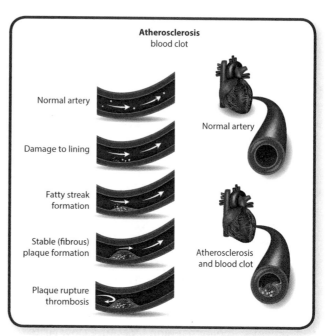

Atherosclerosis blood clot

'Good' and 'Bad' Cholesterol

LDL cholesterol is regarded as being 'bad' cholesterol as it contributes to the formation of plaques in the arteries, which leads to a condition called atherosclerosis. HDL cholesterol is viewed as being 'good' cholesterol. This is because it helps remove LDL cholesterol from the arteries. In reality it is the *excess* of LDL cholesterol that is the problem, not the type.

Atherosclerosis

The arteries transport blood at high pressure away from the heart. It is normal for there to be occasional damage to the lining of the artery lumen. This normally results in inflammation. White blood cells bind to the area. However, if there is a high level of LDL cholesterol being transported in the blood, the white blood cells will take in a high proportion of lipids, including LDL cholesterol. This causes a fatty streak to form and later a plaque, called an **atheroma**. The atheroma will narrow the artery and the artery walls become thick and stiff. This causes a higher blood pressure than normal. This could lead to further damage to the lumen of the artery. If the plaque breaks off a thrombus can form, further blocking the artery. If the blockage is in a coronary artery then a heart attack could occur.

Coronary arteries are most susceptible to blockage from atherosclerosis. This is because they are much smaller than other arteries. Blockages starve the cardiac muscle of oxygen and glucose very quickly, leading to damage or death of the cardiac muscle. If the damage becomes too great, the heart will stop (through a heart attack, or myocardial infarction), and death results.

Strokes occur when the blockages occur in the arteries in the brain.

Lifestyle Factors

It is difficult to identify a definite causal link for CVD. This is because there are so many factors that could be involved in the development of the disease, including diet and lifestyle. As humans carry out individual lives it is impossible to isolate every factor. Instead scientists have to interpret data with a number of variables, trying to find correlations that may help identify causal links.

Scatter diagrams can be used to show whether there are links between lifestyle factors and death from a disease such as CVD. A scatter diagram places the potential cause on the horizontal (x)-axis and the consequence on the vertical (y)-axis.

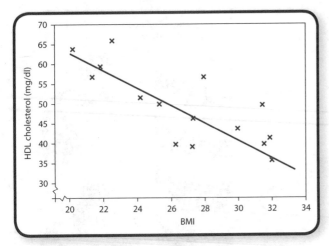

The chart above is exploring the correlation between body mass index (BMI) and level of HDL cholesterol. There is clearly some correlation – the higher the BMI the lower the level of HDL cholesterol. This does not, however, mean that high BMI causes low HDL cholesterol, but there is a correlation that is worth exploring further. Having a high BMI means the person is overweight (above 30 is classed as being obese). It may be the case that they are overweight because they are not exercising and are consuming a diet rich in saturated fats. There will also be exceptions – in this case individuals with a high BMI but also high levels of HDL.

Lifestyle risk factors for CVD include drinking excess alcohol, smoking cigarettes, lack of exercise, and eating foods high in saturated fats.

Diet and Pregnancy

When a woman is pregnant there is a need to alter the normal diet. Increased amounts of protein are needed to provide for the growth of the developing foetus. Calcium levels need to be higher for the foetus to grow bones. If the expectant mother's diet does not have enough then the calcium could be leached from the mother's own bones, which could lead to problems in later life. Iron is needed to ensure that the mother carries enough oxygen to support her developing baby by increasing the amount of haemoglobin. It is important to monitor the amount of vitamin A in the diet if pregnant. Vitamin A, also called retinol, can harm a developing baby. Vitamin A is found in high quantities in liver or liver products, such as pâté. Vitamin C is needed to protect cells and keep them healthy. Folic acid is needed as it prevents defects in the neural tube, which can lead to conditions such as spina bifida. Increased consumption of folic acid is important while a woman is trying to conceive and during the first 12 weeks of pregnancy.

QUICK TEST

1. Describe how the teeth of herbivores are adapted for consuming plant material.

2. What are carnassials?

3. Describe what food groups humans need in a healthy diet.

4. Where would humans obtain the different food groups?

5. How do saturated fats differ from unsaturated fats?

6. What would someone with a BMI of more than 30 typically be classed as?

7. LDL cholesterol is labelled as being 'bad' cholesterol. Why might it have attracted that label?

8. What is the role of HDL cholesterol?

9. What is atherosclerosis?

10. Give three lifestyle factors that increase the risk of cardiovascular disease (CVD).

SUMMARY

- Herbivores consume very tough plant material so their teeth are adapted for grinding.
- Herbivores typically have flat-topped incisors on the lower jaw to tear and pull plants from the ground.
- A horny pad assists with the tearing of plant material.
- Molars and pre-molars have broad, angled surfaces linked to the teeth above or below.
- Sharp enamel ridges grind the tough fibrous material.
- Carnivores use their teeth to kill prey, so canines and incisors are very large, for piercing the skin.
- The pre-molars and molars are modified into teeth called carnassials.
- Carnassials are paired upper and lower teeth that are modified to allow enlarged, self-sharpening edges to pass one another in a shearing manner.
- Humans are omnivores and require a balanced diet.
- Saturated fats only have single covalent bonds between carbon atoms in the fatty acid chains.
- Unsaturated fats have at least one double or triple carbon bond in the fatty acid chain.
- Saturated fats tend to come from animals, unsaturated fats from plants.
- Saturated fats are implicated in a high incidence of cardiovascular disease (CVD).
- Saturated fats are used to make cholesterol.
- LDL cholesterol is essential for making cell membranes. HDL cholesterol is produced to reduce excess LDL cholesterol.
- High levels of LDL cholesterol can lead to atherosclerosis.
- Damage in an artery leads to white blood cells attaching to the artery lining.
- High LDL levels cause a plaque to form which increases blood pressure as the lumen narrows.
- If parts of the plaque break off, a thrombus can form.
- In the coronary arteries this can lead to a myocardial infarction (a heart attack).
- In the brain, this leads to a stroke.
- Atherosclerosis is more likely to have an impact in the coronary arteries as they are narrower than other arteries.
- Lifestyle risk factors include smoking, drinking alcohol, eating saturated fats and lack of exercise.
- These can be plotted on scatter diagrams to see the relationship and help understand causality.

PRACTICE QUESTIONS

1. a) Explain how atherosclerosis can lead to the death of cardiac tissue and a heart attack. **[6 marks]**

   b) Explain the connection between the presence of an atheroma and the risk of thrombosis and stroke. **[3 marks]**

   c) Describe the correlation between the ratio of LDL and HDL cholesterol and the risk of cardiovascular disease. **[3 marks]**

   d) A GP is more interested in the ratio LDL:HDL than the physical quantity of cholesterol. Suggest why this might be the case. **[3 marks]**

The Genetic Code

Nucleic Acids and Nucleotides

Nucleic acids are essential for heredity, the passing on of physical characteristics from one generation to the next. All life on Earth shares the same genetic code.

Nucleotides are the monomers from which nucleic acids (DNA and RNA) are made. DNA (deoxyribonucleic acid) nucleotides are made of a phosphate group, a pentose sugar (deoxyribose) and an organic base. RNA (ribonucleic acid) nucleotides are made of a phosphate group, a pentose sugar (ribose) and an organic base.

Organic Bases

Adenine and guanine are **purine** bases, present in DNA and RNA. They are identified as purines because they consist of two carbon–nitrogen rings joined together.

Cytosine, thymine and uracil are **pyrimidine** bases. They consist of a single carbon–nitrogen ring. Thymine is only found in DNA, being replaced by uracil in RNA.

Nucleotide Structure

The organic base, phosphate molecule and pentose sugar (deoxyribose in DNA, ribose in RNA) are joined to form the nucleotide.

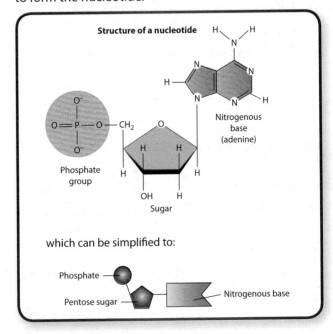

Structure of a nucleotide

Phosphate group

Nitrogenous base (adenine)

Sugar

which can be simplified to:

Phosphate

Pentose sugar

Nitrogenous base

DNA Structure

The nucleotides are arranged with the phosphate groups and pentose sugar units pointing outwards, forming the backbone with the bases in the middle, like rungs of a ladder. DNA molecules consist of two polynucleotide chains that are held together by hydrogen bonds between the bases. There are three hydrogen bonds between G and C and two between A and T.

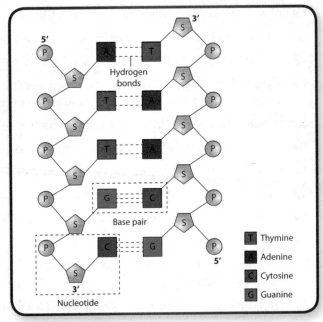

Hydrogen bonds

Base pair

Nucleotide

	T	Thymine
	A	Adenine
	C	Cytosine
	G	Guanine

The two strands twist, forming a **double helix**.

The chains are also **anti-parallel**. The two strands are parallel to each other but run in opposite directions. The ends of the strand are either 5′ (5 prime) as the phosphate group is at the top, or 3′ (3 prime) as the deoxyribose is at the top.

A gene is a section of DNA made of a sequence of bases. The bases form a code that is transcribed and translated to form a functioning protein.

The Genetic Code

Polypeptides are made from a specific order of amino acids. The amino acids are coded by a **triplet** of adjacent bases.

Reading and Interpreting Tables Showing the Genetic Code

Traditionally the genetic code is represented as an RNA **codon** table as it is the messenger RNA (mRNA) sequence that determines the polypeptide structure. The three-letter organic base sequence, or triplet, is converted to a codon in mRNA.

Standard genetic code

1st base	2nd base				3rd base
	U	C	A	G	
U	UUU (Phe/F) Phenylalanine	UCU	UAU (Tyr/Y) Tyrosine	UGU (Cys/C) Cysteine	U
	UUC	UCC (Ser/S) Serine	UAC	UGC	C
	UUA	UCA	UAA Stop	UGA Stop	A
	UUG	UCG	UAG Stop	UGG (Trp/W) Tryptophan	G
C	CUU (Leu/L) Leucine	CCU	CAU (His/H) Histidine	CGU	U
	CUC	CCC (Pro/P) Proline	CAC	CGC (Arg/R) Arginine	C
	CUA	CCA	CAA (Gln/Q) Glutamine	CGA	A
	CUG	CCG	CAG	CGG	G
A	AUU (Ile/I) Isoleucine	ACU	AAU (Asn/N) Asparagine	AGU (Ser/S) Serine	U
	AUC	ACC (Thr/T) Threonine	AAC	AGC	C
	AUA	ACA	AAA (Lys/K) Lysine	AGA (Arg/R) Arginine	A
	AUG (Met/M) Methionine or Start	ACG	AAG	AGG	G
G	GUU (Val/V) Valine	GCU	GAU (Asp/D) Aspartic acid	GGU (Gly/G) Glycine	U
	GUC	GCC (Ala/A) Alanine	GAC	GGC	C
	GUA	GCA	GAA (Glu/E) Glutamic acid	GGA	A
	GUG	GCG	GAG	GGG	G

Each triplet and codon code are non-overlapping. This means that three bases code for one amino acid and then the next three and so on.

The DNA sequence that would code for phenylalanine (Phe or F) would be either AAA or AAG.

AUG codes for 'start' if it is at the beginning of a gene sequence, or methionine (Met or M) if the sequence is already underway.

There are three codes that code for 'stop'. The formation of the polypeptide chain stops at this point.

There are more codons than there are amino acids, 64 in total or 4^3. This means it is a degenerate code. There are multiple codes coding for an amino acid; for example, leucine or L is coded for by six codons. This means that mutations in the DNA sequence, specifically the third base in the triplet code, are less likely to cause a different amino acid to be used.

Transcription

In eukaryotes, the DNA molecule does not leave the nucleus. The genes are transcribed to form pre-mRNA which is then spliced together to form mRNA. The mRNA is small enough to leave the nucleus via nuclear pores. In prokaryotes the DNA is transcribed to form mRNA immediately.

The promoter region is the section of the DNA that initiates the transcription of a gene. Diseases such as cancer can be caused by faulty activation or inactivation of the promoter region.

The DNA is transcribed in the following way:

DNA   3′ AAAGAGGACACT 5′ (template strand)

DNA   5′ TTTCTCCTGTGA 3′ (coding strand)

mRNA   5′ UUUCUCCUGUGA 3′

The mRNA forms from 5′ to 3′ using the template strand (which is read 3′ to 5′). The mRNA molecule formed is complementary to the DNA template and the same as the coding strand (apart from the presence of U instead of T). Tables showing the DNA code for amino acids always indicate the coding strand.

The process of transcription requires enzymes, starting with RNA polymerase which requires ATP.

Exons and Introns

The one gene, one protein hypothesis was devised in the 1940s. However, it is now known that one gene can code for a group of variants of the same type of polypeptide.

During transcription the sections of a DNA nucleotide sequence that become part of the final mRNA molecule are called **exons**. The sections that do not become part of mRNA are called **introns**. Controlling the different exons and introns can lead to a single gene producing a variety of different polypeptides. The initial pre-mRNA contains both exons and introns. Excising the introns leaves the final mRNA molecule.

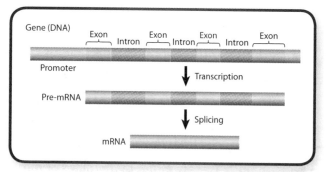

Exons and introns help explain why an organism can form more proteins than the number of genes present in its genome. In humans around 95% of the genes which have exons will lead to different proteins being made.

Translation

Once the mRNA strand leaves the nucleus it arrives in the cell cytoplasm and will be read by ribosomes floating in the cytoplasm or on the rough endoplasmic reticulum.

Transfer RNA (tRNA) molecules have an anticodon formed of three bases. Each tRNA is attached to an amino acid specific to that anticodon. A peptide bond is formed and a polypeptide chain forms.

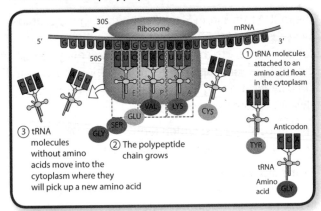

Although the diagram shows one ribosome reading the mRNA sequence, a number can read the same mRNA strand at the same time.

Ribosome Structure

The ribosomes present in eukaryotes are formed of two subunits, the large 50S subunit and a smaller 30S subunit. The S refers to the Svedberg unit, a measure of the rate at which the unit moves towards the bottom of a centrifuge tube. The subunits are made of ribosomal RNA (rRNA). The ribosome has three binding sites. A is where the tRNA binds, and P is where the amino acid attached to the tRNA is chemically joined by a peptide bond to the amino acids forming the polypeptide chain. At the E site the tRNA that now lacks an amino acid is held until being passed back into the cytoplasm.

QUICK TEST

1. What are the components of a nucleotide?

2. How does a nucleotide for RNA differ from a DNA nucleotide?

3. Give two examples of purines (in DNA).

4. Give two examples of pyrimidines (in DNA).

5. If the template strand of DNA reads ATTAACCG, what would the coding strand read and what would the mRNA sequence be?

6. What are exons and introns?

7. What happens at the A, P and E sites on a ribosome?

SUMMARY

- DNA and RNA are nucleic acids essential for heredity.
- All life on Earth shares the same genetic code.
- Nucleotides are the building blocks of nucleic acids.
- DNA nucleotides are comprised of an organic base, a phosphate group and a pentose sugar (deoxyribose).
- In RNA nucleotides the pentose sugar is ribose.
- Organic bases are either pyrimidines or purines.
- Purines (e.g. adenine and guanine) have two carbon–nitrogen rings joined together.
- Pyrimidines (e.g. thymine, cytosine and uracil) consist of a single carbon–nitrogen ring.
- In DNA the bases are adenine (A), thymine (T), guanine (G) and cytosine (C).
- In RNA thymine is replaced by uracil (U).

- DNA is a double helix formed from two anti-parallel strands of polynucleotides.
- Hydrogen bonds form between the complementary base pairs.
- There are two hydrogen bonds between A and T and three bonds between G and C.
- The 5′ end has the phosphate group at the top, and the 3′ end has the deoxyribose at the top.
- A gene is a section of DNA made of a sequence of bases that can be transcribed and translated to form a functioning protein.
- There are 20 naturally occurring amino acids.
- Each amino acid is coded by a triplet of DNA bases.
- Triplets and codons are non-overlapping.
- AUG means 'start', or if the sequence is already being read, then it codes for methionine (Met/M).
- There are three codons that mean 'stop'.
- In transcription, mRNA is formed that matches the coding strand of DNA.
- mRNA can leave the nucleus, unlike DNA.
- The code is read 3′ to 5′ and formed in the 5′ to 3′ direction.
- Genes contain exons and introns.
- Exons are joined together to form the final mRNA molecule. Introns are not translated.
- Ribosomes have a 50S subunit and a 30S subunit.
- In translation, the mRNA feeds into the 30S subunit.
- tRNA with the matching anticodon and with a specific amino acid binds onto the respective mRNA codon at the A site in the 50S subunit.
- At the P site, the amino acid attached to the tRNA is joined by a peptide bond to the amino acids forming the polypeptide chain.
- Having lost its amino acid, the tRNA molecule leaves the ribosome at the E site.
- The tRNA moves into the cytoplasm and picks up a replacement amino acid.

PRACTICE QUESTIONS

1. There are two types of nucleic acid.

a) Complete the table to show the differences between DNA and RNA.

DNA	RNA

[3 marks]

b) A sample of DNA was found to contain 33% cytosine nucleotides. What proportion of the sample was made up of thymine nucleotides? Show your working.

[2 marks]

c) Part of the DNA molecule has the sequence AATTAG. What would the complementary sequence read?

[1 mark]

DNA Replication

Copying DNA

Before cells divide in mitosis, they must first make an exact copy of the DNA.

Semi-conservative replication is the process where an exact copy is made of each DNA strand, using a supply of organic bases, deoxyribose sugars and phosphate molecules (making up the nucleotides).

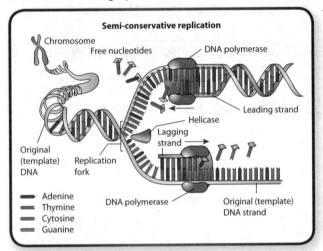

Semi-conservative replication

An enzyme, **helicase**, first unwinds and unzips the DNA molecule. The hydrogen bonds between the bases break, separating the DNA strands. Each complementary strand acts as a template for new nucleotides to join together, forming a new complementary structure.

When replicating in the 3′ to 5′ direction the strand that forms is called the **leading strand**. It is synthesised continuously by the enzyme **DNA polymerase**.

Replicating in the 5′ to 3′ direction the DNA strand that forms is called the **lagging strand**, as it is not synthesised continuously because DNA polymerase can only move along the strand in a 3′ to 5′ direction, synthesising a new strand which has a 5′ to 3′ direction. Instead it is synthesised as a series of small DNA fragments (called **Okazaki fragments**) that have to be joined together by an enzyme called **DNA ligase**.

The enzyme DNA polymerase joins the strands together. There are now two identical copies of the double-stranded DNA. In each DNA molecule, one strand is maintained, the other new, hence the term semi-conservative.

Meselson and Stahl

Meselson and Stahl proved that DNA replication was semi-conservative. There were three possible ways that DNA was thought to be formed:

- **conservative** – where the DNA molecule that formed after replication was completely new
- **dispersive** – where the old and new DNA molecules were both re-formed from new and old DNA
- **semi-conservative** – where the DNA molecules had one strand that was new and the other old.

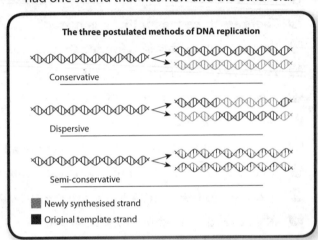

The three postulated methods of DNA replication

Conservative

Dispersive

Semi-conservative

▨ Newly synthesised strand
■ Original template strand

Nitrogen is a major constituent of DNA and there are two isotopes of nitrogen that are common and can easily be used in biological experiments. These are ^{14}N, the most common isotope of nitrogen, which is abundant in the atmosphere, and ^{15}N which is heavier and rarer.

Meselson and Stahl grew cultures of the bacterium *Escherichia coli* in culture medium that contained the isotope ^{15}N for a few generations.

When DNA from the bacteria was extracted and centrifuged in a solution with a salt density gradient the DNA separated out to a point where its density matched the surrounding salt solution. The ^{15}N-grown bacteria produced DNA that had a higher density than ^{14}N-grown bacteria so moved further down the centrifuge tube.

The bacteria were then subcultured into culture medium that contained only ^{14}N. Samples were removed when the bacteria had divided once. Centrifuging the DNA produced a DNA molecule that had an intermediate density to both ^{14}N and ^{15}N DNA. This disproved conservative replication as, if it were taking place, the DNA would have separated into two bands.

To prove whether replication was dispersive or semi-conservative, they monitored the next few cell divisions. On the second division there were two DNA densities measured, one band consistent with DNA comprised of both isotopes and the other consistent with DNA grown only in the presence of ^{14}N. This proved it could not have been dispersive as the mix of light and heavy nitrogen would have still given a single band. Further generations showed the same pattern, with greater amounts of ^{14}N DNA being formed. This evidence proved semi-conservative replication.

Meselson and Stahl's proof of semi-conservative replication
Over four generations the DNA contains ever-increasing proportions of the light ^{14}N, indicating semi-conservative replication must be taking place.

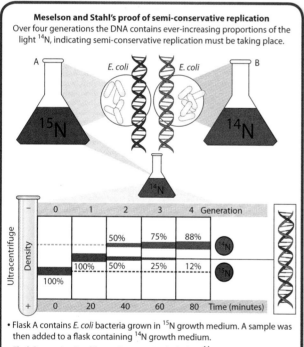

- Flask A contains *E. coli* bacteria grown in ^{15}N growth medium. A sample was then added to a flask containing ^{14}N growth medium.
- Flask B contains *E. coli* bacteria grown in the lighter ^{14}N growth medium.

Replication Accuracy
The replication of DNA can be thought of as a digital process. This is important as errors occurring with replication could easily cause the cell to be unable to carry out essential processes. Even so, errors can and do occur at a rate of around one incorrect base per 10^{10} nucleotides. This is much lower than would be expected if complementary base pairing were the only way of checking fidelity of the copying. Mismatching bases (e.g. A with C) that bond with the wrong partner will occur at a natural rate of 1 in 10^5 nucleotides.

DNA polymerase reduces the error rate to 1 in 10^{10} nucleotides by proofreading each nucleotide against its template strand. If an incorrectly matched base is discovered then the polymerase removes the nucleotide and starts synthesis again.

Even with such a high fidelity of copying, there will still be errors that are not caught. When these result in a new DNA molecule that replicates the error (i.e. it is permanent), they are a **mutation**.

Types of Mutation
Mutations are rare and usually random. They can be caused naturally (through replication errors) or by mutagens – physical and chemical agents that interact with DNA (e.g. ionising radiation, chemicals such as asbestos). There are a number of different types of mutation that can occur.

Substitutions
A **substitution** is the most common type of mutation and is where a base gets swapped with an incorrect base, e.g. A with C. Most are detected and corrected by DNA polymerase.

The effect of this type of mutation depends on the amino acid being coded for and the position of the substitution. If it is the last base in a triplet, then in many instances the amino acid will still be produced as normal.

For example, Phe (F) is coded by the sequence AAA on the template strand. If there is a substitution with the third base to C, Phe will still be made. It is called a silent mutation. If it is changed to either A or G then Leu (L) will be produced instead. Changing to a new amino acid is called a **missense mutation**.

Missense mutations of either the first or second base will have a greater impact as it is less likely that the correct amino acid will be made.

Missense mutations cause a change in the protein produced. This could be beneficial (e.g. the enzyme works slightly better) or it can be detrimental (e.g. sickle-cell anaemia is caused by a single substitution in the β-haemoglobin gene causing a single amino acid to be changed).

If a substitution mutation causes a stop codon instead of the normal amino acid, then it is called a **nonsense mutation**. This will almost certainly lead to a non-functional protein being formed. A polypeptide will still be formed, but depending on where the new stop codon appears, it will be shorter.

Insertions and Deletions

These are more disastrous (and rarer) than substitution mutations.

Insertions involve one or more extra bases being incorporated into a DNA sequence, whereas **deletions** involve removing bases. If the number of bases inserted or deleted is a multiple of three, then the effect will be to create a polypeptide with one extra or one less amino acid present. This will alter the function of the protein formed. For example:

Normal sequence	GCTAAAGCT leads to a three-amino acid polypeptide
Insertion	GCTAAA**GGG**GCT leads to a four-amino acid polypeptide
Deletion	GCTGCT leads to a two-amino acid polypeptide.

If the number of bases added or removed is not a multiple of three, then a **frameshift mutation** has taken place. This completely changes all the amino acids that are produced from the point of the insertion or deletion. Unless the frameshift takes place at the very end of the DNA sequence, the protein will be non-functional. For example:

Normal sequence	GCTAAAGCT leads to a three-amino acid polypeptide
Frameshift	GTAAAGCTC – triplets are different and polypeptide will be formed of different amino acids, and may be shorter or longer as it will continue to be transcribed until a stop codon is reached.

Insertions and deletions can also interrupt DNA replication because they disrupt the double helix structure. This can cause failure of cell division in actively dividing cells.

QUICK TEST

1. What enzyme unzips DNA?

2. What is meant by the term semi-conservative replication?

3. Which strand of DNA is the leading strand?

4. What are Okazaki fragments?

5. How are Okazaki fragments joined together?

6. Who proved semi-conservative replication?

7. What were the other two theories for DNA replication called?

8. What enzyme rejoins DNA strands after replication?

9. Which is the most common type of mutation?

10. What is meant by the term nonsense mutation?

SUMMARY

- DNA replicates through semi-conservative replication.
- Helicase unzips the DNA molecule, breaking hydrogen bonds between bases.
- Each strand acts as a template for new nucleotides to be added.
- The 3′ to 5′ strand is replicated continuously as the leading strand.
- The 5′ to 3′ strand is replicated in Okazaki fragments and is the lagging strand.
- The Okazaki fragments have to be joined together by the enzyme DNA ligase.
- The old and new strands of DNA are then joined together by DNA polymerase.
- Meselson and Stahl proved the semi-conservative replication of DNA.
- Isotopes of nitrogen, ^{14}N and ^{15}N, were used to identify new and old DNA strands.
- *Escherichia coli* was grown in culture medium containing ^{15}N for a few generations.
- The samples were isolated and centrifuged to determine the position of DNA with ^{15}N.
- The samples were then transferred to the ^{14}N-containing medium.
- As the doubling time of *Escherichia coli* was known it was easy to take samples after each division.
- The first experiment disproved conservative replication as, instead of two bands for ^{15}N and ^{14}N, only one intermediate band was made.
- Later experiments disproved dispersive replication, and proved semi-conservative replication.
- Errors in the replication process are prevented by enzymes such as DNA polymerase.
- When an error causes a permanent change in the DNA sequence that is then passed on, it is called a mutation.
- Substitutions are where bases are swapped with incorrect bases.
- Missense mutations cause a change in the final polypeptide.
- Insertions and deletions lead to amino acids being either removed or added.
- These can lead to changes in the function of the final polypeptide.
- Frameshift mutations involve bases being added or removed in non-multiples of three.
- Frameshift mutations often lead to non-functional proteins being formed.

PRACTICE QUESTIONS

1. **a)** What is the role of helicase and of DNA polymerase? [2 marks]

   b) Look at the following DNA sequence.

   ATTCGGCTAGGAACC

   A mutation occurs leading to a new sequence:

   ATTGCTAGGAACCCG

   (i) What type of mutation has occurred? [1 mark]

   (ii) Describe the consequence of this mutation for the polypeptide formed. [2 marks]

Sexual Reproduction

Sexual reproduction involves the production of sex cells (**gametes**) from two different-sex individuals that eventually combine to form a new individual. The new individual inherits characteristics from both parents. This means that the offspring show variation. They resemble the parents but are not identical to them.

Mammalian Reproduction

Gametogenesis is the production of gametes, through meiosis. The production of the mammalian female gamete, or ovum, is called **oogenesis** and the production of sperm, the male gamete, is called **spermatogenesis**.

Oogenesis

Each ovum that is formed during oogenesis is haploid (has half the usual number of chromosomes). In humans, the development of ova occurs in the ovaries. **Oogonia** are all of the female's diploid cells that have the ability to develop into ova. A human female's oogonia are all created when the female is still a foetus. By the time the baby is born, most of the oogonia will have died. The remaining oogonia start meiosis I and become **primary oocytes**. At this point meiosis is paused, the primary oocytes remaining in prophase I. They stay in this paused state until the female begins menstruation. From then on, on an approximately monthly basis, the primary oocytes resume meiosis I.

After the first meiotic division, the chromosomes are divided between daughter cells evenly. However, the majority of the cytoplasm remains in one of the two daughter cells, which becomes a **secondary oocyte**. The one that does not receive the cytoplasm becomes a **polar body**. The polar body allows a primary oocyte to become a haploid cell, reducing its genome by half whilst ensuring the secondary oocyte has the majority of the cytoplasm.

The secondary oocyte undergoes meiosis II and leads to the production of the ovum and a second polar body. The ovum is haploid and has most of the cytoplasm from the original primary oogonium.

Spermatogenesis

Spermatogenesis occurs in **spermatogonia** in the seminiferous tubules in the testes. A diploid spermatogonium divides mitotically to produce a pair of diploid **spermatocytes**. These undergo meiosis I to produce two haploid secondary spermatocytes. These go through meiosis II to produce four haploid spermatids. These then grow a tail and a mitochondria-filled mid-section whilst the genetic material is packed into the acrosome in the head of the spermatozoa.

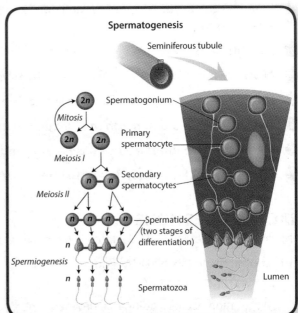

Fertilisation

Ovulation causes an ovum to be released from the ovary. The ovum and associated nurse cells move along the fallopian tube. Fertilisation of the ovum by a spermatozoon usually takes place in the **ampulla** of the fallopian tube (the top section). The ovum generally has to be fertilised within 18 to 24 hours, after which it is destroyed by the fallopian tube. Spermatozoa can survive inside the female reproductive tract for approximately 48 hours. The spermatozoa swim to the ovum. When the first spermatozoon reaches the ovum it comes into contact with the **corona radiata**, an outermost layer of cells which protect the ovum. The corona radiata surrounds the **zona pellucida**, a jelly-like extracellular matrix of glycoproteins. Complementary proteins on the head of the sperm combine with those in the zona pellucida, triggering the **acrosome reaction**. Enzymes are released from the acrosome enabling the sperm cell to pass through. Once the head has breached the zona pellucida, the **cortical reaction** occurs. Cortical granules inside the secondary oocyte move towards the **vitelline membrane** and are then released via exocytosis into the **perivitelline space** and then into the zona pellucida. This causes cross-linking between the protein molecules and the zona pellucida to harden and change electrical charge, preventing the entry of any further spermatozoa.

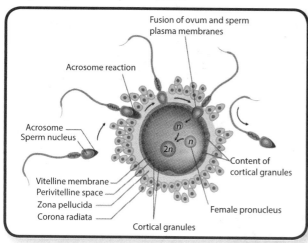

Once the nuclei of the ovum and the sperm fuse, fertilisation has occurred. The fertilised egg, or **zygote**, can now progress through cell division to become an **embryo**.

Cleavage

The zygote undergoes a series of rapid cell divisions converting it into a multicellular structure called a **blastocyst**. The first division occurs approximately 30 hours after fertilisation and forms two cells called **blastomeres**. The polar bodies of the ovum are broken down at this point. The second division takes place

40 hours after fertilisation. After approximately 72 hours the third division takes place, forming an eight-celled mass. By the end of the fourth day after fertilisation the solid mass of blastomeres is called a **morula**, and has usually reached the uterus. The next divisions of the blastomeres lead to the formation of a blastocyst with 64 cells. A space forms inside the blastocyst, called a **blastocoel**. The cells inside the blastocyst divide at different rates as they become specialised. The inner cell mass gives rise to the embryo, whilst the surrounding cells (called the **trophoblast**) help provide nourishment for the embryo and later develop into the **extraembryonic** membranes that form the placenta.

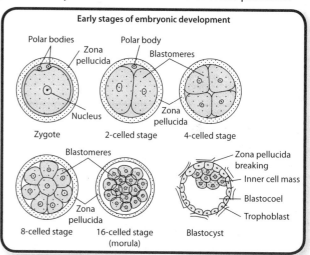

Early stages of embryonic development

Plant Reproduction

The main form of reproduction in plants is sexual reproduction. The flower is the main reproductive organ in plants. There is an enormous variety in the morphology of flowers.

Structure of an Insect-pollinated Flower

An insect-pollinated flower relies on the male gametes, the pollen, being produced by meiosis in the anther. The insect collects the mature pollen grains and transports them to the female stigma of a different flower.

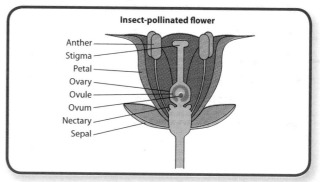

Insect-pollinated flower

Ovule Structure

The ovule of the flower contains an embryo sac. This contains two synergids, which react with the pollen tube to enable it to enter. The ovum will be fertilised to form the embryo and the central cell with two polar nuclei will form the endosperm. The antipodal cells disintegrate after fertilisation.

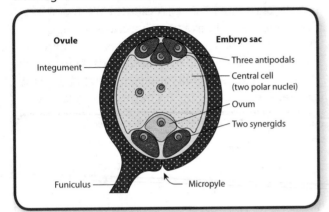

Pollen Tube Formation

A pollen grain contains a vegetative cell that will form the pollen tube, and a generative cell that divides to form two sperm cells. When a pollen grain lands on the stigma of a flower, lipids – specific to the particular plant species – on the surface of the stigma trigger the formation of the pollen tube. The vegetative cell grows to form the pollen tube, which drills down the style until it reaches the ovary, where the female ovule is present. One of the two sperm cells then fertilises the ovum. This will grow into the new plant. The other sperm cell fertilises the polar nuclei of the central cell. The central cell becomes the **endosperm** and serves as the food supply for the developing embryo.

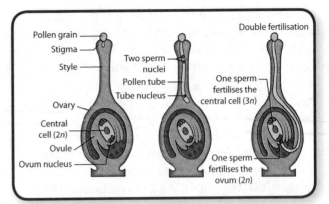

QUICK TEST

1. Define gametogenesis.

2. When does oogenesis initially start?

3. Where does spermatogenesis take place in humans?

4. What cells are formed when a spermatogonium divides mitotically?

5. What is the zona pellucida?

6. What is in the acrosome of a spermatozoon?

7. What are the cells that make up a morula called?

8. How many nuclei are inside a pollen grain?

9. Which cell in the embryo sac produces the embryo of the seed?

10. How many copies of the chromosomes are present in the endosperm?

SUMMARY

- **Sexual reproduction involves the production of male and female sex cells (gametes).**

- **Gametogenesis is the process of the formation of male and female gametes.**

- **Oogenesis is the process of the formation of ova.**

- **Unlike normal meiosis whereby four haploid daughter cells are produced, oogenesis leads to the production of one ovum and two polar bodies.**

- **Oogenesis begins in the developing foetus, with the production of oogonia.**

- The oogonia start meiosis I and become primary oocytes.

- Meiosis then pauses at prophase I until the female begins menstruating.

- From then on, on an approximately monthly basis, the primary oocytes continue through meiosis.

- The first meiotic division leads to the formation of a secondary oocyte, which contains the majority of the cytoplasm, and a polar body.

- The second meiotic division leads to the formation of a haploid ovum and another polar body.

- Spermatogenesis is the process of the production of sperm.

- It occurs in spermatogonia in the seminiferous tubules of the testes.

- A diploid spermatogonium divides mitotically to produce a pair of diploid spermatocytes.

- These undergo meiosis I to produce a pair of haploid secondary spermatocytes.

- Meiosis II leads to the formation of four haploid spermatids, which are then assembled into spermatozoa.

- Ovulation leads to the ovum leaving the ovary into the fallopian tube.

- When a mature spermatozoon reaches the ovum it first makes contact with the corona radiata and then the jelly-like zona pellucida.

- The zona pellucida is made of glycoproteins that react with the proteins in the head of the sperm.

- This causes the acrosome reaction – enzymes are released and digest the zona pellucida, allowing the sperm to move through.

- Once breached, a cortical reaction occurs – granules are released, via exocytosis, that harden the zona pellucida, preventing entry of more sperm.

- When the nuclei fuse, fertilisation has occurred and the fertilised cell becomes a zygote.

- The zygote divides into two blastomeres after 30 hours, four after 40 hours and eight after 72 hours.

- A morula forms and the divisions from that point lead to differences in the structure and the formation of a blastocyst.

- Some of the cells become extraembryonic material (forming the placenta) and the inner cells grow to become the embryo.

- Flowering plants produce pollen.

- When a pollen grain lands on the stigma of a plant of the same species a pollen tube forms.

- The pollen tube has three nuclei – one for the pollen tube and the other two to fertilise the ovum (becoming the embryo) and the central cell (becoming the endosperm).

PRACTICE QUESTIONS

1. **a)** Describe and explain how the events following the acrosome reaction in mammals prevent more than one sperm fertilising an ovum. [4 marks]

    b) Many women with cancer opt to have their ova removed and frozen before treatment starts. Explain, using ideas about oogenesis, why this is a sensible precaution. [4 marks]

Biodiversity

Life on Earth is hugely varied. This variation stems ultimately from mutations in DNA which lead to different genes coding for new or more efficient proteins that enable an organism to survive and pass on those genes to its offspring. **Biodiversity** is an indicator of the variety and diversity of life.

Measuring Biodiversity

There are several types of biodiversity and it is important to be clear which type is being measured.

- **Habitat biodiversity** – the biodiversity occurring in a given habitat, e.g. sand dunes, woodland, meadows, and streams.
- **Species biodiversity** – the species richness and evenness, in other words how many different species are present in a community and how abundant they are.
- **Genetic biodiversity** – a measure of the variation of the genes present in a population of a species.

Sampling Techniques

It is not possible to record all of the organisms in a habitat. Instead, sampling is undertaken that, after mathematical processing, gives an indication of what the true population of an organism is.

There are two types of sampling: random and non-random.

Random Sampling

Random sampling is necessary as it helps remove sampling bias (where the biologist may sample areas that look interesting or easier to count). Techniques that involve random sampling require that the area being sampled is known and mapped out. The locations of the sampling areas are decided by random numbers, generated either by computer or by a random number table. Typically, the numbers are used to identify a point on the map, using the random numbers as grid references. A **quadrat** is placed at that point and the organisms counted using a number of techniques (e.g. counting individuals or measuring the area covered by plants). Alternatively, the random number could generate a starting point for a **line transect**.

Non-random Sampling

- **Systematic sampling** is where the samples are chosen in a regular way, e.g. samples could be taken every 2 metres along a transect line, or at a set time of day. The advantage over random sampling is that it is more likely that a good coverage of an area will be achieved. A grid doesn't have to be used – the sampling just has to be at regular intervals. The disadvantage is that it is more susceptible to bias, with over- or under-representation of a pattern. Transects are used to analyse transitions between microhabitats, e.g. plant succession, intertidal zones.
- **Stratified sampling** is where there are two or more study areas being compared, e.g. two woodlands. The process takes into account the differences in size of the two areas. If 40 samples were to be taken from a study area that contained two types of woodland, one type of woodland covering 80% of the area and one covering 20%, then eight samples would be taken from the smaller woodland area and 32 from the larger woodland area. The advantage of stratified sampling is that the samples can be collected with random or systematic techniques. It can generate more representative results and comparison is easier between subsets of data. The disadvantage is that the proportion of the subsets needs to be known in advance and this must also be accurate.

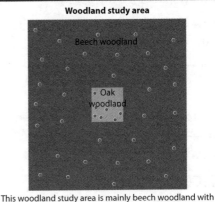

Woodland study area

Beech woodland

Oak woodland

This woodland study area is mainly beech woodland with a small plot of oak woodland in the middle. More samples are taken from the beech woodland than from the oak.

Whichever technique is chosen, it is important to ensure that the range of organisms in a habitat are sampled.

Species Richness and Evenness

Species richness is measured by counting the number of different species in a community. **Species evenness** is the number of individuals of each species (its abundance).

For example, compare two communities, A and B, each with 100 individual trees:
- A – 25 silver beech, 30 red beech, 18 mountain beech, 27 mountain ash
- B – 75 silver beech, 5 red beech, 2 mountain beech, 18 mountain ash.

The species richness in this example is the same, as community A and community B both have four different tree species. The species evenness (or relative abundance) is different, however. In community A it would be easier to see all of the four different species. In community B, however, the focus would be more on the silver beech, with red and mountain beech being much rarer.

Looking at the two communities it seems obvious that community A is more biodiverse than community B. This is not enough for a biological study. Instead biologists have to quantify the difference and see if it is significant or not.

One such method for quantifying this difference is using Simpson's index of diversity. There are, of course, other techniques available.

Simpson's Index of Diversity

Simpson's index of diversity measures the probability that two individuals randomly selected from a sample will belong to the same species. The formula is:

$$D = 1 - \left(\Sigma \left(\frac{n}{N} \right)^2 \right)$$

where Σ = sum of, n = the total number of organisms of a particular species, N = the total number of organisms of all species and D = Simpson's index of diversity.

An alternative version is to use the formula:

$$D = \frac{N(N-1)}{\Sigma n(n-1)}$$

The range of Simpson's index is from 0 (no diversity) to 1 (infinite diversity). In other words, the bigger D gets, the higher the diversity.

Using the example given above for community A:

$$\text{Silver beech} = \left(\frac{25}{100} \right)^2 = 0.0625$$

$$\text{Red beech} = \left(\frac{30}{100} \right)^2 = 0.09$$

$$\text{Mountain beech} = \left(\frac{18}{100} \right)^2 = 0.0324$$

$$\text{Mountain ash} = \left(\frac{27}{100} \right)^2 = 0.0729$$

$$\Sigma = 0.0625 + 0.09 + 0.0324 + 0.0729 = 0.2578$$

$$D = 1 - 0.2578$$

$$= 0.7422$$

$$= 0.74 \text{ (to 2 significant figures).}$$

And for community B:

$$\text{Silver beech} = \left(\frac{75}{100} \right)^2 = 0.5625$$

$$\text{Red beech} = \left(\frac{5}{100} \right)^2 = 0.0025$$

$$\text{Mountain beech} = \left(\frac{2}{100} \right)^2 = 0.0004$$

$$\text{Mountain ash} = \left(\frac{18}{100} \right)^2 = 0.0324$$

$$\Sigma = 0.5625 + 0.025 + 0.0004 + 0.0324 = 0.5978$$

$$D = 1 - 0.5978$$

$$= 0.4022$$

$$= 0.40 \text{ (to 2 significant figures).}$$

This shows that community A has a D of 0.74 compared to a lower D for community B of 0.40.

Calculating Genetic Biodiversity

A species with greater variation in its genome will be in a better position to adapt to environmental change than one which has less. The variation is in the alleles that a species has for its genes. If a gene had only one allele (version) then every individual would express that version of the gene. If there are different alleles, then the genes expressed will differ. The site of the gene on a chromosome is called the gene locus (plural loci). The variant alleles are referred to as being **polymorphic**.

Genetic diversity can be calculated as follows:

Proportion of polymorphic gene loci =

$$\frac{\text{number of polymorphic gene loci}}{\text{total number of loci}}$$

Maintaining Biodiversity

If a species has a wide genetic variation and is abundant, then it will be able to adapt to environmental change.

Higher biodiversity in an area also means that the organisms are more likely to be able to adapt to stresses on the ecosystem. If, for example, a species were to die out in an area of high biodiversity then the feeding relationships would be able to change, e.g. a predator consuming more of a different prey. In an area of low biodiversity such changes are more likely to lead to bigger fluctuations in organism numbers and cause the extinction of other organisms.

Biodiversity is also important as humans have traditionally produced a wide variety of drugs and other chemicals from organisms. If biodiversity is reduced and species become extinct then potential life-saving drugs may disappear along with the species.

How can Biodiversity be Maintained?

Zoos around the world have to be very careful with breeding programmes to ensure that individuals have as wide a variation in their gene pool as possible so that offspring have the lowest number of recessive genes. If the gene pool is too narrow then it might not be possible to save the organism, even with captive breeding programmes.

A kiwi

Once the number of organisms in a programme increases above a certain level then individuals can be released into the wild (with certain protections in place to aid survival).

For example, in New Zealand, kiwi are endangered. Non-native introduced mammals have decimated the population of these flightless birds. Individuals of one rare type of kiwi, the rowi (*Apteryx rowi*), are bred in captivity and then released to certain predator-free islands where they are watched and monitored until adulthood. They are then released properly into the wild.

Governments can pass laws protecting areas of important land, e.g. world conservation sites.

Farming

Farming practices can reduce biodiversity. In the interests of being able to use large farming machinery (such as combine harvesters) and to maximise crop yields, in parts of the world many small fields have been merged to create larger fields. These are mega-farms. Where previously there would have been natural hedgerows separating the small fields, with animals and plants living in the hedgerow habitat, there are now huge monocultures of a crop. Diversity is decreased. Having a single crop grown over a large area also decreases soil biodiversity.

Farmers can prevent loss of biodiversity by growing a greater variety of crops in smaller areas. Planting hedges and trees ensures that there is less chance of the fields becoming barren.

QUICK TEST

1. Define habitat biodiversity.

2. What is species biodiversity?

3. How does genetic biodiversity differ from the other types of biodiversity?

4. Why do ecologists use sampling techniques?

5. What is the advantage of random sampling?

6. What is systematic sampling?

7. What is stratified sampling?

8. Describe species evenness and species richness.

9. Give the formula for Simpson's index of diversity.

10. Why does farming with mega-farms reduce biodiversity?

SUMMARY

- Biodiversity gives an indication of the variety and diversity of life on Earth.
- Habitat biodiversity gives a measure of the biodiversity in a given habitat.
- Species biodiversity gives a measure of the species richness and evenness (how many different species and how abundant they are).
- Genetic biodiversity gives a measure of the variation of the genes present in a population of a species.
- It is not possible to sample every living thing in a habitat.
- Instead, sampling techniques are used that sample smaller parts of the habitat.
- The results can then be scaled up to give an indication of the likely real biodiversity.
- Random sampling is used so that any biases of the researcher are removed.
- Locations of places to sample are generated randomly.
- An issue with random sampling is that if there is a non-random pattern in a sampling area, the random samples may miss this.
- Non-random sampling is where sample locations are chosen in a non-random, regular way.
- Systematic sampling takes samples every set distance from the start or at the same time each day.
- This is better at identifying areas of non-randomness in the population.
- However, it can also introduce bias.
- Stratified sampling takes into account the relative sizes of two or more sampling locations.
- It divides the numbers of samples between the locations.
- Species richness is a measure of the number of different species in an area at a given time.
- Species evenness is a measure of the abundance of each species type.
- Simpson's index of diversity can be used to measure the probability that two individuals randomly selected from an area will come from the same species.
- The range of Simpson's index is from 0 (no diversity) to 1 (infinite diversity).
- Governments can help protect biodiversity by protecting key ecological areas.
- Farmers can help to increase biodiversity by growing more varied crops in smaller fields, and by replacing hedgerows.

PRACTICE QUESTIONS

1. An ecologist is sampling two different rivers, A and B. The results are shown in the table.

   a) For each river calculate the Simpson's index. Use $D = 1 - \left(\Sigma\left(\frac{n}{N}\right)^2\right)$. Show your working. **[6 marks]**

   b) What do the results tell you about the diversity of the two rivers? **[3 marks]**

River A		River B	
Fish	**Number**	**Fish**	**Number**
Rainbow trout	230	Rainbow trout	339
Brown trout	345	Brown trout	180
Catfish	25	Catfish	0
Carp	1970	Carp	2370
Steelheads	213	Steelheads	21
Pike	31	Pike	33
Total	2814	**Total**	2943

Evolution

Classification

All life on Earth can be classified into groups. Classification is the sorting of organisms into different categories. The earliest method of classification was based on grouping by similar **morphological** (body plan) characteristics. Modern technology has enabled DNA sequencing and bioinformatics to determine the **phylogenetic relationship** of organisms.

Binomial Classification

The system used to identify organisms scientifically is the **binomial system**, devised by Carl Linnaeus in the 18th century.

All life can be sorted into the following hierarchy:
- Domain/kingdom, phylum, class, order, family, genus and species. Note that the convention is to write the genus and species in italics or underline it, e.g. *Homo sapiens* or <u>Homo sapiens</u>.

For example, a lion can be classified as:
- Eukaryota, Animalia, Chordata, Mammalia, Carnivora, Felidae, *Panthera leo*.

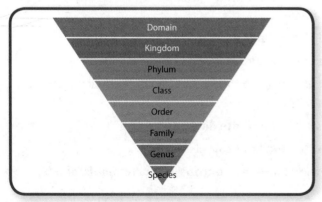

Domain

There are three domains – the Archaea, the Bacteria and the Eukaryota. The domain system is based on the rRNA possessed by organisms and is gaining in prevalence. It was devised by Carl Woese and colleagues in 1977. There are still discussions about how to arrange the classification of organisms.

Kingdom

An alternative starting point for classification separates organisms into one of five kingdoms – Animalia, Plantae, Fungi, Protoctista and Prokaryotae.

If using with the domain system, then the Prokaryotae are subdivided into the kingdoms Archaebacteria and Eubacteria. This system was devised in 1969 and is currently the most widely used classification system.

Species

The final name for an organism is the species. A species is defined as a group of organisms with similar characteristics that can interbreed and produce fertile offspring. This is a definition created by biologists and there are exceptions and grey areas. Generally, if two organisms can successfully breed together, then they should be in the same species.

For example, horses and donkeys are very similar to each other. They can breed and reproduce, with a mule being the product. Mules, however, are sterile. So the horse and donkey are separate species. Given enough time and evolutionary changes there might come a point when the cross will not even lead to the birth of mules.

Even with the species definition it can still be difficult to allocate an organism to a species. Within the species there is often a lot of variation. For example, trees grown in one location (e.g. a windswept mountain) might have morphological differences to those grown in another (e.g. dense woodland).

Ring Species

Ring species is a term used to describe two populations of a species living in the same geographical area that cannot interbreed. However, there is a ring of populations separated by a geographical barrier that *can* interbreed.

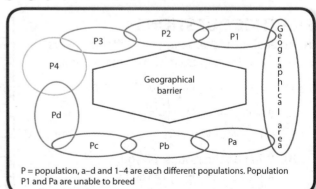

P = population, a–d and 1–4 are each different populations. Population P1 and Pa are unable to breed

Morphological Convergence

Over very long timescales it is possible for organisms to develop similar morphological characteristics, due to evolution through natural selection.

For example, bats evolved wings that enabled them to fly, which led some people to misidentify them as birds.

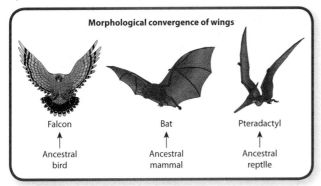

Morphological convergence of wings

Falcon ↑ Ancestral bird

Bat ↑ Ancestral mammal

Pteradactyl ↑ Ancestral reptlle

Another example is the mulgaras. These are marsupial carnivores related to Tasmanian devils, and are found in Australia. They are very similar to the placental mouse.

This means that, although classifying organisms according to their morphology has been very useful, there is an unacceptable level of errors. Instead, scientists have had to look at the genetics of organisms to be sure of connections. This leads to phylogenetic classification, which categorises organisms based on the genes they possess.

Gel Electrophoresis

Some organisms appear very similar and could be placed in the same genus.

Genetic analysis can show whether an organism is really related to another. Samples of DNA are obtained and then subjected to gel electrophoresis. The samples of DNA are broken into smaller fragments using specific cutting enzymes called restriction endonucleases. The samples are loaded onto a gel made of polyacrylamide and subjected to an electric current. This separates the fragments according to size and charge. The phosphate groups present in the DNA mean the fragments are negatively charged and so move to the positive anode. The larger fragments move more slowly than the smaller fragments. The result is a pattern of bands, or DNA profile. The patterns can be compared to assess how related the species are.

Variations of this technique exist, e.g. looking at mitochondrial DNA (which varies less than normal DNA) and separating proteins.

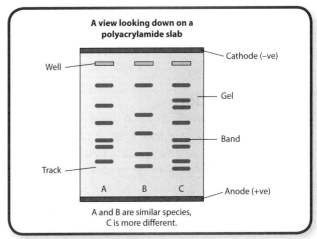

A view looking down on a polyacrylamide slab

Well — Cathode (−ve)

Gel

Band

Track

A   B   C   Anode (+ve)

A and B are similar species, C is more different.

A version of this technique, called DNA fingerprinting, can be used to determine paternity and to help determine the guilt or innocence of a person when a crime has been committed.

Genetic methods have the advantage that the remains of extinct organisms can also be analysed (subject to there being enough DNA for the analysis).

Typically, mitochondrial gene variants are used to map relatedness in animals (e.g. the gene encoding cytochrome oxidase 1). In plants genes coding for chloroplasts are used instead.

Bioinformatics

Analysing the DNA from organisms involves the interpretation of huge sequences of DNA. It is easier to identify the amino acids that would be produced from the DNA and to use single letters for those amino acids (e.g. F for phenylalanine). Bioinformatics involves passing the polypeptide sequences through computer databases. Natural selection may have led to changes to the polypeptide sequence, including the insertion of new introns that are not present in other species. Algorithms are used to match up the relevant sections of DNA. The information derived from bioinformatics can be used to create phylogenetic trees.

For example, this technique has been used to work out the familial relationship between mammoths (now extinct) and Indian and African elephants, to answer the question of which is more closely related to the ancestral mammoth.

Phylogenetic Trees

All life on Earth shares a common ancestor. This means that all life is related. Relationships can be shown by plotting a phylogenetic tree. A phylogenetic tree enables the reader to work out how related organisms are to one another based on their genetic make-up, and to see how the species evolved over time.

Natural Selection

We have seen that all life on Earth shares a common ancestor – all genetic evidence points to this fact, and there is no evidence suggesting otherwise. The great diversity of life is the result of evolution through natural selection.

Evolution is the process by which organisms change over time. Natural selection is the method that leads to evolution.

An organism has its genetic code. Over time mutations take place, at a very low rate. The successful mutations lead to the organism surviving long enough to pass on its genes to its offspring (along with the mutated version or **allele** for the gene). Proteins formed from the new alleles will vary from the original protein and may be more or less effective. Under certain environmental pressures the new version of the protein may enable the organism to survive better than those that do not produce it. Over time, the allele coding for that protein will increase in frequency in the population.

Adaptations

The genetic variation of organisms leads to a variety of different proteins being formed. Those proteins alter the anatomy and physiology of an organism. They can also alter behaviour. The adaptations enable an organism to survive in a particular environment. For example, organisms living in very cold conditions may have evolved proteins that can work more effectively under cold conditions. The way an organism fits into an ecosystem is called its **niche**. This includes its interactions with the environment and other organisms.

Directional Selection

This is where an adaptation is selected for, leading to those organisms that carry the adaptation increasing throughout a population. This can be seen in the response of a population of bacteria to an antibiotic.

Initially, when the mainly non-resistant bacteria are exposed to the antibiotic the non-resistant bacteria die before they can reproduce, and decline in number. This leaves those carrying the adaptation for resistance and these resistant bacteria reproduce and increase in number.

How does Speciation Occur?

In any species there is variety between individuals. The variation is due to the genes possessed by that species and the number of different alleles. The more alleles, the more genetically varied the species is. Members of the same species can freely interbreed and produce fertile offspring.

If the populations of a species become isolated from each other then, over time, mutations leading to new alleles will arise and spread through the populations. If the new alleles prevent individuals from each population from producing fertile offspring then a new species will have been formed.

Geographical Isolation

This is where populations are separated by a geographical barrier. This includes creation of an island, where water acts as a barrier to breeding between populations.

Temporal Isolation

This is where populations of the same species are awake at different times, so there is no opportunity for breeding between populations.

QUICK TEST

1. What is the binomial system of classification?
2. What are the three domains?
3. Give the definition of the term species.
4. Explain what is meant by a ring species.
5. Describe morphological convergence.
6. How is a phylogenetic tree created?
7. How does genetic diversity help protect a species from environmental change?

- All organisms on Earth can be sorted into groups based on their morphology or their genetic make-up.
- The system of binomial classification gives every organism a genus and a species name.
- It was devised in the 18th century by Carl Linnaeus.
- A species is defined as being a population of organisms that can freely interbreed and produce fertile offspring.
- A ring species is a term used to describe two populations of a species living in the same geographical area that cannot interbreed. However, there is a ring of populations separated by a geographical barrier that *can* interbreed.
- Systems based on morphology can have problems – organisms can appear to be in the same group when they are not, e.g. bats and birds (both having wings).
- Analysing the gene sequences of organisms enables a phylogenetic tree to be drawn.
- The genes being analysed are separated through gel electrophoresis.
- In animals it is common to use the gene variants encoding the mitochondrial enzyme cytochrome oxidase 1.
- In plants the genes coding for chloroplasts are used instead.
- Bioinformatics is the analysis of the DNA from organisms to create a phylogenetic tree.
- Evidence from phylogenetic trees points to all life on Earth sharing a single common ancestor.
- Natural selection selects for characteristics that help organisms survive and pass on their genes.
- Over time the alleles coding for the beneficial characteristic spread in the species.
- The greater the genetic diversity in a species the more likely it is that the species will be able to survive environmental changes.
- The alleles for a gene produce different proteins which can alter metabolism and even behaviour.
- If a population becomes geographically or temporally isolated from other populations of the same species then the build-up of unique alleles could lead to the populations being unable to produce fertile offspring.
- If this occurs, a new species will have arisen.

PRACTICE QUESTIONS

1. The words below show the names and taxons used to classify one species of elephant, the Indian elephant:

    Order Proboscidea **Domain** Eukaryota **Genus** *Elephas* **Kingdom** Animalia

    Phylum Chordata **Class** Mammalia **Species** *maximus* **Family** Elephantidae

    a) Write the classifications in the correct hierarchical order.   **[4 marks]**

    b) Scientists tried to find out the relationship of Asian and Indian elephants to the extinct woolly mammoth.

        What does the phylogenetic tree (right) tell you about the relationship of the Asian and Indian elephants to the mammoth?   **[2 marks]**

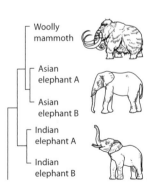

Woolly mammoth

Asian elephant A

Asian elephant B

Indian elephant A

Indian elephant B

Disease

A disease is a disorder of a tissue, organ or organ system. When an organism has a disease, symptoms may become evident. Symptoms can be the result of a **metabolic pathway** being affected, leading to the failure of a particular enzyme or to the growth of cells in the wrong place.

Transmission of disease can be direct, through physical contact with an infected person, or indirect, where there is no direct contact. Contact occurs from contaminated surfaces or objects, or via vectors.

Types of Diseases

- **Pathogen borne** – caused by other living organisms infecting the host
- **Genetic** – passed on through genes from parent to offspring
- **Dietary** – caused by the diet
- **Environmental** – the environment interferes with the normal metabolic processes
- **Autoimmune** – the immune system develops a fault and starts attacking the organism's own cells.

Pathogen-borne Disease

Organisms are surrounded by pathogens. A pathogen is a disease-causing agent, e.g. a bacterium, fungus, protist or virus. For a pathogen the internal environments of plants and animals provide protection and a ready source of nutrients. Animals additionally provide a means of transport to new locations. Many pathogens are spread by a vector which carries them from one organism to another. Organisms have evolved defences against pathogens, and medical intervention can be used to support natural defences.

Bacterial-borne Diseases

Tuberculosis (TB) is a disease of humans caused by the bacterium *Mycobacterium tuberculosis*. It is spread directly by droplets coughed or sneezed by an infected individual. The moist, warm surface of the alveoli in the lungs is an ideal entry point for the bacterium.

Bacterial meningitis is caused by direct bacterial infection, and affects the brain and spinal cord. The bacteria involved normally cause other diseases (e.g. *Haemophilus influenzae* and *Streptococcus pneumoniae* that cause influenza and pneumonia) but as they have infected the brain they have a different impact on the host. The bacteria are directly passed on through exchange of respiratory and throat secretions (e.g. through kissing).

Ring rot is a bacterial disease in plants, such as potatoes (caused by *Clavibacter michiganensis*) and tomatoes. It is passed on directly through wounds acquired during the farming process and from infected seed. It can devastate a crop and lead to starvation.

Viral-borne Diseases

HIV (human immunodeficiency virus) is the name given to the virus that causes AIDS (acquired immune deficiency syndrome) in humans. Transmission is direct, via the exchange of body fluids, contaminated needles used in **intravenous** drug use, or the transfusion of infected blood.

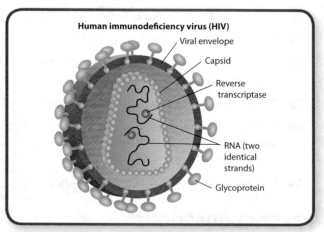

Human immunodeficiency virus (HIV)

- Viral envelope
- Capsid
- Reverse transcriptase
- RNA (two identical strands)
- Glycoprotein

Influenza, or flu, is caused by one of the Orthomyxoviridae, a group of RNA viruses that can infect vertebrates, including birds and mammals. There are three genera of influenza viruses, A, B and C, of which A is the most virulent, causing the most deaths in humans. It is spread directly through droplets produced when coughing and sneezing. Symptoms include a high fever, runny nose, sore throat and aching muscles.

Tobacco mosaic virus (TMV) is a virus that causes disease in a wide range of plants, including tobacco and potatoes. It causes a mosaic-like mottling of the leaves, reducing the effectiveness of photosynthesis and so reducing crop yields. It is transmitted directly via people handling infected plants.

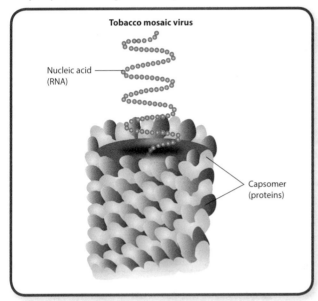

Tobacco mosaic virus

Nucleic acid (RNA)

Capsomer (proteins)

Protist-borne Diseases

Malaria is a disease of the blood caused by a member of the Protoctista in the genus *Plasmodium*. *Plasmodium* is transmitted indirectly via a vector, a female *Anopheles* mosquito.

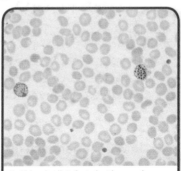

Red blood cells infected with a number of *Plasmodium* show up clearly against uninfected red blood cells when stains are used

Potato/tomato late blight is caused by *Phytophthora infestans*, originally thought to be a fungus but now known to be a protist. It caused the Great Potato Famine in Ireland in 1845 in which over a million people died. The disease causes the leaves to die and the potatoes to turn into a foul, inedible mush. It is passed on through infected plant material, e.g. storing infected potatoes and using them to start the following year's crop.

Fungal Diseases

Black sigatoka is a disease of bananas caused by a fungus called *Mycosphaerella fijiensis*. It causes a significant decrease in leaf area and loss of yield. It is transmitted by spores that are blown by the wind.

Ringworm in cattle is caused by *Trichophyton verrucosum*. It is directly transmitted from infected animals. Providing dry conditions for the cows is one way to reduce the risk of infection.

Athlete's foot is a fungal infection by the human ringworm fungi. Transmission is indirectly through spores present in communal areas. Damp, humid conditions (e.g. not drying the skin after washing) enable the spores to germinate and the fungus to grow on the skin.

Plant Defences

Plants lack an immune system comparable to animals. Instead they have developed a wide range of chemical- and protein-based methods of combating infection by preventing the pathogen from entering in the first place.

Plants with particular genes can produce chemicals that prevent growth of pathogens, e.g. antimicrobials. Other plants have systems to limit the spread of infection, e.g. through **callose** deposition in the cell wall. The laying down of callose, a polysaccharide, closes the plasmodesmata, forming a barrier to symplastic movement of pathogens.

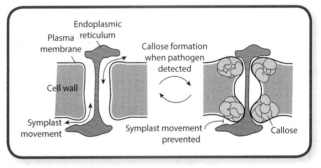

Endoplasmic reticulum

Plasma membrane

Callose formation when pathogen detected

Cell wall

Symplast movement

Symplast movement prevented

Callose

Non-specific Animal Defence

Animals have a number of ways of preventing infection that do not rely on an immune system.

Skin

The skin is a thick barrier to entry by pathogens into the body. It is a waterproof mechanical barrier. The skin is naturally covered in microorganisms, some of which would be pathogens if they could enter it. They can only do this if the skin is broken or damaged.

Mucous Membranes

The skin cannot cover all of the body. There are parts which have to be exposed, e.g. the nostrils, eyelids, ears, trachea, genitals and anus. Thin mucous membranes surround the organs and line the various cavities in the body (e.g. stomach). They prevent entry of pathogens into the organs. Some membranes also produce a thick mucus to trap pathogens.

Expulsive Reflexes

When the throat or nasal passage are exposed to irritants, including pathogens, the response is to sneeze or cough. This expels the pathogens.

Blood Clotting

If the skin is broken, the blood clots, sealing the site of the injury and preventing further infection from the outside.

1. Platelets present in the blood form a plug, blocking the skin breach. They release clotting factors, such as thromboplastin.

2. Prothrombin, which is a constituent of blood plasma, is converted to its active form, thrombin (catalysed by thromboplastin).

3. The thrombin structurally alters the soluble protein fibrinogen, causing it to form a string-like mesh made of insoluble fibrin. The mesh traps red blood cells that form a scab.

The dry surface of a scab provides a temporary waterproof layer.

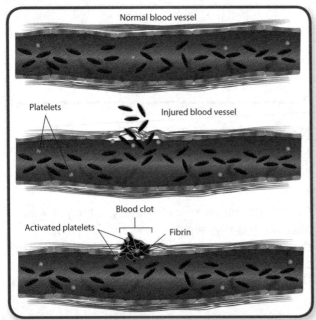

Normal blood vessel

Platelets

Injured blood vessel

Activated platelets

Blood clot

Fibrin

Wound Repair

The next step is to repair the wound and grow new cells to reseal the skin barrier.

Inflammation

Inflammation is a protective response to infection. The purpose is to provide the materials needed to repair the damaged cells, eliminate the cause of the problem (the pathogen), and set up the required conditions so that the immune system can function.

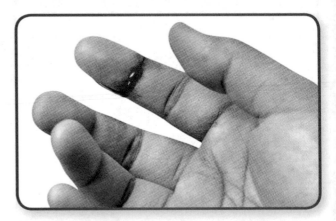

QUICK TEST

1. What is a disease?

2. There are a number of ways an organism can get a disease. One way is through pathogens. Give three other types of disease.

3. Give three examples of bacterial pathogens.

4. How is HIV transmitted?

5. What is a typical consequence of a crop being infected with a disease?

6. How can plants protect against infection?

7. How does the skin of an animal protect against disease?

8. How do expulsive reflexes help prevent infection?

9. Describe the sequence that takes place when the skin is cut and a clot forms.

10. How does a scab help protect the skin against further infection?

- A disease is a disorder of a tissue, organ or organ system.

- Symptoms can be the result of a metabolic pathway being affected leading to the failure of an enzyme or growth of cells in the wrong place.

- Types of diseases include:
  - pathogen borne – living organisms infecting the host
  - genetic – passed on through genes from parent to offspring
  - environmental – a factor in the environment interferes with the body's metabolic processes
  - autoimmune – the immune system develops a fault and starts attacking the organism's own cells.

- Bacterial-borne pathogens include tuberculosis (TB), bacterial meningitis and ring rot.

- Viral-borne pathogens include HIV, influenza and tobacco mosaic virus (TMV).

- Protist-borne pathogens include malaria and potato/tomato late blight.

- Fungal-borne pathogens include black sigatoka, ringworm and athlete's foot.

- Plants have developed a range of chemical- and protein-based methods to combat infection.

- Plants can produce antimicrobial compounds. They can also form callose at cell walls, that closes the plasmodesmata to limit the spread of infection.

- Animal skin acts as a physical barrier and has its own microbial fauna that helps defend against pathogens.

- Mucous membranes occur where the skin cannot seal the body. Mucus traps invading pathogens.

- Expulsive reflexes help to remove irritants and pathogens if they enter the throat and nasal passage.

- Blood clotting occurs when the skin is cut or pierced, to rapidly seal the breakage.

- Platelets form a plug, releasing thromboplastin; prothrombin is converted to thrombin, catalysed by thromboplastin; thrombin alters the structure of fibrinogen causing it to form a mesh made of fibrin.

- A scab is formed, sealing the breach.

PRACTICE QUESTIONS

1. a) In the table on the right give an example of a disease caused by an organism from each of the kingdoms shown. **[3 marks]**

    b) A boy cuts his hand on a branch. Describe the process of blood clotting. **[3 marks]**

Kingdom	Disease
Protoctista	
Prokaryotae	
Fungi	

2. In 1845 there was a famine in Ireland, known as the Great Potato Famine. A million people died and another million left the country to find food elsewhere.

    a) The disease was caused by *Phytophthora infestans*. What type of organism is *Phytophthora infestans*? **[1 mark]**

    b) Plants do not have immune systems like animals. Give two ways plants can attempt to prevent or slow infection, and say how they work. **[2 marks]**

Immune Response 1

Phagocytes

Phagocytes are a type of white blood cell involved in primary, non-specific defence (the primary immune system). They protect the body by ingesting harmful foreign particles, bacteria and dead or dying cells. They move to the sites of infection through capillaries, tissue fluid and lymph as well as being found in plasma. Neutrophils, eosinophils and monocytes are all types of phagocyte.

Neutrophils are among the first cells to reach the site of injury or infection. They are involved with inflammation and are the main component of pus. They ingest foreign particles and microorganisms.

Neutrophil

Eosinophils are involved in combating parasites in the body. They are also involved in allergic reactions.

Eosinophil

Monocytes are the largest of all white blood cells. They respond to inflammation signals and move to the inflammation site. They become macrophages (antigen-presenting cells).

Monocyte

Lymphocytes

Lymphocytes are a subtype of white blood cell. They are subdivided into different types. The natural killer cells attack viruses and cancer cells and are part of the primary immune response.

Lymphocytes

Cytokines

When neutrophils arrive at the site of injury or infection they release **cytokines**. Cytokines promote blood flow to the injury. The increase in blood flow leads to the reddening of the skin and an increase in temperature associated with inflammation.

Phagocytosis

Phagocytes recognise foreign bodies or pathogens by the presence of chemicals called **opsonins** on the surface. Opsonins (from the Greek for 'prepare for eating') are a protein that attaches to a pathogen. If a foreign body has opsonins then it will be attacked by phagocytes and ingested.

Phagolysosomes

A vesicle forms around an ingested particle or pathogen, called a **phagosome**. This merges with a lysosome, which contains a variety of enzymes and proteins to destroy the foreign body. The combined phagosome and lysosome is called a **phagolysosome**. Once the particle has been digested, the fragments are excreted into the blood.

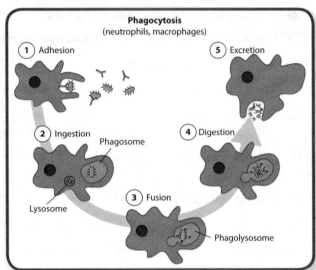

Phagocytosis
(neutrophils, macrophages)

1. Adhesion
5. Excretion
2. Ingestion — Phagosome
4. Digestion
Lysosome
3. Fusion
Phagolysosome

Adaptive Immune Response

Vertebrates uniquely have a second immune system that complements and builds upon the primary non-specific defence of other animals. This is called **adaptive immunity** (or acquired immunity). This involves the integration of a wide variety of receptors that can identify and then target specific pathogens for destruction. Adaptive means that the response is improved by previous exposure to the infecting pathogen. This also means that the response is slower than the primary non-specific defence. The adaptive immune response has two stages, primary and secondary.

Primary Immune Response

The primary response is where the immune system encounters the invading foreign body for the first time and produces antibodies. It can be as fast as a few days but typically can take weeks or even months.

Lymphocytes

There are three types of lymphocytes. In addition to the natural killer cells, there are also B-lymphocytes and T-lymphocytes. B-lymphocytes produce antibodies (the humoral response). T-lymphocytes are part of the cell-mediated response working with macrophages (a cell type formed from monocytes).

Any substance that causes a response by either B- or T-lymphocytes is called an **antigen**.

B-lymphocyte Recognition

On each B-lymphocyte is a Y-shaped molecule, the antigen receptor, with an antigen binding site. This will vary between B-lymphocytes and will bind to specific antigens, like a lock and key. When an antigen binds to the antigen binding site on the antigen receptor it causes a soluble form of the receptor, called an **antibody**, to be released. This is the function of B-lymphocytes, to release millions of antibodies when an antigen is encountered.

Antibodies

Antibodies have the same Y-shaped receptor as the antigen receptor. The receptor will bind onto the antigen of a foreign body. They can recognise free-floating antigens as well as those on the surface of a foreign body.

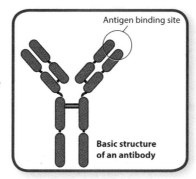

Antigen binding site

Basic structure of an antibody

T-lymphocytes

T-lymphocytes also have an antigen receptor. This is a single site, compared to the double site present in B-lymphocytes. They develop in the thymus, hence their name. There are a variety of different T-lymphocytes, often called T-cells (e.g. T-helper cells, T-killer cells).

Macrophages

Macrophages consume foreign bodies and then present antigen fragments on their cell surface membranes.

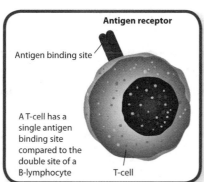

Antigen receptor

Antigen binding site

A T-cell has a single antigen binding site compared to the double site of a B-lymphocyte

T-cell

Clonal Selection

When a T-helper cell with the correct specificity encounters the macrophage, it binds onto the antigen that has been presented. Interleukin, a type of cytokine, is secreted by the macrophage and this causes the T-helper cell to divide by mitosis, producing a number of clones. All the clones have an identical antigen receptor and binding site. They will also clone if they bind to the antigens of the same foreign body (clonal expansion).

T-cell Response

The use of cytokines, such as interleukin, is an example of cell signalling. The clones release interleukin, causing more B-lymphocytes and T-killer cells to be activated.

T-killer Cells

T-killer cells bind to an antigen and then release molecules that will kill the infected cell, breaking down enzymes and the membrane.

B-lymphocyte Differentiation

Once the interleukins are released by the T-helper cells and B-lymphocytes, the B-lymphocyte will go through mitosis creating more B-lymphocytes. These will differentiate into plasma cells and B-memory cells.

Plasma Cells

Some B-lymphocytes differentiate into plasma cells. The function of the plasma cells is to massively increase the output of antibodies, releasing thousands of antibody molecules every second.

B-memory Cells

These are specialised B-lymphocytes that produce multiple copies of the antigen receptor on their cell surface. They will be used in the secondary immune response (see next topic).

T-memory Cells

Like B-memory cells, T-memory cells develop from T-cells that have encountered an antigen. They express the antigen receptor across the cell. They are used for the secondary immune response.

T-regulator Cells

These are essential for stopping the immune response, ensuring that, once the infection has been dealt with, the system reverts to normal.

QUICK TEST

1. What are phagocytes?

2. Describe the process of phagocytosis.

3. What are the three types of phagocytes called?

4. What are cytokines used for?

5. What is the name of the chemicals present on the surface of pathogens that are recognised by phagocytes?

6. How do B-lymphocytes recognise a pathogen?

7. What function do macrophages carry out?

8. What do interleukins do?

9. What is the role of T-killer and T-regulator cells?

10. How does the secondary immune response protect against future infection?

SUMMARY

- **Phagocytes are a type of white blood cell. They ingest foreign particles, bacteria and dead or dying cells.**

- **Phagocytes can be divided into neutrophils, eosinophils and monocytes.**

- **Neutrophils arrive first to the site of infection or injury.**

- **Eosinophils combat parasites in the body and are involved in allergic reactions.**

- **Monocytes are the largest of all white blood cells and respond to inflammation signals.**

- **Monocytes eventually become macrophages (antigen-presenting cells).**

- **Lymphocytes can become different types of cells with different specialisms.**

- **Cytokines are chemicals released by neutrophils at the site of injury or infection.**

- **Cytokines promote blood flow to the injury, causing inflammation (reddening of skin and swelling).**

- **Phagocytes recognise foreign bodies or pathogens by the presence of opsonins on their surface.**

- **During phagocytosis a vesicle surrounds the foreign body, called a phagosome.**

- **This merges with a lysosome, which contains digestive enzymes, forming a phagolysosome.**

- **Digested fragments are expelled from the phagocyte.**

- **Vertebrates have a second immune system that complements and builds on the primary immune response.**

- **This is called adaptive or acquired immunity and means the organism is prepared to fight the same pathogen again if the body is reinfected.**

- The first time the secondary immune system responds to infection lymphocytes are produced.

- Antigens cause B- or T-lymphocytes to be stimulated.

- B-lymphocytes have a Y-shaped antigen receptor which has a double site and matches a specific antigen.

- When the correct antigen binds, millions of a soluble form of the receptor are released into the blood (antibodies).

- T-lymphocytes have an antigen receptor, which has a single site.

- Macrophages consume foreign bodies and then present the antigen fragments on their cell surface membranes.

- A T-helper cell with the matching antigen receptor binds onto the antigen on the macrophage.

- Interleukins are released, causing the T-helper cells to divide, forming many clones all with the same antigen site.

- The interleukin also signals more B-lymphocytes and T-killer cells to arrive.

- T-killer cells bind to the antigen and release molecules to kill the infected cell.

- The interleukins also cause the B-lymphocytes to divide and make plasma cells and B-memory cells.

- Plasma cells massively increase the output of antibodies.

- B- and T-memory cells remain in the blood with the pathogen's antigen receptor on their surface to start the secondary response should the organism get reinfected.

- T-regulator cells are produced to stop the immune response once it has successfully combated the infection.

PRACTICE QUESTIONS

1. A girl caught a bacterial infection. The graph shows the progress of her illness.

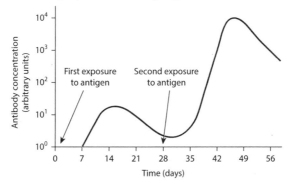

a) Explain why it took 7 days before the first antibodies were produced. **[4 marks]**

b) Which cells in the immune system do the following:

- Produce antibodies [2]

- Present antibody fragments [1]

- Release interleukins [1] **[4 marks]**

Immune Response 2

At the end of the primary immune response, a number of B- and T-memory cells were formed. These move throughout the body. If the body is invaded by the same (or a very similar) invading pathogen the **secondary immune response** is initiated. This is much faster than the primary immune response, taking only three to four days.

This is because the body already contains B- and T-memory cells that can quickly identify the foreign antigen and lead to rapid plasma and killer T-cell production.

Active Immunity

The secondary immune response is an example of **active immunity**. Immunity is achieved after the immune system has come into contact

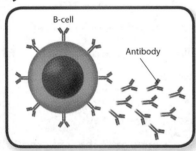

B-cell

Antibody

with a pathogen or its antigen. Once the B- and T-memory cells are present the immunity may last for years or even for the vertebrate's entire life.

The antibodies are presented on the outer surface of the cell. Antibodies are also released into the blood.

Passive Immunity

Passive immunity is immunity that hasn't come from the organism's own immune response to infection. In humans, antibodies produced by a pregnant mother can pass through the placenta into the developing foetus. This means that when the baby is born it already has some antibodies to the same pathogens that the mother had been subjected to. This also means that the baby receives antibodies against the pathogens present in the environment the mother has been in. Antibodies are also passed on to the baby via breast milk. The antibodies provided by the mother last from three to six months.

Passive immunity can also be provided by injections of antibodies. For example, antidotes to snake and spider bites are created by injecting the venom into

a host, such as a horse or goat. The animal undergoes an immune response, producing antibodies. These are then harvested and used to inject into a patient. Another example is with the disease Ebola. In the outbreak of 2015, patients who survived had samples of their blood removed and this was then injected, after being analysed, into other patients who still had the disease.

Natural and Artificial Immunity

Immunity can be:

● **natural** – from actively developing antibodies and B- and T-memory cells, or passively acquiring antibodies from the mother
● **artificial** – from being vaccinated (active immunity) or through injection with antibodies directly.

Vaccination

The development of vaccination has had a huge impact on worldwide health. There are a number of different forms of vaccine, with the most effective being ones that are most similar to those that cause the actual disease.

● **Live vaccine** – This is where a weakened (or attenuated) form of the pathogen is used. The weakened version is not pathogenic and does not cause the disease in the individual. Examples include the vaccines for measles, mumps and rubella. This type of vaccine relies on the weakened virus reproducing in the person's body. Although it does not cause the disease, if the person has a weakened immune system there could be problems.
● **Dead microorganisms** – This is where the microorganism, which has been killed using radiation or heat treatment, is used as the vaccine. The microorganisms cannot reproduce, so the entire dose is given in the vaccination. Examples include influenza, polio and rabies.
● **Pathogen fragments** – A variation of the dead microorganisms vaccine, this is where the pathogen has been killed and broken into fragments. Typically the fragments used are from the polysaccharide units making up the capsule of the microorganism. Examples include meningitis and pneumonia.

The body responds to the injected pathogens and antigens by stimulating the adaptive immune response. After a week or so the body will have produced antibodies and B- and T-memory cells. If the vaccinated individual were to come across the real disease, they would immediately implement the secondary immune response against that pathogen. This is **artificial immunity**.

Booster Vaccinations

With certain vaccines there is a requirement for the person to receive booster vaccines over a period of time. Live vaccines tend to be effective with one dose, with no need for boosters. Dead microorganisms and pathogen fragments need boosters. This is because the first injection just 'primes' the immune system. The protective immune response only happens after one or two more injections of the vaccine.

Vaccination Issues

Unfortunately pathogens evolve and show antigenic variation. This means that over time vaccinations cease to be effective against the new variants of pathogen. When that happens, the vaccine ceases to be effective and people who were vaccinated against the old variant are no longer immune to the new one.

Thus over time changes need to be made to vaccines. The more frequently the pathogen changes its antigenic properties, the less effective a specific vaccine becomes. Diseases such as rubella and measles have a low rate of change so the vaccines given to young children protect them for a lifetime. Influenza has a high mutation rate so vaccines have to be given annually.

Live vaccines can in theory potentially revert to becoming the **virulent** form. To date this has only happened with live polio vaccine, which is now no longer given for this reason.

Ethical Issues

Ever since the first person was vaccinated with the cowpox virus which conferred resistance against the similar but virulent disease smallpox, there have been ethical issues with vaccination. In a very small number of people, vaccination can cause adverse reactions. However, these are outweighed by the benefits to the far larger number who would suffer with the real disease. This is not much consolation for the sufferer of a vaccine reaction, however.

As an example, girls in the UK are now given the Human Papilloma Virus (HPV) vaccine to prevent cervical cancer. Cervical cancer kills a large number of women, so the vaccine saves lives. However, the vaccine can cause side effects, such as temporary fever, headache, nausea and muscle pain. It is judged that the benefit of preventing cervical cancer outweighs the inconvenience of the temporary side effects.

Vaccination Programmes

To be effective, vaccination programmes need to ensure that the majority of a population are vaccinated. This is the **critical vaccination level**. This will vary for each disease based on the effectiveness of the immunity provided by the vaccine. There will also be people who are unable to receive the vaccination because they are ill or have other medical issues (e.g. a compromised immune system that does not function correctly). Above the critical vaccination level the disease will not infect those who have been vaccinated, as well as those who could not have the vaccine or who chose not to be vaccinated. Above the critical vaccination level the unvaccinated population is effectively immune (this is called **herd immunity**). However, if the vaccinations drop below the critical vaccination level then the people who have not been vaccinated may get the disease. If an epidemic occurs, the people who have been vaccinated become at risk as the disease has a greater chance of mutating.

The critical vaccination levels for several diseases are shown in the table.

Disease	Critical vaccination level (%)	
	Reproductive rate of disease variant	
	Low	High
Measles	90	95
Rubella (German measles)	85	90
Influenza A	35	75

The table indicates that measles has a very high critical vaccination level. Even with variants with a low reproductive rate, 90% of the population still need to be vaccinated to confer herd immunity on the whole population.

Global Programmes

It is difficult to ensure that everyone is vaccinated. Some people in less economically developed countries might not be aware of the need for, or hear about, a vaccination programme. There is also the difficulty of keeping the vaccine cool enough (often they are refrigerated). Once the vaccine arrives in the country it is often very difficult to distribute it to those who need it. Even then, the population may not be healthy enough to take the vaccine. If food is short, those who should be vaccinated will lack protein in their diet, needed to ensure their immune systems work and the relevant immune cells can be grown. Programmes are often coordinated by the World Health Organization.

Autoimmune Diseases

Autoimmune diseases are those where the body's immune system starts to attack self instead of non-self. The immune response may be restricted to particular organs or involve a tissue wherever it is in the body.

Examples include:

- **diabetes mellitus type 1** – the immune system attacks and destroys the insulin-producing cells in the pancreas
- **psoriasis** – the immune system attacks skin cells, causing itchy, red scaly patches to appear.

With autoimmune diseases it has been important to understand how the immune system works. This means that more effective treatments (such as medicines) can be developed.

Sources of Medicines

Even though vertebrates have a very powerful immune system, it does not always immediately cure infections by pathogens. Medicines are chemical drugs that can treat or prevent disease or ensure that a patient survives an infection and can produce their own antibodies and memory cells. Some medicines effect the replacement of a missing metabolic pathway component. They can also provide relief from the symptoms of illness.

Medicines are often discovered in microorganisms and plants. For example, the antibiotic penicillin was found, like many antibiotics, in a mould (*Penicillium*).

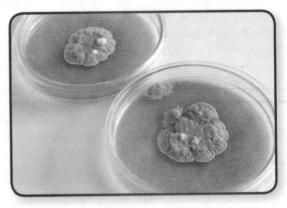

Digoxin, used to treat irregular heart rhythms, was discovered in the foxglove (*Digitalis*), and the main ingredient of aspirin, salicylic acid, was first extracted from the bark of the willow tree.

Most medicines in use have been extracted from a biological source. As more pathogens become resistant to current medical treatments, it becomes important to find new medical drugs. This means that there is a need to preserve biodiversity. For example, there are likely to be many new drugs hidden within plants and animals living in the Amazon rainforest. If humans continue cutting down the forest and burning it to create more space for farming, then there is a real danger that these potential drugs will be lost forever.

QUICK TEST

1. How long does active immunity last?
2. What is meant by passive immunity?
3. How does a baby initially acquire passive immunity?
4. How does the antidote to rattlesnake venom get made?
5. What is artificial immunity?
6. What are the three types of vaccine?
7. Which type gives immunity for the life of the individual?
8. What is the critical vaccination level?
9. What causes a vaccine to stop being effective?
10. Why can't 100% of a population be vaccinated?

- Active immunity (e.g. the secondary immune response) can last for the life of the vertebrate.

- Passive immunity is where the immunity has been passed on to the organism, not from its own immune response.

- Antibodies to pathogens which the mother has acquired can be passed on to the foetus developing in the uterus and in breast milk.

- The advantage is the baby is immune to pathogens present in the environment the mother has been in.

- Passive immunity can also be passed on through injection of antibodies.

- Anti-venoms are produced by injecting venom into a large organism, such as a horse.

- The horse's immune system produces antibodies that are then harvested and injected as the anti-venom.

- Natural immunity occurs from developing antibodies, B- or T-memory cells or passively acquiring antibodies from the mother.

- Artificial immunity is from being vaccinated or through injections with antibodies directly.

- Vaccines can be live, dead or made of pathogen fragments.

- Booster vaccinations need to take place if a live vaccine has not been used.

- This is because the immune system is only primed with the first injection, and further injections are needed to ensure the immune system has fully responded.

- Live vaccines can potentially revert back to the virulent form (although this is extremely rare).

- Vaccination carries risks and therefore giving a vaccine has an ethical dimension.

- Lack of refrigeration, lack of transport channels and poor health of target groups reduces uptake in vaccination programmes.

- The critical vaccination level gives an indication of how many of a population need to be vaccinated to confer herd immunity (protection of unvaccinated individuals).

- Some people choose not to be vaccinated, and others cannot be vaccinated due to health issues, even if they wanted to be.

PRACTICE QUESTIONS

1. The World Health Organization administers vaccination programmes in countries where much of the population is malnourished.

   Look at the graph on the right.

   a) Explain how diet affects vaccination effectiveness. **[1 mark]**

   b) Suggest the reasons for the difference in effectiveness. **[2 marks]**

   c) Why doesn't the amount of antibodies detected rise continuously? **[1 mark]**

   d) The critical vaccination level for another disease, rubella (German measles), is reported as being between 85 and 90%. What does this mean in terms of running a vaccination programme for rubella? **[3 marks]**

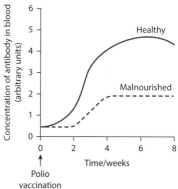

Antibiotics and Stem Cells

Antibiotics

Antibiotics are chemicals that act on bacteria, either killing them (**bactericidal**) or preventing their growth (**bacteriostatic**). Antibiotics were discovered by Alexander Fleming in 1928. His discovery of penicillin led to the ability to treat diseases and injuries that previously would have been unsurvivable.

Antibiotics target bacteria in one of three ways:
- causing the bacterial cell wall to fail
- preventing damaged bacterial DNA from being repaired
- preventing the bacteria from producing the metabolic components needed for growth.

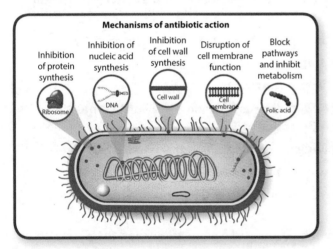

Key to the use of antibiotics is that bacterial cells are structurally different from human cells. Bacteria are prokaryotic, having a peptidoglycan cell wall and DNA floating freely in the cell. Because eukaryotic cells do not have these structures, antibiotics do not affect them. Bacteria can be divided into Gram positive and Gram negative, depending on whether they take up the Gram stain into their cell walls. Gram-positive cells have much thicker cell walls than Gram-negative ones.

Antibiotics are part of a group called **antimicrobials**. These include chemicals that can kill other microorganisms, such as fungi and protoctistans.

Resistance

There are not many classes of antibiotics. Over time the bacteria evolve to become resistant to the antibiotic. Bacteria that are resistant to all known antibiotics are on the increase, which means that eventually, unless new antibiotics are discovered, humans will once again die from bacterial infections.

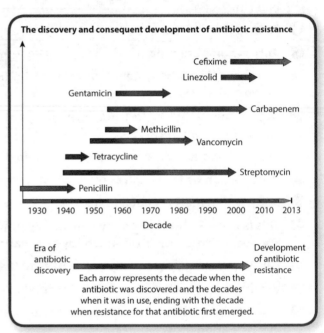

The issue occurs because people taking antibiotics often fail to finish the course. This means that bacteria remain in the individual and can become resistant, passing on the genes to other members of the population via plasmid transfer.

The disease tuberculosis (TB) is an example where the pathogen has developed resistance to treatment as well as the vaccine. Tuberculosis has to be treated over many months and it is easy for those who are receiving the long course of antibiotics to feel that they are well and stop taking them. This gives the opportunity for resistant varieties of TB to spread.

There are a small number of bacteria that are resistant to most antibiotics. Methicillin-resistant *Staphylococcus aureus* (MRSA) is often found in hospitals and has developed resistance against most available antibiotic treatments. Again, its spread has occurred due to a number of factors:

- prescribing antibiotics when unnecessary, e.g. for the common cold, caused by a virus
- cheap availability of antibiotics over the Internet from grey markets
- overuse of antibiotics in farm animals
- people not completing antibiotic courses.

Personalised Medicine

By using genetic analyses it is now possible to identify the genes present in a person. This means that in some cases it is possible to have personalised medicine. Some medicines may not work if a person carries a particular allele. For example, warfarin is a blood-thinning chemical used to treat thrombosis (the formation of blood clots). Some people have a genetic lack of sensitivity to warfarin so they need a higher dose to have the desired effect. Others carry alleles for an increased sensitivity to the drug that means a smaller quantity is needed for the effect. If a genetic analysis has been done, the patient can receive the correct treatment fast and have it work correctly.

Stem Cells

One promising avenue for treating disease is through using stem cells. Stem cells are cells that are undifferentiated and can be triggered to form specific, specialised cells.

Potency

There are different types of stem cell. **Totipotent** cells can become any type of cell, including extraembryonic or placental cells. This means that a totipotent cell could be taken and used to grow a new human being. A zygote, the cell formed after fertilisation, is the first stem cell of a developing body. The first few cells formed through the first two cell divisions are also totipotent.

Pluripotent stem cells are cells that can develop into any cell in the body. The embryonic stem cells formed after the first two cell divisions fit into this category.

Multipotent stem cells can develop into more than one type of cell, but are more limited than pluripotent stem cells. These tend to produce a cell line, e.g. **haematopoietic** stem cells in bone marrow can form a number of different blood cells – red, white and platelets.

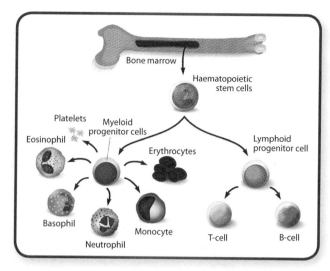

The haematopoietic stem cells give rise to progenitor cells, either lymphoid or myeloid progenitor cells. Lymphoid progenitor cells produce the T-cells and B-cells which are involved in the secondary immune system. Myeloid progenitor cells produce red blood cells as well as platelets and neutrophils.

Uses of Stem Cells

Stem cells and their ability to differentiate into different cell types have opened up the possibility of their use for treating certain diseases and injuries.

It is possible to use stem cells to grow tissues such as epithelial cells to use in skin grafts. If the stem cell has come from the patient then there will not be issues with organ rejection. Organ rejection is where the body's immune system attacks the newly transplanted tissue or organ. Typically people who have received a donated organ or tissue have to take immune suppressant drugs that stop the immune system from attacking the transplant. However, this means that the patient is more likely to suffer from infection.

Embryonic stem cells are useful in medicine because they can become any cell in the body. Embryonic stem cells are currently being investigated for their potential to help cure diseases such as Parkinson's disease. There is, however, an ethical issue with embryonic stem cells. They can only be obtained from embryos undergoing the first few cell divisions. Typically these are embryos that have not been used for implantation after *in vitro* fertilisation. However, there are some religious organisations who do not agree with the use of the cells, even though there is no chance that the embryo would ever develop into a human being.

Scientists are now investigating the possibility of being able to make a cell pluripotent. Induced pluripotent stem cells would remove the need for using embryonic stem cells and potentially open up the opportunity for a patient to use their own cells to make the induced pluripotent cells. This would mean that the cells would be recognised by the body as self and would not be attacked by the immune system.

One problem with the use of stem cells is that they can potentially become cancerous. A cancer is a cell that divides uncontrollably. Until the risk is significantly reduced, this strategy is still in the research phase.

QUICK TEST

1. What name is given to antibiotics that kill bacteria?

2. What name is given to antibiotics that stop the growth of bacteria?

3. Give three ways in which bacteria are targeted by antibiotics.

4. A bacterium is Gram positive. What does this tell you about its cell wall?

5. What would the consequence be if bacteria become resistant to all antibiotics?

6. Explain why TB has become resistant to treatment with antibiotics.

7. Why do doctors not prescribe antibiotics for the common cold?

8. What are totipotent cells?

9. What are extraembryonic cells?

10. How does the potency of haematopoietic cells differ from that of embryonic stem cells?

SUMMARY

- Antibiotics are chemicals that have a negative effect on bacteria.
- Bactericidal antibiotics kill the bacteria.
- Bacteriostatic antibiotics stop the bacteria growing.
- Antibiotics only affect bacterial cells as they are prokaryotic and human cells are eukaryotic.
- Bacteria can be classified by whether their cell wall is thick or thin.
- Thick cell walls take in Gram stain and are Gram positive.
- Thin walls don't take in Gram stain and are Gram negative.
- Antimicrobials act in a similar way to antibiotics but are effective against fungi and protoctistans.
- Over time bacteria evolve resistance to antibiotics.
- Over the last century fewer antibiotics have been discovered.
- If bacteria become resistant to all antibiotics then people will start dying of common bacterial infections.
- A major cause of resistance is people failing to complete a course of antibiotics.

- This happens because the antibiotic course has to be followed for a very long time, but because people feel better long before the end of the course they stop taking the medicine.

- A few bacteria mutate and in the presence of antibiotics only the antibiotic-resistant ones survive.

- If the course is not finished, the resistance will be able to be passed on to non-resistant bacteria, making them immune.

- Tuberculosis is an example of a disease where this has occurred.

- MRSA is another example where the pathogen is now resistant to most antibiotics.

- Apart from failing to complete the course of antibiotics, resistance can also be caused by:
  - prescribing antibiotics when they are not necessary
  - cheap availability of antibiotics over the Internet
  - overuse of antibiotics in farm animals.

- Individual genetic analysis means that drugs can be targeted and given at the correct dose.

- Stem cells are cells that can differentiate into other cells.

- Totipotent cells can become any type of cell, including extraembryonic cells.

- Pluripotent cells can become any cell (apart from extraembryonic).

- Multipotent cells can produce a range of different cells in the same line.

- Haematopoietic cells in bone marrow produce a range of blood cells.

- Stem cells are being investigated for their potential to treat diseases such as Parkinson's disease.

PRACTICE QUESTIONS

1. Antibiotics were first used in medicine in the 1930s. Over the next 40 years a large number of antibiotics were discovered in a relatively short time frame.

   Look at the chart on the right. It shows the year of first deployment and the year that resistance first started.

   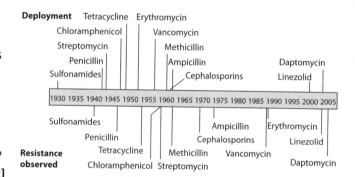

   a) What is meant by the term antibiotic resistance?
   [1 mark]

   b) With the first antibiotics in the early 20th century, how long was the interval between deployment and the development of resistance? Use the table to record your answers.

Antibiotic	Length of time before resistance
Chloramphenicol	
Streptomycin	
Sulfonamides	

   [3 marks]

   c) There was a gap where no new antibiotics were discovered, then two new antibiotics were deployed. How does the length of time before resistance developed compare to the antibiotics discovered before 1970?

   [1 mark]

Answers

Day 1

Water

QUICK TEST (Page 7)
1. δ negative (delta negative).
2. Hydrogen bonding causes water molecules to join/stick together.
3. Accept:

$$O^{\delta-}$$
$$\delta+ H \qquad H \delta+$$

4. It can dissolve a wider range of solutes/substances than any other solvent.
5. The water molecules form a crystal structure where they are arranged in a hexagonal shape. This means that the water molecules are further apart from one another than in liquid form.
6. Hydrolysis is the chemical process by which water is used to break a bond in a molecule.
7. Water can absorb a lot of energy before turning from a liquid into a gas. Therefore when someone is sweating, the evaporation removes some heat without requiring an excessive quantity of water.
8. Surface tension.
9. 4.2 J/g °C.
10. As water has a high specific heat capacity, it means that a lot of energy has to be supplied before the water temperature will rise. This means that the sea will absorb a lot of heat energy from the Sun before changing temperature. Organisms living in the sea will not have to adapt to regularly changing temperatures. The temperatures will be constant most of the time.
11. If the specific heat capacity of water were lower then organisms would experience a far wider range of water temperatures. This would limit the range of organisms in water.
12. Hydrogen bonding.

PRACTICE QUESTIONS (Page 7)
1. a) (i) Condensation reaction [1].
   (ii)

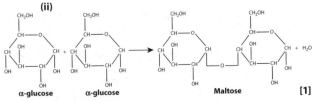

α-glucose   α-glucose   Maltose   [1]

   b) (i) Hydrolysis [1].
      (ii) Water/H_2O [1].
2. a) Water is a polar molecule. This means that the water molecules can surround other polar molecules, such as ions [1]. With Mg^{2+} the oxygen atoms will face the Mg^{2+} ion and with PO_4^{3-} the hydrogen atoms will face the ion. This creates a hydration shell around each ion [1].

   b)

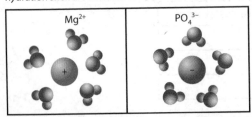

[4 marks: 2 marks for each correct arrangement] [Could also accept Mg^{2+} in centre instead of +, and PO_4^{3-} instead of –. Also accept majority of oxygen atoms pointing towards nucleus for Mg^{2+} and majority of hydrogens pointing towards nucleus for PO_4^{3-}]

Carbohydrates

QUICK TEST (Page 10)
1. A bond between a carbon atom on one sugar and a carbon atom on the other sugar, with oxygen in between (i.e. C—O—C).
2. C, H and O.
3. It can form up to four covalent bonds with other atoms.
4. Triose, pentose and hexose sugars.
5. Lactose.
6. α-glucose and fructose.
7. Amylopectin and amylose.
8. It is an unbranched, straight, molecule with hydrogen bonding between the cellulose molecules. This makes it very strong.

PRACTICE QUESTIONS (Page 11)
1. a) A drawing of maltose [1] and water (accept H_2O) [1]:

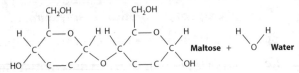

   b) A condensation reaction [1].
2.

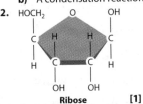

Ribose   [1]

Lipids

QUICK TEST (Page 15)
1. In lipids, the proportion of oxygen to the carbon and hydrogen is lower than in carbohydrates.
2. Ester bond.
3.

$$\overset{O}{\underset{\|}{}}$$
$$-C-O$$

4. Fats are solid whilst oils are liquid.
5. They are hydrophobic.
6. Through a hydrolysis reaction, adding water.
7. A saturated fat has no double or triple bonds between carbon atoms in the fatty acid chains.
8. An unsaturated fat has at least one double or triple bond between carbon atoms in the fatty acid chains.
9. The double or triple bonds in an unsaturated fat cause a 'kink' to appear in the fatty acid chain. This makes unsaturated fats less able to form solids.
10. Temperature insulation/Electrical insulation around neurones/Support around organs/Energy store.

PRACTICE QUESTIONS (Page 15)
1. a)

An ester bond
$$R-C-O-CH_2$$
$$R-C-O-CH$$
$$R-C-O-CH_2 \quad [1]$$

   b) A circle drawn connecting the COO arrangement on any one of the three ester bonds [1].
   c) The R represents the carbon chain, which can be any length [1].

d) If the triglyceride is an oil at 20°C, this must mean that it has a double or triple carbon bond in one or more of the fatty acid chains [1]. The triglyceride is said to be unsaturated [1]. The double or triple bond causes a kink in the chain making it more difficult for the triglyceride to form a solid [1].

e) Phospholipid [1].

Proteins
QUICK TEST (Page 19)
1. Peptide bond.
2.

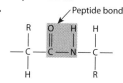

3. An amine group, NH_2, a carboxylic acid group, COOH, and an R group.
4. 20.
5. Animals have to eat other animals and plants.
6. The primary structure is the order of amino acids in the polypeptide.
7. α-helices and β-pleated sheets.
8. Disulfide bridges/Hydrogen bonding/Ionic bonds/Hydrophobic and hydrophilic interactions.
9. The quaternary (4°) structure includes more than one subunit.
10. Fibrous and globular.

PRACTICE QUESTIONS (Page 19)
1. **a)**

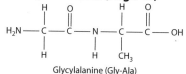

Glycylalanine (Gly-Ala)

[2 marks: 1 mark for glycine and alanine in correct order; 1 mark for peptide bond correctly drawn]

b) Peptide bond [1].

c) Circle drawn around CONH atoms [1].

2. **a)** 13 [1].

b)

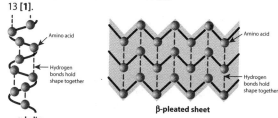

[3 marks: 1 mark for correct helix; 1 mark for correct pleated sheet; 1 mark for showing H-bonding on both]

c) Fibrous proteins are insoluble whereas globular proteins are soluble [1].

Enzymes
QUICK TEST (Page 22)
1. Enzymes are globular proteins that catalyse metabolic reactions.
2. Any example of a catabolic reaction (where a molecule is broken down), e.g. starch to maltose with amylase, proteins to amino acids with peptidases, etc.
3. Any example of an anabolic reaction (where a molecule is built up), e.g. glucose converted into starch, glucose converted into glycogen, etc.

4. A competitive inhibitor attaches to the active site of an enzyme so that the actual substrate cannot fit.
5. A non-competitive inhibitor alters the shape of the active site from a distance.
6. High temperatures cause the disulfide bridges and hydrogen bonds to permanently break, causing the shape of the enzyme to be irreversibly altered.
7. pH affects the active site by altering its shape. Unlike with temperature, the change is not permanent.
8. Enzymes reduce activation energy.
9. A holoenzyme is the combination of the enzyme and any non-protein groups, such as co-factors and prosthetic groups.
10. Any example of a coenzyme, including vitamin C (ascorbic acid).

PRACTICE QUESTIONS (Page 23)
1. Enzymes have an active site [1] that only fits one specific substrate, like a lock and key [1].
2. The active site of the enzyme is flexible/changes shape/is structurally altered [1] when the substrate interacts with it [1]. With the lock and key hypothesis, the active site is fixed and does not change shape [1].
3. Enzymes have an active site which a specific substrate will fit into [1]. A competitive inhibitor is a substance with a similar shape to the substrate that can fit into it, blocking the substrate from binding [1]. Competitive inhibition is temporary [1]. A non-competitive inhibitor acts from a distance, by altering the action of the active site indirectly so that the substrate can no longer fit correctly [1]. An enzyme–substrate complex can form but the product formation is prevented [1]. Note: Labelled drawings may be marked if they cover the points above.

Day 2
Eukaryotes
QUICK TEST (Page 27)
1. DNA is held in a nucleus.
2. Rough endoplasmic reticulum is the site of protein synthesis.
3. Smooth endoplasmic reticulum is the site of lipid synthesis.
4. The Golgi apparatus is the site where molecules are packaged into vesicles so that they can pass through the cell surface membrane.
5. Plant cells possess a cellulose cell wall, have a large sap-filled vacuole and have chloroplasts.
6.

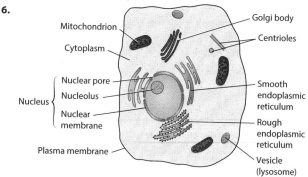

7.

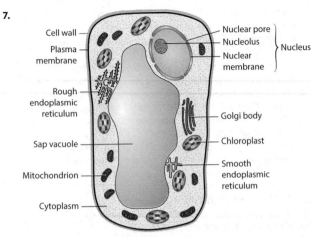

8. They have membrane-bound organelles.
9. The chloroplast.
10. Inside the mitochondria.

PRACTICE QUESTIONS (Page 27)

1. **a)**

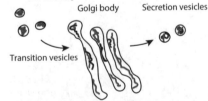

   [1]

   b) Rough endoplasmic reticulum has thousands of ribosomes attached to the membranes **[1]** whereas smooth endoplasmic reticulum does not have any **[1]**.

2. **a)** The nucleus stores DNA to allow it to be decoded and replicated when the cell divides **[1]**.

   b)

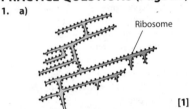

   Nucleolus (RNA and ribosomes made here)

   Nuclear pore (mRNA moves out here)

   [3 marks: 1 mark for pores; 1 mark for nucleolus; 1 mark for labels]

3.

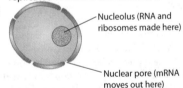

   Golgi body   Secretion vesicles

   Transition vesicles

   [2 marks: 1 mark for transition vesicles to Golgi body; 1 mark for Golgi body to secretion vesicles]

4. **a)** Lack of cell wall **[1]**, chloroplasts **[1]** and large cell vacuole **[1]**.
   b) The centrioles **[1]**.

Prokaryotes

QUICK TEST (Page 31)

1. Prokaryotes do not have membrane-bound organelles, including a nucleus.
2. A nucleoid is the main loop of DNA that is present in bacteria.

3. Peptidoglycan/murein.
4. That it is thicker as it takes the Gram stain.
5. The prokaryotic ribosome is smaller, 70S, compared to the 80S-sized eukaryotic one.
6. A circular section of DNA that can be passed on independently.
7. They are acellular and cannot reproduce by themselves.
8. Genetic material, a capsid and an attachment protein.
9. They use the cellular machinery of the host cell.
10. An electron microscope.

PRACTICE QUESTIONS (Page 31)

1. **a)** Bacteria have a cell wall made of peptidoglycan/murein **[1]** which provides structural integrity and ensures the cell is rigid and stable **[1]**.

   b) (i) How thick the cell wall is/Whether the cell wall is thick (Gram positive) or thin (Gram negative) **[1]**.

   (ii) The use of Gram stain is common to sort and identify bacteria **[1]**. If the bacterium does not take in Gram stain then it will not be identified as quickly/could be misidentified/would need further tests to establish what the infection was from **[1]**.

2. Tobacco mosaic virus is optimised to infect cells and get the cell to reproduce its genetic information **[1]**. By removing the TMV's genetic material and replacing it with the desired genetic material **[1]**, the cell then transcribes and translates the DNA, making the desired missing protein **[1]**.

Methods of Studying Cells

QUICK TEST (Page 35)

1. The resolution is the resolving power, i.e. the minimum distance at which two objects can be seen as separate entities.
2. Magnifying power = objective magnification × eyepiece magnification.
3. Magnification = $\dfrac{\text{size of image}}{\text{size of real object}}$.
4. Stains make transparent parts stand out, to identify different areas.
5. ×1000 and 200 nm.
6. ×250 000 and 0.5 nm.
7. Samples for SEM are coated with gold or gold and platinum.
8. In cell fractionation cells are separated from their tissues.
9. Cells are centrifuged to separate the different cell types based on density.
10. They will need to use ultracentrifugation to separate cell organelles and components.

PRACTICE QUESTIONS (Page 35)

1. **a)** The virus and phospholipid bilayer **[1]** would not be observed with a light microscope. This is because the resolving power of a light microscope is too low/200 nm **[1]**. The virus and phospholipid bilayer is much smaller than that resolving power **[1]**.

   b) Any three from: A TEM uses a beam of electrons instead of a beam of visible light; the image is not real; it has to be displayed on a fluorescent screen/computer; the lenses are not made of glass but are electromagnets. **[3 marks: 1 mark for each point made]**

2. This would be an ideal answer worth 6 marks:

The invention of the light microscope enabled the viewer to see objects that normally could not be seen with the unaided eye. This led to the discovery of cells and larger cell structures. Light microscopes, however, can only magnify up to ×1000 and resolve objects as small as 200 nm. The advent of electron microscopy meant that scientists could observe what was in the cell, resolving down to 0.5 nm and a magnification of ×250 000. As the technology improves it is possible to see smaller and smaller objects.

Cell Division

QUICK TEST (Page 39)
1. Cell differentiation is where the cells specialise so that they can carry out a specific function.
2. G1.
3. They are never going to divide, so they do not need to make the machinery for reproducing DNA.
4. The synthesis of DNA by semi-conservative replication.
5. Prophase, metaphase, anaphase, telophase.
6. Cyclins and cyclin-dependent kinases.
7. A tumour may form/cancer may develop.
8. Meiosis has two cell divisions leading to four haploid cells whereas mitosis has only one division and leads to diploid cells.
9. A homologous chromosome is one of a pair of chromosomes, either the one from the mother or the one from the father.
10. During crossing over sections of the arms of the homologous chromosomes overlap and swap, so the chromosomes have different genetic information.

PRACTICE QUESTIONS (Page 39)
1. a) A is a cell in anaphase [1] because the chromosomes are being pulled to opposite poles of the cell [1]. B is a cell in prophase [1] because the chromosomes have just become visible [1].
   b) The stages of meiosis are prophase I, metaphase I, anaphase I and telophase I, prophase II, metaphase II, anaphase II and telophase II. [2 marks: 1 mark for all phases; 1 mark for correct order]
2. Most cells once differentiated [1] do not need to divide again [1].

Day 3

Cell Transport
QUICK TEST (Page 42)
1.

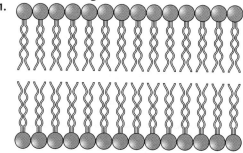

2. The phosphate heads are hydrophilic/the lipid tails are hydrophobic.
3. Integral proteins are permanent fixtures in the cell surface membrane whereas peripheral proteins are non-permanent.
4. Transmembrane proteins allow molecules to pass in and out of the cell through a central channel.

5. Glycoproteins and glycolipids are involved in cell to cell interactions and act as markers for cell identification.
6. Cholesterol is required to restrict the movement of transmembrane proteins, giving the cell membrane stability.
7. Diffusion is the movement of particles down a concentration gradient in liquid or gas.
8. Osmosis is the movement of water down a gradient of water potential, from higher water potential to lower water potential, across a partially permeable membrane.
9. They both transport molecules against a concentration gradient, low to high concentration.
10. If surface area were increased, the transport rate would be greater.
11. If the number of carrier proteins were reduced, the transport rate would decrease.
12. The steeper the gradient, the greater the rate of transport.

PRACTICE QUESTIONS (Page 43)
1. a) A = phospholipid bilayer [1], B = hydrophilic head/phosphate group [1], C = hydrophobic tail/fatty acid chain [1], D = peripheral proteins [1], E = integral protein [1].
   b) Glycoproteins and glycolipids are used for cell signalling/ communication [1].
   c) Cholesterol maintains the integrity of the membrane [1] by restricting the movement of the protein components of the membrane [1]. It also helps in cell signalling [1].

Gas Exchange 1
QUICK TEST (Page 46)
1. The higher the surface area compared to the volume, the quicker the rate of diffusion.
2. Single-celled organisms have a very high surface area to volume ratio so can absorb materials for respiration and metabolism over their cell surface membranes.
3. If a cell keeps growing in size, its surface area to volume ratio decreases. This means that, although substances can diffuse in and out, the central part of the cell may not be able to receive the nutrients it needs or remove toxic waste products.
4. The steeper the gradient, the greater the rate of diffusion.
5. Increased surface area, moist surfaces, decreased pathway.
6. Air enters the spiracles. It then enters tracheoles that are filled with a fluid. The tracheoles extend into the insect, coming into contact with the cells deep inside.
7. Gills have a very large surface area to volume ratio, with gill segments.
8. In counter-current flow, water and blood flow in opposite directions and water always passes blood with a higher oxygen concentration. This ensures that there is always a diffusion gradient for oxygen to move down.
9. Air enters through an opening called a stoma (plural stomata). The opening and closing of a stoma is controlled by guard cells either side of it.
10. Spongy mesophyll is a plant tissue found in the lower part of the leaf. It is comprised of spongy mesophyll cells and a large number of spaces which air can move around in.

PRACTICE QUESTIONS (Page 47)
1. a) The body wall of an insect is covered in an impermeable wax [1].
   b) In a flying insect, the fluid would be forced into the muscle cells [1] as this reduces the diffusion pathway, ensuring the muscle cells get the oxygen they need [1].
2. a) A gill from a bony fish is made of bony struts [1]; these have a large number of gill segments [1] that create a very large surface area for water to move over [1].

b) **Any four from:** Fish swim continually to ensure flow of water over the gills; when the water flows over the gills it flows in the opposite direction to the blood; this is called counter-current flow and ensures that the maximum amount of oxygen is extracted from the water by maintaining a concentration gradient from the water to the blood; fish haemoglobin has a very high affinity for oxygen. **[4 marks: 1 mark for each point made]**

Gas Exchange 2
QUICK TEST (Page 51)
1. Air is breathed in through the mouth. It passes into the trachea and moves down to the bronchi. It will move into either the left or right bronchus. Next it moves into smaller bronchioles which ultimately end in the alveoli.
2. Alveoli are grape-like structures/air sacs which are coated with a surfactant and covered in capillaries. They are the site of gas exchange.
3. Instead of being one large, single surface the alveoli increase the surface area of the lungs. They have a thin epithelium.
4. Gases can diffuse through liquids easily. The surfactant also reduces surface tension.
5. During inhalation the intercostal muscles contract causing the ribs to move upwards and outwards. The diaphragm contracts, moving downwards. This creates a lower pressure inside the lungs compared to the outside air. Air moves into the lungs down a pressure gradient.
6. During exhalation the intercostal muscles relax causing the ribs to move downwards and inwards. The diaphragm relaxes, moving upwards and forming a dome shape. This creates a higher pressure inside the lungs compared to the outside air. Air moves out of the lungs down a pressure gradient.
7. CO_2 will move from the blood into the alveoli.
8. This is because the concentration of CO_2 in the blood is much higher than the concentration in the air inside the alveolus. The CO_2 moves down a concentration gradient.
9. Tidal volume is the volume of air that is breathed in and out in normal breathing at rest.
10. The residual volume is the volume of air that always remains after the maximum possible amount of air has been breathed out.

PRACTICE QUESTIONS (Page 51)
1. **a)** i = trachea **[1]**, ii = (external) intercostal muscles **[1]**, iii = ribs **[1]**, iv = diaphragm **[1]**.
   b) When breathing in, the air outside is at a higher pressure than the air inside, so moves down a gradient of pressure **[1]**. When breathing out, the air inside the lung is at a higher pressure than the air outside the lung, so moves down the gradient of pressure **[1]**.
2. The tidal volume should stay the same **[1]**; this is because it is the gas exchange that is affected not the volume of gas breathed in **[1]**.

Energy from Respiration
QUICK TEST (Page 54)
1. VO_2max is a measure of the maximum rate of oxygen consumption.
2. VO_2max is a better way to measure ventilation because it reflects the amount of O_2 that has actually been used by the body rather than the amount of air breathed in or out.
3. The unfit or unhealthy, or people with respiratory disorders/diseases.

4.

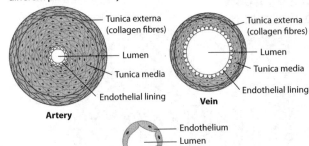

5. ATP uses ribose and has three phosphates attached to the sugar whereas a DNA adenine nucleotide uses deoxyribose and has only one phosphate attached.
6. Metabolism/Cell structure and movement/Cell signalling.
7. $ATP + H_2O \rightarrow ADP +$ inorganic phosphate, P_i.
8. P_i is used to phosphorylate other compounds, such as sugars.
9. Anaerobic respiration yields a much lower amount of ATP.
10. Lung cancer reduces the surface area of the lungs, reducing gas exchange.

PRACTICE QUESTIONS (Page 55)
1. **a)** Phosphorylate means that an inorganic phosphate ion/PO_4^{3-}/P_i **[1]** is added to activate a protein **[1]**.
   b) Hydrolysis **[1]**.
   c) If the CDK–cyclin protein complex could not be activated the cell cycle would stop and not progress **[1]**.
   d) $ADP + P_i \rightarrow ATP + H_2O$ **[1]**.

Day 4
Mass Transport
QUICK TEST (Page 58)
1. Mass transport systems allow substances required for metabolism to be moved deep inside an organism.
2. Haemolymph.
3. Insects, crustaceans, molluscs.
4. It allows hydraulic control of body parts and removes heat efficiently.
5. Haemolymph is 90% plasma, with amino acids, proteins and sugars. The remaining 10% is comprised of haemocytes used for clotting and defence.
6. The blood travels in a closed system and does not leave the blood vessels.
7. The blood pressure in a fish decreases as it moves around the body.
8. Two advantages are that blood pressure can be altered to meet increased metabolic demands, and that blood flow is faster to the different parts of the body.
9.

10. Valves in veins prevent the backflow of blood.

PRACTICE QUESTIONS (Page 59)

1. **a)** Veins contain semi-lunar valves **[1]**. These prevent the backflow of blood **[1]**. If these fail then the blood will pool at the next available valve **[1]**, causing an unsightly bulge.
   b) Humans have a double circulatory system whereas fish have a single circulatory system **[1]**. Blood moves through the heart of a mammal twice whereas it moves through a fish's heart once for every circuit of the body **[1]**.

Transporting Blood
QUICK TEST (Page 62)

1. 50–60%.
2. Mammalian haemoglobin is a quaternary globular protein made up of two α units and two β units as well as four non-protein haem prosthetic groups tightly associated to the protein.
3. Carbonic anhydrase is an enzyme that catalyses the conversion of carbon dioxide and water into bicarbonate and protons (and vice versa).
4. $HCO_3^- + H^+ \rightarrow H_2CO_3 \rightarrow CO_2 + H_2O$.
5.

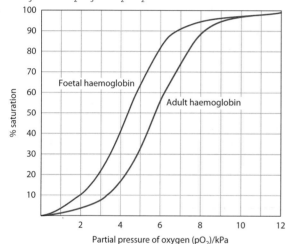

6. Foetal haemoglobin is adapted to bind to O_2 at lower partial pressures compared to adult haemoglobin. This is because the foetus is receiving lower O_2 from the mother through the placenta.
7. Oncotic pressure is the pressure in the capillaries in a capillary bed due to the blood containing a high proportion of proteins.
8. The pressure from the heart overcomes oncotic pressure, forcing fluid into the capillary bed. At the end of the capillary bed the pressure from the heart is less than oncotic pressure, so fluid moves back into the capillary.
9. Tissue fluid has the same composition as plasma apart from not having any red blood cells and albumin proteins.

PRACTICE QUESTIONS (Page 63)

1. **a)** A = arteriole **[1]**, B = capillary **[1]**, C = lymphatic/lymph vessel **[1]**, D = venule **[1]**.
   b) The blood entering the capillary bed from the arteriole is at a high pressure which is greater than the oncotic pressure **[1]**. The fluid moves into the area around the cells down the pressure gradient **[1]**.
   c) The fluid in C has the same composition as the tissue fluid **[1]** but includes white blood cells and fat droplets **[1]**.

Controlling Heart Rate
QUICK TEST (Page 66)

1. Systole means contraction of heart muscle, diastole means relaxation of heart muscle.
2. Stage 1 ventricular diastole, atrial systole; Stage 2 ventricular systole, atrial diastole; Stage 3 atrial and ventricular diastole.
3. The 'lub' sound is caused by the atrioventricular valves closing; the 'dub' sound is caused by the semi-lunar valves closing.
4. Factors include high or low blood pressure, stress, adrenaline, whether the organism is sleeping or hibernating, doing exercise, etc.
5. The SAN and AVN (the heart pacemakers) keep the cardiac muscle contracting in time.
6. The medulla oblongata sends electrical nerve impulses to the SAN and AVN via the sympathetic and vagus nerves.
7. The SAN is located in the wall of the right atrium.
8. The Purkinje fibres transmit the signal to get the ventricles to contract.
9. Someone with brachycardia has a very slow resting heart rate of less than 60 bpm. The ECG would show a normal cardiac sequence but over a much longer time.
10. Fibrillation is where the cardiac muscle is contracting randomly, in effect quivering. Unless it is reset the person will die of heart failure.

PRACTICE QUESTIONS (Page 67)

1. **a)** Patient B needs to be treated first **[1]** as the ECG shows that his/her heart is undergoing fibrillations **[1]**. This means that the heart is not pumping blood around the body **[1]** because all the cardiac muscles are contracting and relaxing at random intervals **[1]**.
   b) A **[1]**.
   c) C **[1]**.
   d) During the QRS complex, the ventricles depolarise **[1]** which triggers the main pumping contractions **[1]**.

Plant Transport
QUICK TEST (Page 70)

1. Root hairs have a very high surface area to volume ratio, to maximise movement of water into the cell.
2. The water potential of the root hair cell is greater than the first cell next to it. The water moves into the next cell by osmosis. The amount of water in the cell sap has increased, making it have a higher water potential than the next cell in sequence. This process continues until the cortex is reached.
3. Via apoplast, via symplast and via the vacuoles.
4. The lignin in xylem vessels strengthens the xylem and makes it waterproof.
5. If the companion cell were to die, so would the sieve tube as the companion cell supplies the sieve tube with all metabolic needs.
6. Water is cohesive and adhesive.
7. Xerophytes are plants that survive in very dry conditions.

PRACTICE QUESTIONS (Page 71)

1. **a)** **Any three from:** Leaf is rolled to trap air inside/prevent water loss; hairs present to minimise turbulence; stomata in the curls of the leaf to prevent excess water loss; waxy cuticle to prevent water loss. **[3 marks: 1 mark for each point made]**
   b) Xerophytes **[1]**.
   c) A potometer **[1]**.

Day 5

Nutrition

QUICK TEST (Page 75)

1. Three from maintaining cells, growth, fighting diseases and reproduction.
2. Digestion is the process of breaking down large molecules into molecules that are small enough to pass into cells through the cell surface membrane.
3. Carbohydrases.
4. Maltose molecules.
5. Maltase is bound to the cell surface membrane in the ileum.
6. Glycerol and free fatty acids.
7. They target the peptide bond between amino acids.
8. Exopeptidases catalyse the breakdown of the peptide bonds at the amine or carboxylic acid terminals of the polypeptide chain, whereas endopeptidases catalyse the breaking of the bond between amino acids in the polypeptide chain.
9. When sodium ions and glucose are present a conformational change occurs in the carrier molecule, drawing them into the cell. This is co-transport.
10. Fats are transported across the cell surface membrane in structures called micelles.

PRACTICE QUESTIONS (Page 75)

1. **a)** Pepsin [1].
   b) Glycerol and free fatty acids [1].
   c) In the brush border cells of the villi in the small intestine/ileum [1].
   d) **(i)** Phosphorylation [1].
   (ii) The peptidases would otherwise be able to digest essential proteins in the cell [1]. Requiring activation before use enables control of where the peptidases will act [1].

Modelling Digestion

QUICK TEST (Page 79)

1. Cellulose.
2. The visking tubing is partially permeable, meaning particles less than the diameter of the pores can pass through while those that are larger cannot.
3. A gradient of water potential means that water of a higher water potential will move, via osmosis, to an area of lower water potential (water with more dissolved solutes).
4. The visking tubing will start to swell as water from the area of higher water potential (outside the visking tubing) moves to an area of lower water potential (the glucose solution inside the visking tubing).
5. The visking tubing will start to shrink as water from the area of higher water potential (inside the visking tubing) moves to an area of lower water potential (the glucose solution).
6. Drops of iodine dissolved in potassium iodide solution are added to the sample being tested. If the sample contains starch, then the colour changes from brown to a dark blue/purple colour.
7. I_3^- ions.
8. Sodium citrate forms a complex with the Cu^{2+} preventing them from converting to Cu^+ ions.
9. Sucrose is not a reducing sugar, so the colour at the end of the experiment would be blue, the same as at the start.
10. Purple.

PRACTICE QUESTIONS (Page 79)

1. **a)** Add drops of I_2/KI solution/iodine dissolved in potassium iodide solution [1]. If starch is present the solution turns from a brown colour to deep blue/purple [1].
   b) Grind the meat up and add to deionised water [1]. Add Biuret reagent and leave for 5 minutes [1]. If protein is present, the solution changes colour from blue to purple [1].
   c) Take the sample and mix with ethanol/alcohol [1]. Once the solids have settled out, decant the layer of alcohol into water [1]. If a milky white suspension is formed, fats were present [1].

Trophy

QUICK TEST (Page 82)

1. An autotroph is an organism that can make complex organic compounds using simple substances in their environment.
2. Photoautotrophs use energy from light for metabolic reactions, chemoautotrophs get their energy from the oxidation of electron donors in the environment (e.g. hydrogen sulfide).
3. Heterotrophs obtain their energy from consuming other organisms.
4. A fungus grows in the food source. It secretes digestive enzymes via vesicles. These digest the food externally. The cells of the hyphae then absorb the dissolved nutrients via diffusion.
5. Amoebae feed via phagocytosis. They surround the food into a phagosome. This then merges with a lysosome to form a phagolysosome. Enzymes inside the phagolysosome break down the food into smaller particles that are absorbed by diffusion.
6. An internal tube for digestion means that the cells in the tube can be differentiated to perform different roles, e.g. secreting particular enzymes, absorbing particular nutrients.
7. A cow has a number of stomach-like rumens where bacteria work on digesting the plant material.
8. Bacteria and protozoans.
9. The carnivore digestive system is far shorter than a herbivore's because protein is relatively easy to digest.
10. Parasites take their nutrition from the host, which has already digested the food.

PRACTICE QUESTIONS (Page 83)

1. **a)** A = hooks (in two whorls) [1], B = suckers [1].
   b) The hooks and suckers are used to attach the tapeworm to the lining of the intestine [1] and prevent it from being dislodged [1].
   c) A thin surface minimises the diffusion pathway, increasing the rate of diffusion [1]. The elongated body ensures that the tapeworm can absorb the maximum quantity of nutrients passing through the host's digestive system [1].

Dentition and Diet

QUICK TEST (Page 86)

1. Herbivore teeth typically have flat-topped incisors on the lower jaw to tear and pull plants from the ground. Molars and pre-molars have broad, angled surfaces linked to the teeth above or below. Sharp enamel ridges grind the tough fibrous material.
2. Carnassials are paired upper and lower teeth that are modified to allow enlarged, self-sharpening edges to pass one another in a shearing manner.
3. Humans need fibre, vitamins and minerals, carbohydrates, protein and fat in their diet.

4. Fibre and vitamins and minerals from fruit and vegetables; carbohydrates from pasta, bread, rice; protein from meat or plant protein such as soya and beans; fats from meat, oily fish, dairy products and nuts.
5. Saturated fats only have single bonds between carbon atoms whereas unsaturated fats have at least one double or triple bond between carbon atoms.
6. Someone with a BMI of more than 30 would typically be classed as 'obese'.
7. LDL cholesterol is essential for creating cell surface membranes. Too much, however, can lead to atherosclerosis.
8. HDL cholesterol is released to reduce the amount of LDL cholesterol in the blood.
9. Atherosclerosis can follow damage to an artery if there is a high level of LDL cholesterol in the blood. A plaque, or atheroma, forms which blocks the artery. This causes higher blood pressure and can starve an organ, such as the heart, of nutrients and oxygen.
10. Three from: smoking, drinking excess alcohol, eating saturated fats and lack of exercise.

PRACTICE QUESTIONS (Page 87)

1. a) This would be an ideal answer worth 6 marks:

    Atherosclerosis starts with the formation of a fatty plaque inside an artery. Arteries transport oxygenated blood away from the heart at a high pressure. The presence of a plaque attracts white blood cells and, if LDL cholesterol is present, the plaque becomes an atheroma, reducing the blood flow and increasing blood pressure. The coronary arteries supply the cardiac muscle with oxygen and nutrients. They are smaller than the other arteries in the body, so an atheroma has a greater effect. The cardiac muscle receives less oxygen and this can cause the muscle cells to die or to start contracting out of sync. If this happens then it will trigger a myocardial infarction (a heart attack).

   b) When an atheroma has built up there is a risk that the increased pressure could cause a part of the atheroma to break off [1]. If this is in the arteries in the brain then it can trigger a stroke, as the section of the brain involved is starved of oxygen [1]. If the clot, or thrombosis, appears in other arteries it will block the artery and the patient will suffer pain as the artery involved fails to supply tissues with oxygen [1].

   c) LDL cholesterol is needed for cell surface membranes [1]. However, if the diet is high in cholesterol, too much LDL will be in the bloodstream. HDL cholesterol is produced to convert excess LDL cholesterol into HDL cholesterol [1]. Too high a level of LDL cholesterol means that there is a much greater chance of atherosclerosis occurring (and hence the increased risk of CVD) [1].

   d) If the ratio LDL:HDL is high it means that there is too much LDL cholesterol and the body is not correcting for it [1]. If the LDL:HDL is lower it shows the body is able to reduce available LDL [1]. The ratio is independent of the physical mass [1].

Day 6

The Genetic Code

QUICK TEST (Page 90)

1. A phosphate group, a pentose sugar and a base.
2. The pentose sugar is ribose instead of deoxyribose and thymine is replaced by uracil (U).

3. DNA purines are adenine (A) and guanine (G).
4. DNA pyrimidines are thymine (T) and cytosine (C).
5. Template strand = ATTAACCG
   Coding strand = TAATTGGC
   mRNA = AUUAACCG
6. During transcription, exons are the sections of a DNA nucleotide sequence that become part of the final mRNA molecule. Introns are the sections that do not become part of the final mRNA.
7. The A site is where the tRNA attaches to the ribosome and translates the mRNA, the P site is where the amino acids are joined by peptide bonds, and the E site is where the tRNA exits the ribosome.

PRACTICE QUESTIONS (Page 91)

1. a) **Any three from each column:**

DNA	RNA
Double stranded	Single stranded
Contains deoxyribose	Contains ribose
Contains thymine as a potential nucleotide/ATGC	Contains uracil as a potential nucleotide/AUGC
Only one type of DNA	A number of types of RNA: mRNA, tRNA, rRNA, etc.
Helical	Not helical

   [3 marks: 1 mark for each complete row]

   b) 33% C, therefore 33% G, = 66% [1]. Remainder 34% A and T/2 = 17% thymine [1].

   c) TTAATC [1].

DNA Replication

QUICK TEST (Page 94)

1. DNA helicase.
2. Semi-conservative replication is the process where an exact copy is made of each DNA strand, using a supply of organic bases, deoxyribose sugars and phosphate molecules (making up the nucleotides). One (old) strand is used as the template for the new strand.
3. The leading strand is the strand of DNA that forms when DNA is transcribed from 3' to 5'.
4. Okazaki fragments are the sections of DNA that have been replicated from the strand in the 5' to 3' direction.
5. Okazaki fragments are joined together by the enzyme DNA ligase.
6. Meselson and Stahl proved the semi-conservative nature of DNA replication.
7. The other two theories were conservative replication and dispersive replication.
8. DNA polymerase.
9. The most common mutation is a substitution mutation.
10. It is where a stop codon is coded for instead of the normal amino acid. This is usually shorter than the original protein.

PRACTICE QUESTIONS (Page 95)

1. a) Helicase is the enzyme that unzips the DNA [1]. DNA polymerase is the enzyme that joins DNA strands together [1].

   b) (i) A frameshift mutation [1].
      (ii) The polypeptide will be completely different from the point ATT [1] and will not function [1].

Sexual Reproduction

QUICK TEST (Page 98)
1. Gametogenesis is the production of gametes, through meiosis.
2. In the foetus.
3. In spermatogonia in the seminiferous tubules in the testes.
4. Spermatocytes.
5. A jelly-like layer surrounding the ovum which hardens after the cortical reaction to prevent entry of more sperm.
6. Enzymes that dissolve the zona pellucida.
7. Blastomeres.
8. Three (tube nucleus and two sperm nuclei).
9. Ovum.
10. Three/3n.

PRACTICE QUESTIONS (Page 99)
1. a) **Any four from:** The sperm cell, having passed through the zona pellucida, fuses with the ovum cell membrane; this initiates the cortical reaction; where cortical granules inside the secondary oocyte move towards the membrane; and are released through exocytosis; this leads to the zona pellucida hardening/thickening; and changing electrical charge.
   [4 marks: 1 mark for each point made]
   b) **Any four from:** The majority of a female's oogonia are produced when she is a foetus; they become primary oocytes and stay in prophase of meiosis I until the female begins menstruating; they then move through meiosis producing a (secondary) oocyte and two polar bodies; if a woman undergoes chemo- or radiotherapy there is a danger that the DNA in the oocytes will be disrupted/mutated, preventing the formation of viable ova; freezing the ova means they can be replaced after treatment has finished. **[4 marks: 1 mark for each point made]**

Biodiversity

QUICK TEST (Page 102)
1. Habitat biodiversity means the biodiversity occurring in a given habitat, e.g. sand dunes, woodland, meadows, streams.
2. Species biodiversity is the species richness and evenness, in other words how many different species are present in a community and how abundant they are.
3. Genetic biodiversity is a measure of the variety of genes in a population rather than the number of individuals of a population or species.
4. Sampling techniques are used as in most scenarios it is impossible to record every living thing in an area. Sampling makes it a manageable process.
5. Random sampling removes bias.
6. Systematic sampling takes samples every set distance from the start or at the same time each day.
7. Stratified sampling takes into account the relative sizes of two or more sampling locations.
8. Species evenness is a measure of the abundance of a species whereas species richness is a measure of the number of different species in an area at a given time.
9. $D = 1 - \left(\sum\left(\frac{n}{N}\right)^2\right)$
   or
   $D = \frac{N(N-1)}{\sum n(n-1)}$
10. Mega-farms rely on growing a monoculture in a massive field. This removes hedgerows and alters the composition of the soil in terms of mineral nutrients/fertility.

PRACTICE QUESTIONS (Page 103)
1. a) For river A:

Fish	Number	Working
Rainbow trout	230	$\left(\frac{230}{2814}\right)^2 = 0.00668$
Brown trout	345	$\left(\frac{345}{2814}\right)^2 = 0.0150$
Catfish	25	$\left(\frac{25}{2814}\right)^2 = 0.0000789$
Carp	1970	$\left(\frac{1970}{2814}\right)^2 = 0.490$
Steelheads	213	$\left(\frac{213}{2814}\right)^2 = 0.00573$
Pike	31	$\left(\frac{31}{2814}\right)^2 = 0.000121$

$\sum = 0.00668 + 0.0150 + 0.0000789 + 0.490 + 0.00573 + 0.000121 = 0.518$
$D = 1 - 0.518 = 0.482 = \mathbf{0.48}$ (to 2 significant figures)

For river B:

Fish	Number	Working
Rainbow trout	339	$\left(\frac{339}{2943}\right)^2 = 0.0133$
Brown trout	180	$\left(\frac{180}{2943}\right)^2 = 0.00374$
Catfish	0	$\left(\frac{0}{2943}\right)^2 = 0$
Carp	2370	$\left(\frac{2370}{2943}\right)^2 = 0.649$
Steelheads	21	$\left(\frac{21}{2943}\right)^2 = 0.0000509$
Pike	33	$\left(\frac{33}{2943}\right)^2 = 0.000126$

$\sum = 0.0133 + 0.00374 + 0 + 0.649 + 0.0000509 + 0.000126$
$= 0.666$
$D = 1 - 0.666 = 0.334 = \mathbf{0.33}$ (to 2 significant figures)
[6 marks: 2 marks for each table; 1 mark for each set of correct workings]
   b) The results indicate that river A is more diverse than river B **[1]**, as river A has a higher Simpson's diversity index (D) of 0.48 **[1]**, compared to river B's 0.33 **[1]**.

Evolution

QUICK TEST (Page 106)
1. Binomial classification gives every organism a two-part name made up of its genus and species name.
2. Archaea, Bacteria and Eukaryota.
3. Individuals of a population that can freely breed and produce fertile offspring.
4. A term used to describe two populations of a species living in the same geographical area that cannot interbreed. However, there is a ring of populations separated by a geographical barrier that *can* interbreed.
5. Over very long timescales it is possible for organisms to develop similar morphological characteristics (e.g. eyes, wings, etc.), due to evolution through natural selection.
6. A phylogenetic tree is created by analysing the DNA of members of each species and placing them according to similarities and differences in their DNA.
7. The more varied the alleles are, the more likely it is that individuals will be able to cope with environmental changes.

PRACTICE QUESTIONS (Page 107)

1. a) Domain – Eukaryota; Kingdom – Animalia; Phylum – Chordata; Class – Mammalia; Order – Proboscidea; Family – Elephantidae; Genus – *Elephas*; Species – *maximus*. **[4 marks: 1 mark for every two names and taxons in the correct order]**
   b) Asian elephants are descended from a common ancestor of the woolly mammoth/are more closely related to woolly mammoths **[1]**. Indian elephants diverged from an earlier common ancestor/are not as closely related to the woolly mammoth as the Asian elephant is **[1]**.

Day 7

Disease

QUICK TEST (Page 110)

1. A disease is a disorder of a tissue, organ or organ system.
2. Any three from genetic, dietary, environmental and autoimmune.
3. Three examples of bacterial pathogens are: tuberculosis/TB, bacterial meningitis and ring rot.
4. HIV is transmitted by exchange of body fluids, sharing contaminated needles and transfusion of infected blood.
5. Low crop yield.
6. Plants can secrete antimicrobials and then form callose, closing the plasmodesmata.
7. Animal skin is a thick barrier to entry by pathogens into the body. It is a waterproof mechanical barrier. The skin is naturally covered in microorganisms, some of which would be pathogens if they could enter the skin. This helps prevent entry of disease.
8. Expulsive reflexes happen when the throat or nasal passage are exposed to irritants, including pathogens. The response is to sneeze or cough, and this removes the pathogen from the body.
9. If the skin is broken blood clots, sealing the site of the injury and preventing further infection from the outside. Platelets present in the blood form a plug, blocking the skin breach. They release clotting factors, such as thromboplastin. Prothrombin, which is a constituent of blood plasma, is converted to its active form, thrombin (catalysed by thromboplastin). The thrombin structurally alters the soluble protein fibrinogen, causing it to form a string-like mesh made of insoluble fibrin. The mesh traps red blood cells, forming a scab.
10. A scab is waterproof, sealing the wound so that pathogens cannot get in.

PRACTICE QUESTIONS (Page 111)

1. a)

Kingdom	Disease
Protoctista	Potato/tomato blight; malaria
Prokaryotae	Tuberculosis/TB; bacterial meningitis; ring rot
Fungi	Black sigatoka; ringworm; athlete's foot

[3 marks: 1 mark for each complete row]
   b) Platelets present in the blood form a plug, blocking the skin breach. They release clotting factors, such as thromboplastin **[1]**. Prothrombin, which is a constituent of blood plasma, is converted to its active form, thrombin (catalysed by thromboplastin) **[1]**. The thrombin structurally alters the soluble protein fibrinogen, causing it to form a string-like mesh made of insoluble fibrin. The mesh traps red blood cells, forming a scab **[1]**.

2. a) A protist/protoctistan **[1]**.
   b) Plants can produce antimicrobial chemicals to kill the bacteria **[1]**. The passage of the pathogen through the plant can be slowed by the formation of callus material at the plasmodesmata **[1]**.

Immune Response 1

QUICK TEST (Page 114)

1. Phagocytes are a type of white blood cell involved in the primary non-specific defence (the primary immune system). They protect the body by ingesting harmful foreign particles, bacteria and dead or dying cells. They move to the sites of infection through capillaries, tissue fluid and lymph as well as being found in plasma.
2. Phagocytosis occurs when a vesicle forms around an ingested particle or pathogen, called a phagosome. This merges with a lysosome, which contains a variety of enzymes and proteins to destroy the foreign body. The combined phagosome and lysosome is called a phagolysosome. Once digested, the fragments are excreted into the blood.
3. Neutrophils, eosinophils and monocytes.
4. Cytokines promote blood flow to the injury. The increase in blood flow leads to a reddening of the skin and an increase in temperature associated with inflammation.
5. Opsonins/antigens.
6. B-lymphocytes recognise a pathogen by its specific antigen that fits its antigen receptor site.
7. Macrophages consume foreign bodies and then present antigen fragments on their cell surface membranes.
8. Interleukins cause more B-lymphocytes and T-killer cells to be activated.
9. T-killer cells bind to an antigen and then release molecules that will kill the infected cell, breaking down enzymes and the membrane. T-regulator cells ensure that, once the infection has been dealt with, the system reverts to normal.
10. The secondary immune response protects against future infection through B-memory and T-memory cells remaining in the blood with the pathogen's antigen receptors on their surface, ready to start the secondary response should the organism get reinfected.

PRACTICE QUESTIONS (Page 115)

1. a) The first time the pathogen entered the body the immune system had not come across it before so there were no antibodies in the blood **[1]**. There is a delay as the immune system first has to recognise the invading pathogen, with cells such as B- and T-lymphocytes detecting the antigens on the pathogen **[1]** and then triggering other immune cells to make the antibodies which kill the pathogen **[1]**. These remain in the blood to attack the same invading pathogen if it enters the body again in a second infection **[1]**.
   b) Produce antibodies – B-lymphocytes **[1]** and plasma cells **[1]**. Present antibody fragments – macrophages **[1]**. Release interleukins – T-helper cells **[1]**.

Immune Response 2

QUICK TEST (Page 118)

1. The life of the organism.
2. Passive immunity is where the immunity has been passed on to the organism, not from its own immune response.
3. From the mother's blood during pregnancy and through breast milk after being born.

4. The venom from the rattlesnake is injected into a horse, the horse's immune system responds by making antibodies, the antibodies are harvested and then injected into a person who has been bitten by a rattlesnake.
5. Artificial immunity is from being vaccinated or through having injections with antibodies directly.
6. Live vaccine, dead microorganisms and fragments of microorganisms.
7. Live vaccine.
8. The percentage of the population that needs to be vaccinated so that those who are not vaccinated are protected by herd immunity.
9. Evolution of the pathogen so the immune system no longer recognises it.
10. Some individuals are not well enough to receive the vaccine, e.g. immune compromised individuals.

PRACTICE QUESTIONS (Page 119)

1. **a)** A poor diet causes vaccination to be less effective because malnutrition means the body doesn't have enough nutrients (particularly protein) to make antibodies [1].
   b) The reason for this is that the body needs to manufacture cells in the immune system [1]. This requires energy and resources (e.g. protein) [1].
   c) There will come a point where the immune system has generated enough antibodies to keep the individual protected, and making more would be a waste of the body's resources [1].
   d) Rubella has a high critical vaccination level, which means at least 85% of the population need to be successfully vaccinated [1]. This might be difficult to achieve if the population is difficult to get to [1] or the population is malnourished [1].

Antibiotics and Stem Cells

QUICK TEST (Page 122)

1. Bactericidal.
2. Bacteriostatic.
3. Causing the cell wall to fail/Preventing bacterial DNA from being repaired/Preventing production of metabolic components.

4. The cell wall must be thick as it has taken in the Gram stain.
5. People would die from bacterial infections that are currently treatable.
6. The disease requires treatment with antibiotics over a very long period. The patient often feels better well before the end of the course, so stops taking the antibiotics. This allows bacteria that have evolved resistance against the antibiotic to pass on the characteristic in plasmids to other bacteria that have not been completely destroyed as the treatment has stopped. This leads to the trait being passed on in the general population.
7. The common cold is caused by a virus.
8. Cells that can become any type of cell, including extraembryonic cells.
9. The cells that make the placenta/placental cells.
10. Unlike embryonic stem cells that can be used to grow any type of cell, haematopoietic cells are multipotent so can create a range of cell types within a cell line. Haematopoietic cells produce different blood cells.

PRACTICE QUESTIONS (Page 123)

1. **a)** Antibiotic resistance is where the bacteria have evolved to become resistant to the antibiotic [1].
   b)

Antibiotic	Length of time before resistance
Chloramphenicol	10 years ± 2
Streptomycin	15 years ± 3
Sulfonamides	10 years ± 2

[3 marks: 1 mark for each complete row]
   c) The time between discovery and resistance appears to be far shorter than in the majority of earlier antibiotics [1].

Index

acrosome reaction 97
active immunity 116–19
active transport 41–2, 68
adaptations 106
adaptive immunity 112–15
adenosine triphosphate 40–1, 52–3
adhesion 4–6, 69
aerobic respiration 52–3
alveoli 48–9
amino acids 16–19, 60, 73
amylose/amylopectin 9–10, 72, 76
anaerobic respiration 53
antibiotics 120
antibodies/antigens 60, 113
apoplastic transport 68
arteries/arterioles 57–8, 85
asexual reproduction 37
atherosclerosis 13, 85
atria 62, 64–6
atrioventricular node 65
attachment proteins 29–30
autoimmune diseases 108, 118
autonomic nervous system 65
autotrophs 80

B-lymphocytes 113, 116
bacteria 28–31, 37, 108, 120
Benedict's reagent 76–7
binary fission 37
binomial classification 104
biodiversity 100–3
Biuret test 77
blastocoel 97
blastocyst 97
blastomeres 97
blood 60–3, 110, 112–13, 116
breathing 48–50
bronchioles/bronchi 48
Bundle of His 65

capillaries 48, 58, 60
capsid 29–30, 108
capsule 28
carbohydrates 5, 8–11, 40, 72, 84
carbon dioxide 44–6, 48–9, 60–1
carbon monoxide 53
carbonic anhydrase 60–1
cardiac cycle 62, 64–6
cardiovascular system 52, 56–7, 84–6
carnivores 82, 84
carrier proteins 41–2
Casparian strip 68
cell cycle 36–9
cell fractionation 33–4
cell surface membranes 24, 40–3, 44
cell walls 10, 24–5, 28
cellular transport 40–3, 53
centrifugation 34
chemoautotrophs 80
chloroplasts 24–5
cholesterol 13, 40, 85–6
chromosomes 24, 28, 36–8
circulatory systems 56–71

cleavage 97
clonal selection 113
clotting 110
co-factors 17, 21
co-transport 42, 73
codons 88–9
coenzymes 21
cohesion 4–6
competitive inhibitors 22
concentration 21, 40–1
condensation reactions 5, 9–10, 12, 53
corona radiata 97
cortical reaction 97
cytoplasm 24–5, 28, 69

deletion mutations 94
dentition 84
diet 84–7, 108
differential staining 32
diffusion 40–1, 44–5, 76
digestion 72–83
directional selection 106
disaccharides 8–9, 72, 77
disease 108–23
diversity 100–7
DNA 24, 29–30, 36–8, 88–95, 105–6
duodenum 72

electrolytes 60
electron microscopes 24, 32–3
emulsion test 77
endocytosis 53
endoplasmic reticulum 24–5
endosperm 98
environmental diseases 108
enzymes 17, 20–3, 53, 60–1, 72–3, 92–3
eosinophils 112
eukaryotes 24–7
evolution 104–7
exocytosis 53, 80
exons 89

facilitated diffusion 41
fats 12–15, 60, 72–3, 77, 84–5
fertilisation 38, 96–7
fibrillation 65–6
fish 45–6, 57
flower structure 97
fluid-mosaic model 40
food tests 76–7
fractionation 33–4
frameshift mutations 94
fungi 80, 109

gametes 96
gametogenesis 96
gas exchange 44–51
gel electrophoresis 105
genetic biodiversity 100–1
genetic code 88–91
genetic diseases 108
genetic recombination 37
geographical isolation 106

gills 45–6
glucose 5, 8–9, 10, 42, 60, 73, 76
D-glyceraldehyde 8
glycogen 10
glycolipids 40
glycoproteins 40, 108
Golgi apparatus 24–5
Gram negative/positive 28

habitat biodiversity 100–1
haemocoel 56
haemoglobin 17, 46, 48, 53, 60–1
haemolymph 56
heart 61–2, 64–7
helicases 92–3
herbivores 81–2, 84
heterotrophs 80–2
histones 24
HIV 29–30, 108
holozoic nutrition 80–2
hormones 60, 85
humans 29–30, 48–50, 81, 85–6, 108, 116–18
hydrogen bonds 4, 16–17
hydrolysis 5, 41, 53
hydrophilic/hydrophobic 12–13, 40
hydrophytes 70
hyphae 80

ileum 42
immune responses 112–19
independent assortment 38
induced fit model 20–1
inflammation 110
inhibition of enzymes 22
inorganic ions 5, 42, 53
insects 45, 56
insertion mutations 94
integral (intrinsic) proteins 40–2
interstitial fluid 45, 61
introns 89
iodine–potassium iodide test 76

lagging/leading strands 92
leaves 46
lenses 32–3
lifestyle 85–6
lipids 12–15, 60, 72–3, 77, 84–5
lock and key model 21
lungs 48–50
lymphatic system 61
lymphocytes 60, 112–13, 116
lysosomes 24–5

macrophages 113
mass transport 56–71
medicines 118, 120
meiosis 37–8
messenger RNA 24, 88–90
metabolism 5, 22, 53
micelles 73
microscopy 32–3
missense mutations 93
mitochondria 24–5

mitosis 36–7
monosaccharides 8, 77
morphology 104–5
morula 97
mucous membranes 110
mutations 93–4, 106

natural selection 106
niches 106
non-competitive inhibitors 22
non-reducing sugars 77
nonsense mutations 94
nucleic acids 88–95
nucleoids 28
nucleus 24
nutrition 72–87

Okazaki fragments 92
oncotic pressure 60
oogenesis 96
optical microscopy 32
osmosis 13, 41, 69
ovule structure 98
oxygen 44–6, 48–9, 60–1

parasites 82
partially permeable membranes 41, 76
passive immunity 116
pathogens 29–30, 108–9, 120
peptides see proteins
peripheral (extrinsic) proteins 40
phagocytosis 80–1, 112
phloem 69–70
phospholipids 13, 24, 40
photoautotrophs 80
phylogenetics 104, 106
plants 24, 46, 56, 68–71, 80, 97–8, 109
plasma 60
plasma membranes 24–5, 28–9, 40–3
plasmids 28
plasmodesmata 68–9

pollen tube formation 98
polypeptides 16–19, 73
polysaccharides 9–10, 72
potometers 70
pregnancy 86
primary immune responses 112–13
prokaryotes 28–31, 37
prosthetic groups 17, 21
proteins 5, 16–19, 20–3, 40–2, 53, 60, 73, 77,
    84, 90
protists 109
purine/pyrimidine bases 88

red blood cells 60–1
reducing sugars 76–7
replication 92–5
reproduction 37–8, 96–9
respiration 8, 52–4
ribosomes 24–5, 28, 90
ring species 104
RNA 24, 29–30, 88–90
roots 68–9

saccharides 5, 8–11, 76–7, 84, 88
sampling 100–1
saprophytes 80
secondary immune responses 116–19
semi-conservative replication 36, 92–3
serum albumin 60
sexual reproduction 96–9
Simpson's index of diversity 101
single-celled organisms 44, 80, 108, 120
sinoatrial node 65–6
sodium ions 42
species 100–1, 104–7
spermatogenesis 96
spindle fibres 36–8
spiracles 45
staining 32–3
starch 9–10, 72, 76
stem cells 121–2

stomata 46, 69–70
stratified sampling 100
substitution mutations 93–4
sugars 5, 8–11, 76–7, 84, 88
surface area to volume 44
symplastic transport 68–70
systematic sampling 100

T-lymphocytes 113, 116
teeth 84
temporal isolation 106
tissue fluid 45, 61
trachea/tracheoles 45, 48
transcription 89
transfer RNA 24, 90
translation 90
translocation 69–70
transpiration 4, 69–70
triglycerides 12–15, 60, 72–3, 77, 84–5
trophy 80–3

ultracentrifugation 34

vaccination 116–18
vacuoles 24–5, 68
valves 58
variation 38
vascular system 56, 68–71
veins 58
ventilation 48–50
ventricles 62, 64–6
vesicles 24–5
viruses 29–30, 108–9

water 4–7, 13, 41, 60, 68–70

xerophytes 70
xylem 68–9

zona pellucida 97
zygote 97

Acknowledgements

The author and publisher are grateful to the copyright holders for permission to use quoted materials and images.

Cover & P1: © Tossaporn Sakkabanchorn/Shutterstock.com

All other images are © Shutterstock.com and © HarperCollins*Publishers* Ltd

Every effort has been made to trace copyright holders and obtain their permission for the use of copyright material. The author and publisher will gladly receive information enabling them to rectify any error or omission in subsequent editions. All facts are correct at time of going to press.

Published by Letts Educational
An imprint of HarperCollins*Publishers*
1 London Bridge Street
London SE1 9GF

ISBN: 9780008179069

First published 2016

10 9 8 7 6 5 4 3 2 1

© HarperCollins*Publishers* Limited 2016

British Library Cataloguing in Publication Data.
A CIP record of this book is available from the British Library.

Series Concept and Development: Emily Linnett and Katherine Wilkinson
Commissioning and Series Editor: Chantal Addy
Author: Eliot Attridge
Project Manager and Editorial: Erica Schwarz
Index: Indexing Specialists (UK) Ltd.
Cover Design: Paul Oates
Inside Concept Design: Ian Wrigley and Paul Oates
Text Design, Layout and Artwork: Q2A Media
Production: Lyndsey Rogers
Printed in Italy by Grafica Veneta SpA

MIX
Paper from responsible sources
FSC™ C007454
www.fsc.org